Justice and Fairness in International Negotiation

International negotiations have become increasingly significant in international affairs, as the number of parties involved have grown, and regional and global decison-making fora have multiplied. Cecilia Albin examines the role of considerations of justice and fairness in these negotiations. She asks when and why parties act on such considerations, how they are defined and operationalised, and what impact they have upon actual decision-making. She argues that negotiators do not simply pursue their narrow interests or those of their countries, but regularly take principles of justice and fairness into account. These principles come into play at an early stage, as talks are structured and agendas set; in the bargaining process itself; and in the implementation of and compliance with agreements. The analysis is based on cases in four important areas: the environment (air pollution); international trade (the GATT/WTO); ethnic conflict (the Israeli–Palestinian conflict); and arms control (nuclear non-proliferation). Drawing on a mass of empirical data, including a large number of interviews, this book relates the abstract debate over international norms and ethics to the realities of international relations.

CECILIA ALBIN is Lecturer in Politics at the University of Reading, where she is also Director of the Centre for International Security and Non-Proliferation and Deputy Director of the Graduate School of European and International Studies. She was previously Deputy Director of the Global Security Programme at the University of Cambridge

CAMBRIDGE STUDIES IN INTERNATIONAL RELATIONS: 74

Justice and Fairness in International Negotiation

Cambridge Studies in International Relations is a joint initiative of Cambridge University Press and the British International Studies Association (BISA). The series will include a wide range of material, from undergraduate textbooks and surveys to research-based monographs and collaborative volumes. The aim of the series is to publish the best new scholarship in International Studies from Europe, North America and the rest of the world.

Justice and Fairness
in International Negotiation

Cecilia Albin

CAMBRIDGE
UNIVERSITY PRESS

PUBLISHED BY THE PRESS SYNDICATE OF THE UNIVERSITY OF CAMBRIDGE
The Pitt Building, Trumpington Street, Cambridge, United Kingdom

CAMBRIDGE UNIVERSITY PRESS
The Edinburgh Building, Cambridge CB2 2RU, UK   www.cup.cam.ac.uk
40 West 20th Street, New York, NY 10011–4211, USA   www.cup.org
10 Stamford Road, Oakleigh, Melbourne 3166, Australia
Ruiz de Alarcón 13, 28014 Madrid, Spain

First published 2001

Printed in the United Kingdom at the University Press, Cambridge

Typeset in Palatino 10 / 12.5pt   [CE]

A catalogue record for this book is available from the British Library

ISBN 0521 79328 9 hardback
ISBN 0521 79725 X paperback

Contents

Figure

Preface and acknowledgments

Every staff member faces a roughly comparable pile of exam scripts each year in my department, irrespective of seniority and other responsibilities. Perfectly equal loads are not practical, but the 'burden' of marking is distributed as equally as is possible. A little further back cakes and ice cream bricks, seemingly all too rarely served, were divided between my siblings and myself according to the 'divide-and-choose' method in order to avoid argument. Of course, the idea of fairness operating in both cases can be disputed (after all, someone has to be head of department) and each method can be abused (there are ways to divide the cake to one's own advantage, as I discovered). The frequent use of these and many other methods exemplifies nonetheless the important role which equity considerations play in ordinary everyday life, in the distribution of resources and burdens. Procedures and allocations have to be seen as reasonably fair if they are to win respect and approval, and prevent conflict.

These sorts of ideas are well established in certain fields, notably in social-psychological research on interpersonal conflict and bargaining situations and in public policy research on 'fair division'. They are not new to anyone who has lived in a family, and should perhaps not be new to anyone who has worked in an academic department. They are, however, quite new to the way of thinking about and analysing international negotiations.

As this book sees daylight, I have many to thank for ending up with such an interesting project and for being able to complete it. The project began at the International Institute for Applied Systems Analysis (IIASA) in Austria, where I held a research post from 1991 to 1993. In the blissful surroundings of the Institute, there was no shortage of inspiration or time to work through diverse literatures on the role of justice and fairness in different areas of human affairs. I learnt particularly from studies by social psychologists on bargaining and conflict resolution in interpersonal and intrasocietal contexts, and was at the same time struck by the dearth of any comparable research in the area of international negotiation. When the analytical framework for a research project began to take shape (now in chapter 2 of this book), I benefited from interaction with scholars who regularly visited or worked at IIASA including Peyton Young, the late Jeffrey Z. Rubin, I. William Zartman and Bertram I. Spector. Lively representation of profoundly sceptical views about the role of justice and fairness in international affairs was not lacking either. In fact, an IIASA committee member threatened to resign if this project was allowed to proceed! The Institute being the home of world-class research on the science of air pollution, it was also here that I did the preliminary work on the case of the European acid rain negotiations (presented in chapter 3).

As the project moved with me to Cambridge University in 1993, it was more exposed to ideas from outside the negotiation field. Although this study is about the meaning and impact of justice and fairness considerations at the micro-level, in actual bargaining situations, my most useful and interesting discussions were with political theorists and philosophers. A generous grant over eighteen months from the United States Institute of Peace, Washington, DC (grant number USIP-109–96F) made it possible to complete the extensive research on the case studies. Among other things, the grant funded a research assistant, Liora Zion, to work on this project. I am very grateful for her exceptionally dedicated and professional assistance. The Global Security Fellows Initiative and Newnham College, Cambridge, financed sabbatical leaves to enable me to concentrate on this project, as well as some research expenses, including a field trip to Israel and the Palestinian territories. Anonymous referees enlisted by Cambridge University Press provided critical comments on draft chapters of the book, which challenged me to rethink the approach taken and improved the final product. I thank Richard Bellamy for helping out in refining that approach at a time when it made a real difference and the Department of Politics at Reading University, where I eventually wrote up the study, for a stimulating and congenial research environment.

The heart of this book draws on the insights and experiences of senior international negotiators. These remain poorly documented and analysed, despite the surge in writing on bargaining and conflict resolution over the past three decades. Detailed empirical research, particularly comparative research with coverage of several cases and issue areas, on what actually happens inside the international negotiating room and why, is still all too scarce. This work could therefore not have been done without access to a large number of practitioners. I am deeply grateful to all those (listed in the list of references at the end of the book) who agreed to be interviewed at length, and twice or more when required; who themselves or through colleagues provided additional information, documentation and advice on their respective areas of work; and who generally took much interest in the project. I especially wish to thank Lars Björkbom, the long-standing Chair of the acid rain talks within the UN Economic Commission for Europe (Geneva). Apart from agreeing to numerous interviews and responding scrupulously to the steady flow of questions over the years, he also commented in detail on several drafts of chapter 3. Richard Self, the chief US negotiator on services in the Uruguay Round of the GATT, provided extensive and valuable comments on chapter 4. Hannelore Hoppe, Chief of the Weapons of Mass Destruction Branch in the UN Department for Disarmament Affairs (New York), read and suggested improvements to chapter 6. As it is customary and important to point out, the author is responsible for any remaining flaws in these or other parts of the manuscript.

An earlier and briefer version of chapter 3 was published as a chapter entitled, 'Justice and Fairness in the Battle Against Acid Rain', in A. J. Coates (ed.), *International Justice* (Ashgate Publishers, London, 2000). An earlier version of chapter 5 was published as a journal article, entitled 'When the Weak Confront the Strong. Justice, Fairness, and Power in the Israel–PLO Interim Talks', in *International Negotiation* (Kluwer Law International), Vol. 4, No. 2, 1999, pp. 327–67. Expanded and updated versions of these published pieces are included here, with the permission of Ashgate and Kluwer Law.

Abbreviations

BAT	best available technology
BATNA	best alternative to a negotiated agreement
CAP	Common Agricultural Policy (of the EC/EU)
CTBT	Comprehensive Test Ban Treaty
DoP	Declaration of Principles on Interim Self-Government Arrangements (the Israel–PLO Accord of 13 September 1993 or the 'Oslo Accords')
EC	European Community
EU	European Union
FRG	Federal Republic of Germany
GATS	General Agreement on Trade in Services
GATT	General Agreement on Tariffs and Trade
GDP	gross domestic product
GNP	gross national product
IAEA	International Atomic Energy Agency
LDCs	less developed countries
LRTAP	Convention on Long-Range Transboundary Air Pollution
MFN	most-favoured nation
NAM	Non-Aligned movement
NGO	non-governmental organisation
NNWS	non-nuclear weapons states
NO_x	nitrogen oxides
NPT	Nuclear Non-Proliferation Treaty
NWS	nuclear weapons states
OECD	Organization for Economic Cooperation and Development
PLO	Palestine Liberation Organization
RAINS	Regional Acidification Information and Simulation (computer model)

SO$_2$	sulphur dioxide
UNCED	United Nations Conference on Environment and Development
UN-ECE	United Nations Economic Commission for Europe
VAT	value added tax
VOCs	volatile organic compounds
WTO	World Trade Organization

1 Introduction

A strife of interests masquerading as a contest of principles. The conduct of public affairs for private advantage.[1]

An expanded role for international negotiation

Justice and fairness are not considerations that naturally come to mind when we think of international negotiation. This is, after all, a political activity driven by the objectives of individual countries and the prospect of mutual gains. That negotiation is all about the pursuit of narrow self-interests, with the backup of whatever power and skills can be mustered, is a common notion with well-established roots. Yet issues of justice are a major cause of conflict. Disagreements over justice, like conflicts of interests, can turn violent and lead to wars.[2] They all too often undermine the capacity of negotiation to produce acceptable and durable solutions to disputes.

Negotiation is a joint decision-making process in which parties, with initially opposing positions and conflicting interests, arrive at a mutually beneficial and satisfactory agreement. It normally includes dialogue with problem-solving and discussion on merits, as well as bargaining and the exchange of concessions with the use of competitive tactics.[3] More than other tools such as arbitration and adjudica-

---

[1] A. Bierce, *The Enlarged Devil's Dictionary* (1967).
[2] For a discussion of how considerations of justice can play a role in the outbreak of wars, see Welch (1993).
[3] Traditional negotiation analysis distinguishes between distributive and integrative processes (Walton and McKersie, 1965; Pruitt, 1981). The former refers to competitive, 'win–lose' bargaining in which selfish parties seek merely to maximise their own gains. The latter refers to 'win–win' negotiations in which parties cooperate to identify or create solutions of high joint gains which eliminate the need for costly concessions.

1

tion, this is a flexible method of resolving differences which leaves the parties themselves with considerable control over the process and the outcome. Every party usually exercises leverage based on a variety of sources, and at the very least based on its ability to threaten to walk away from the table. Negotiation can bring on board new and needed parties by virtue of promising them 'gains from trade'. It can result in the creation or identification of new solutions to shared problems, and lend legitimacy to and facilitate the implementation of them as they have been agreed in a process of deliberation. Negotiation is used not only to produce agreement on the division or exchange of particular resources or burdens, but also to establish and reform institutions, regimes and regulations that will help to govern future relations between parties.

Governments have always relied on this activity to manage their relations. In the last three decades, however, growing interdependence among states and the recognition of a range of new threats to human survival and well-being have increased dramatically the significance, scope and complexity of international negotiation. Among the factors which have driven this expansion are the transborder nature of the threats, the need for voluntary multilateral cooperation and coordinated measures to tackle them, and the insufficiency or ambiguity of existing international regulations. Today negotiation is the principal means of collective decision-making, rule-making and dispute settlement in the management of transboundary issues. More broadly, it is fundamental to all efforts to achieve a measure of stability and order in the post-Cold War era. Environmental degradation, trade, arms control, economic integration and development, ethnic-sectarian conflict, the break-up and succession of states, and human rights are only some of the questions with which international negotiators now grapple.

Issues of justice and fairness lie at the heart of problems in every one of these areas. Global climate change, for example, threatens many countries with devastation primarily due to the actions of other states. Yet negotiations concerned with this problem keep stumbling over the dilemma of how to distribute the formidable costs of cutting greenhouse gas emissions. Who should have to reduce their emissions

In fact, most negotiations include both integrative and distributive processes, but few analyses have explored the interplay between the two. Exceptions include Lax and Sebenius (1986) and Zartman and Berman (1982).

2

and who should pay for it, given the resource inequalities and sharp differences in past and current emission levels (responsibility for the problem) between states? How much should emissions be cut and by what time, considering that reductions in the near term are prone to hamper the economic development of poorer countries? The cooperation of these countries will clearly be required to stabilise rising emission levels. But it is unlikely to be forthcoming unless industrialised states, as the principal atmospheric polluters to date, address at least some of the requests for justice advanced by the developing world.[4] Compensatory justice, expressed through preferential treatment of less developed countries (LDCs) in the form of exemptions and financial and technical assistance, was a cornerstone of the 1987 Montreal Protocol on Substances that Deplete the Ozone Layer, one of the most successful environmental agreements ever negotiated.

The growing dilemma of siting toxic nuclear waste and other hazardous facilities is partly the result of perceived injustices arising from inadequate representation or regard for all affected parties and interests in negotiations both within and between countries.[5] Contentious arguments about economic justice underlie negotiations over debt relief and repayments between industrialised states and international financial institutions on the one hand, and poor debtor nations on the other. Talks within the General Agreement on Tariffs and Trade (GATT) and, more recently, the World Trade Organization (WTO) have repeatedly been brought to the brink of collapse by bitter conflicts over unfair trade practices involving the EC, the US, Japan, LDCs, import-competing domestic producers and other parties. Charges that many countries remained too protectionist and were getting a 'free ride' on the open markets of others led the Uruguay Round of the GATT to treat cardinal GATT norms as negotiable rather than automatic obligations. Some observers have pointed to this development as a danger to the global trading system, whose strength has been built over the decades on unqualified application of these norms. In other areas, including in talks over nuclear non-proliferation, charges of free-riding and inadequate implementation of prior agreements continue to shape the bargaining process.[6]

---

[4] This is discussed further in Shue (1992).
[5] See *Risk: Health, Safety and Environment*, Vol. 7, No. 2, 1996 (issue devoted to fairness issues in siting decisions, based on a symposium held at the International Institute for Applied Systems Analysis, Laxenburg, Austria).
[6] See further chapter 6.

Is there a place for justice and fairness?

Ethical issues thus arise in international bargaining. But under what circumstances, if any, do such considerations genuinely constrain the behaviour of negotiators? What is their motive for behaving justly? What criteria are used, or should be used, to recognise when justice has been done? A review of the pertinent literatures, particularly on justice and on international relations, quickly reveals how debated and contested these questions are.[7] It is not an intention here, nor a possibility, to provide a comprehensive survey of these debates. This and the following chapters will instead refer to the literature selectively, as required, to explain concepts and arguments which are central to this study.

The predominant notion from the time of Plato to the present has been that the bounds of justice coincide with state boundaries and that it is not, and cannot be, an issue in relations between or across states. Principles of distributive justice apply to the contemporary members of a single group or society with shared values and opportunities for mutually beneficial cooperation, and specifically to the distribution of the cooperative gains among those members (Rawls, 1971). There is indeed an extensive record of the influential role played by concepts of justice and fairness in interpersonal and intrasocietal negotiations, particularly in the social-psychological literature (Deutsch, 1973; Bartos, 1974; Lind and Tyler, 1988; Benton and Druckman, 1973; see also Young, 1994).

By contrast, work exploring when and how such concepts matter in international negotiation is very limited. It generally deals with isolated case studies and offers a variety of conflicting propositions (Druckman and Harris, 1990; Albin, 1997a; Zartman, 1995; Zartman *et al.*, 1996). Predominant approaches have honoured the Realist tradition and its arguments about the limited applicability of morality to state conduct and interstate relations. These point to conditions in international affairs such as different rules of conduct and ethical notions among states (the absence of a shared moral purpose and of agreed ethical criteria), the lack of a supranational authority capable of ensuring compliance with norms, and states' inevitable tendency to

---

[7] Barry (1995) points out that theories of justice can be distinguished on the basis of their answers to three questions: what is the motive for behaving justly? What are the criteria for a just set of rules? Why would somebody with the specified motive comply with rules which are just according to the specified criteria?

pursue their own interests and define any moral obligations narrowly in terms of these and duties to their respective peoples. The approaches have thus focused on the role of power and self-interest in international bargaining (Snyder and Diesing, 1977; Habeeb, 1988). A party's readiness to make concessions and accept a particular deal is supposedly based on a calculation of its relative strength *vis-à-vis* the other side. Parties bargain to secure all they can acquire rather than their 'just' or 'fair' share, which may be more or less. The outcome will largely reflect the relative distribution of power, particularly in cases of asymmetry. 'Power' is defined in a number of ways ranging from conventional military and economic resources to the possession of skills, access to information and the exercise of leadership.[8] A key element is certainly the value of a party's best alternative to a negotiated agreement, or 'BATNA' (Fisher and Ury, 1981). The higher that value the less dependent the party is on reaching an agreement and the more it can afford to concede little, take risks and wait out the other side. It cannot be so abusive as to remove all incentives to negotiate, but may appease a weaker party by offering some advantage over a continued state of conflict on unequal terms.

The exploitation of power advantages and the constant striving to maximise self-interest do not imply that international negotiations are necessarily considered amoral or unprincipled. First, the classic Realist view holds that the selfishness of states is grounded in and justified by a moral responsibility of national leaders to the security and well-being of their own populations. Even if state action was subject to some universal moral principles, no leader can be required to adhere to such principles or help another leader fulfil her duties when this compromises his primary moral obligations towards his own people (Morgenthau, 1971, 1948). Secondly, even the staunchest Realist would hold that the voluntary conclusion of an agreement creates an obligation to honour it. Justice is achieved when parties comply with whatever terms they have accepted freely and rationally.

The intellectual roots of this minimalist view are found foremost in the moral theory of Thomas Hobbes.[9] In the Hobbesian 'state of nature', men as selfish competitors for scarce resources share an interest in agreeing to constrain their behaviour, to avoid mutually destructive conflict. Until such an agreement has been reached, men

[8] This is further discussed in chapter 5.
[9] See Hobbes (1991).

are effectively at war and have no obligations: they possess unlimited 'natural rights' and liberties to do whatever they can to preserve and please themselves, including at the expense of the lives and property of others. The concept of natural rights, and Hobbes' argument that there are no independent criteria of justice or fairness, mean that such considerations are inapplicable to the process of negotiation and to the terms of any agreement. Until an agreement is concluded, there are no constraints on what a party may do or take to better its own situation other than the limits of its own strength. However, an agreement creates obligations of compliance, for supposedly free parties have themselves chosen to conclude it and to constrain their actions accordingly, in the expectation of mutual benefit. As long as enough parties comply to maintain the collective benefits of the agreement, it is morally binding as well as rational (self-serving) to implement it. Any gains to be had from 'cheating' (failing to comply while benefiting from the compliance by others) will be undermined by the long-term consequences of being excluded from future cooperative ventures.[10] There can never be conflict between justice and power or self-interest for negotiated agreements will reflect the balance of forces, and justice as much as rationality require that they be honoured.

One major theory, defining justice as 'mutual advantage', is founded on these Hobbesian and Realist premises. Arrangements are just if based on terms which the parties themselves have established and agreed to honour. They must be mutually beneficial, since parties strive to maximise their own gains. So justice cannot involve a pure redistribution of resources, nor involve parties which are unable to reciprocate and contribute to the joint gains. For David Gauthier, a representative of this school of thought, the starting positions for negotiations, and the tactics and leverage used, may well reflect power inequalities which result from the parties' own legitimate resources and efforts to better themselves. Acquisitions may be illegitimate if, for example, they were acquired by exploiting another party's resources. However, Gauthier argues that in certain circumstances agreements may legitimately reflect such situations as well. First, one party may exploit another's resources if this is required to

---

[10] According to Hobbes, humans are unable to internalise this logic and to abandon voluntarily the goal of maximising short-term self-interests. Hence the need for a sovereign ruler to formulate moral codes, and to enforce agreements on mutual constraints which leave all parties better off than in a state of non-cooperation.

avoid worsening its own situation, or if adequate compensation is provided. Secondly, if the confiscation of resources is to be considered unjust in the first place the deprived party must be the legitimate owner of them (having acquired them through its own labour), must have been using (or intended to use) them, and must have been affected negatively by their removal. Thirdly, mutual gains from negotiation is considered a practical necessity which must override other considerations whenever they are conflicting. Past injustices can therefore be corrected or compensated for, only as far as it is consistent with offering all parties gains from an agreement (Gauthier, 1986). Whatever their specific terms, agreements are thus considered legitimate chiefly by being mutually advantageous and by virtue of having been concluded voluntarily.

In this approach, the motivation to behave justly is entirely self-serving and calculating. The acceptance of principles of justice is viewed as a necessary compromise between egoistic parties who are too equal to pursue their interests without regard for the other or to do injustice without suffering unacceptable costs. The adherence to moral constraints depends on the existence of a balance of power in this sense: 'We care for morality, not for its own sake, but because we lack the strength to dominate our fellows or the self-sufficiency to avoid interaction with them. The person who could secure her ends either independently of others or by subordinating them would never agree to the constraints of morality. She would be irrational – mad' (Gauthier, 1986, p. 307).

Realist-inspired approaches face considerable challenges. A substantial body of literature on international relations, political theory and political philosophy now points to the explanatory power of norms rather than 'realism' (Nardin, 1983; Frost, 1986; Beitz, 1979; Rittberger, 1993). It examines why and how norms and normative regimes, including concepts of justice and fairness, influence state conduct and interstate relations.[11] International negotiation is used to build regimes in particular issue areas (Spector, Sjöstedt and Zartman, 1994). As this book's case study on international trade talks illustrates, once they are well established, negotiation is itself influenced by the

---

[11] The concept of 'regime' is defined as a set of principles, norms, rules and decision making procedures, implicit and explicit, around which actors' expectations converge in a given issue area of international affairs (Krasner, 1983). 'Norms' are rules or standards of behaviour defined in terms of rights and obligations (Brown, 1997). These include, but are not limited to, concepts of justice and fairness.

principles and norms which the regimes embody. One analyst points out that the conditions in international affairs on which Realist arguments are based exist also in interpersonal and intersocietal relations, without for that matter eroding the role of morality in those relations and that widely accepted norms, moral and legal, are indeed generally observed in the international arena (Barry, 1989b). States usually adhere to norms because doing so overlaps with rather than contradicts their interests, broadly defined, in an age of interdependence.

Brian Barry's theory, probably the most serious attack to date on the notion of justice as mutual advantage, holds similarly that concern about justice is driven by a desire to defend one's actions on impartial grounds which others cannot reasonably reject and which can elicit voluntary agreement and cooperation (Barry, 1989a, 1995). He admits that such a desire and a habit of considering the interests of others are more likely to be cultivated in largely equal parties owing to their experience of interdependence and their need to secure the collaboration of others. It is a broadly held view that the absence of sharp power inequalities enhances the motivation to negotiate and otherwise act justly, while their presence may exclude a role for justice.

What is a just and fair agreement? Competing criteria

How do we know when justice has been done? How is a just solution to be distinguished from an unjust one? The matter of what criteria should be (or are in fact) used to answer these questions is deeply contested. It raises issues about how such values relate to the bargaining process and what power inequalities and self-interests, if any, may be reflected in arrangements which are to be accepted as just or fair. There are basically three types of standards, further discussed in chapter 2, which can be employed: internal, external, and impartial ones.

Internal or *contextual criteria* are intrinsic to the situation at hand. Realist-inspired approaches, including that of justice as 'mutual advantage', rely on these criteria. This is also the case of the few models in the traditional negotiation literature which are at all concerned with this subject. They stress the 'rational' or selfish purposes of negotiation, the absence of one overarching or universal standard by which to judge agreements, and often the value of each party's BATNA as the basis for determining the meaning of justice or fairness. In game-theoretical approaches such as those originally put forward by Nash (1950) and Braithwaite (1955), the nature of a just and fair outcome is defined inside the negotiation process without reference to any external criteria. The most permissive approach regards *any* outcome as just by virtue of it having been agreed, with no constraints imposed on the standards applied or methods used. Parties can bargain to acquire everything possible given their weight and tactical advantages (Zartman, 1995). More specific contextual criteria are also used. Many pose enormous challenges regarding application because of the practical difficulties of measuring gains, BATNAs and so forth in any common unit. One group of standards is based on the premise that parties should gain to about the same extent from a negotiated agreement. In Nash's famous concept, a fair solution yields to each party one half of the maximum gains it can rationally expect to receive (Nash, 1950). In another notion, a just agreement should give parties the value of their respective BATNAs and divide the remaining benefits proportionally to the worth of their contributions to the cooperative venture (Gauthier, 1986).

External criteria here refer to major principles of distributive justice. Their general substantial content is independent of any particular negotiation or allocation to be judged. Principles which are prominent in both the literature and actual practice include equality, proportionality, compensatory justice and need. The principle of *equality* requires parties to receive identical or comparable rewards and burdens. The original Aristotelian notion stresses the importance of unequal (proportional) treatment of unequals as much as the equal treatment of equals.[12] In other words, parties should be treated the same only if they are indeed equal in all respects relevant to the distribution. Equality in this interpretation means denial of discriminatory treatment on indefensible grounds rather than equal treatment of everyone *per se*.

The principle raises the question of what exactly is to be treated equally, and of how an outcome of actual equality is to be achieved when the parties are unequal to begin with. Divergent resources and preferences mean that parties in practice gain unequal levels of utility from acquiring the same goods in equal amounts. A common interpretation is equality of utility or welfare. It requires measuring and

---

[12] See notably Aristotle's *Nicomachean Ethics*.

comparing individual experiences of welfare from consuming particular goods, and distributing them accordingly to ensure equality of well-being. Rawls (1982) argues that this, if at all possible, is not necessarily desirable or fair. The proposition that resources should be distributed to render people's 'functioning capabilities' the same also poses problems of measurement and comparison (Sen, 1992). They are bypassed in the notion of equality as 'equal shares', which refers to the uniform distribution of resources regardless of differences in preferences, needs, contributions or other considerations (Pruitt, 1981). One approach to intergenerational equality sets out three obligations of current generations to future ones: the conservation of options through preservation of the diversity of the natural and cultural resource base; the conservation of quality through maintenance of the quality of the planet; and the conservation of access through the provision of equal access to the earth's resources (Weiss, 1989).

A second major criterion of distributive justice is *proportionality*, which holds that resources should be allocated in proportion to relevant inputs. Justice is achieved when each party's ratio of inputs to rewards or burdens is the same, and injustice is experienced in relation to these ratios rather than in absolute terms. The principle originates in Aristotle's argument for distribution in proportion to merit when relevant inequalities among parties justify deviation from the equality principle. Two types of input are particularly relevant: assets (e.g., skills, intelligence, wealth, income, status) and contributions (i.e., actions and efforts adding value to the collective or disputed goods). The proportionality norm is similar to the concept of *desert* (Barry, 1965; Sidgwick, 1901). In some versions of this concept, parties deserve rewards and burdens only for efforts and actions which are voluntary and deliberate. The more positive (or negative) contributions a party makes intentionally, the more rewards (or burdens) it merits.

There are numerous interpretations of the proportionality norm. Those which distribute resources and burdens proportionally so as to achieve an outcome of equality in some respect are frequently confused with equality norms. 'Equal sharing of responsibility' and 'equal sacrifices' entail that parties make concessions and accept burdens in proportion to their ability to do so, which may be measured by level of economic development and national income (Kelley, Beckman and Fisher, 1967). Thus all parties will in a sense bear equal costs from their respective standpoints. Others argue that distributive justice and fair division are achieved when net rewards (e.g., money, education) are allocated in direct proportion to investments (e.g., time spent, risks taken) so that everyone's ratio of profit to investment is the same (Adams, 1965; Walster, Walster and Berscheid, 1978). The 'opportunities' norm, by contrast, equates equity with a form of efficiency by allocating resources in proportion to how well each party can use and benefit from them.

Another principle is *compensatory justice*. It stipulates that resources should be distributed to indemnify undue costs inflicted upon a party in the past or the present. At times it is mistakenly used synonymously with a fourth criterion, that of *needs*. While compensatory justice involves claims based on actions resulting in unjust burdens, needs are based on some supposed general standard to which people or nations are entitled. Compensatory justice ignores possessions (or lack of these), but the needs principle holds that resources should be allocated relative to the strength of need so that the least endowed party gets the greatest share. Often driven by the past, compensatory justice links resource distributions only to identifiable wrongdoings and may therefore reward the already well endowed. The needs norm, by contrast, focuses on the present and aims to meet basic wants irrespective of their origins. But both criteria are comparative: is the compensation adequate for the inflicted harm? Who is the most needy? Neither includes considerations of contributions. And neither aims to erase inequalities or to establish an outcome of equality between parties *per se*: the objective is to rectify specific injustices or to ensure a basic level of well-being. A compensatory approach to world poverty might, for example, aim to remedy any economic and developmental damage done to Third World countries which take steps to protect the environment. A needs-driven distribution would instead target the world's poorest peoples or countries regardless of their preparedness to participate in environmental protectionism.

A third set of approaches, arising from the philosophical literature, employ so-called *impartial standards*. These delineate requirements which a negotiation process and an agreement must fulfil in order to be taken to be just and fair. They limit what interests may be pursued and what kind of power may be exercised, if any. The purest expression of impartiality is John Rawls' well-known theory of 'justice as fairness'. His argument that principles of justice are only those which parties would select and agree upon if they were ignorant of their own identity and position is meant to purge the bargaining process of all inequalities in individual resources and advantages, including skills and power. The parties are denied any information about their own interests and circumstances because it is taken to be irrelevant to, and is likely to bias, the choice of principle (Rawls, 1958, 1971). The need for a 'veil of ignorance' arises from the assumption that parties are motivated by a narrow interest to maximise their own gains. Discussion and negotiation remain essential behind the veil, but clearly take a form radically different from any common practice.

This notion, so important in the philosophical literature, cannot be operationalised in actual international encounters which fail to meet the Rawlsian criteria of a fair selection situation. It stands in contrast to Brian Barry's theory of justice as impartiality, which draws on that of Thomas Scanlon. In Barry's and Scanlon's approach, the motivation is to be able to justify one's behaviour on reasonable grounds. Here, justice is 'what can freely be agreed on' by parties who are equally well placed, notably in the sense of being able to reject and veto an agreement (Barry, 1995, p. 51; see also Scanlon, 1982). It can be justified and defended on impartial grounds, and cannot be reasonably rejected by an outside observer or a party looking beyond its own narrow self-interests. The core criterion is the voluntary acceptance by parties of whatever arrangements are proposed, and their acceptability from a more general detached viewpoint. What is just elicits consent without the use of threats or rewards, so there is no place for negotiations which take place in a coercive or manipulative context. Agreements held in place by force are clearly seen as illegitimate. Moreover, the value of non-agreement points or BATNAs, however acquired, has no role in determining the nature of just distributions (Barry, 1989a). Justice as impartiality is advocated particularly when there are conflicting conceptions of the good which cannot be resolved through rational reasoning (Barry, 1995). Others express a looser notion which entails constraining the use of power and the pursuit of self-interest. It is a common view that the initial bargaining positions, the starting point for negotiations, and any leverage utilised in bargaining should only reflect a party's own legitimate endowments and efforts to better itself, without taking advantage of another. Strategic advantages and strong BATNAs acquired through activities which worsened the bargaining position or overall situation of another party cannot be exploited or define a party's stake in negotiations, if just agreements are to result (Shue, 1992).

The approach of this study

What justice is and requires is thus disputed. The same arrangement may be perfectly appropriate by one set of criteria, and devoid of all moral content and acceptability by another. Of course, the dispute exists not only in the literature. It is very much alive in the world of international negotiation. Different principles affect parties differently. The fact that a single standard rarely emerges as salient and unchallenged means that several competing criteria are often invoked, for reasons which may involve genuine ethical conceptions as well as tactical calculations. There is a virtual consensus on one score, however, despite different understandings of what is just and fair: negotiations and agreements which parties perceive as such are far more likely to be accepted and to lead to successful outcomes. Therefore, the way in which competing ethical notions are handled in the process often has a direct impact on its results.

The purpose of this book is to investigate empirically when, why and how justice and fairness matter in international negotiation. What motivates negotiators to take such considerations into account? What content do they give to these concepts in complex political talks, and how do they tackle conflicting ideas of what is right or reasonable in particular situations? The book seeks to illuminate what conditions and circumstances permit justice and fairness to play a role, what effect these values have on the bargaining process and how, if at all, they filter through to and influence the formulation of the terms of international agreements. In doing so the book will shed light on two larger questions: how do other influential factors such as power relations, domestic politics and interests, and access to knowledge and information (or lack of it) interact with and affect the role of justice and fairness? And how important are these concepts for the effectiveness of international negotiation? The heart of the study consists of detailed case studies drawn from four major areas of international relations: trade, the environment, ethnic and territorial conflict, and arms proliferation and regulation.

It is not an objective to address questions posed by political philosophers about the nature of a just social order, or the formulation of principles for the conduct of negotiations and the distribution of resources in society. These intellectual debates are obviously significant. They fall outside the scope of this work, however, because it focuses on forces which actually drive the dynamics of international negotiations. Discussions in the literature on theories of justice, and on norms in international relations, usually take place at a too general or too abstract level to be helpful in this area. Young (1994) argues that major theories of justice fail to explain even how domestic societies, in practice, define the concept and resolve problems regarding the distribution of public resources and burdens. The treatment of justice and fairness in the negotiation literature is very limited, as chapter 2 notes in more detail. The aim then is to illuminate the meaning given to these concepts and their impact at the micro-level, in real bargaining situations. The emphasis therefore falls on examining empirically what parties perceive as just and fair in particular contexts, and when and how they act upon those conceptions.

This does not mean that justice and fairness become solely contextual or subjective notions accepted at face value, as the next section below will show. Nor are they assumed always to be important, for they are sometimes washed out in the negotiation process by other considerations. Finally, these concepts are not taken to be influential only when negotiators refer to or consciously think of them. The extent to which the language of equity is actually used in international negotiations varies between issue areas and countries. Such references are common in, for example, climate change and recent trade negotiations. They are peripheral or even absent in the language of arms control talks; yet, the duty of compliance with freely negotiated agreements is one principle among others which is taken very seriously because of its implications for national and international security. In all the negotiations covered in this volume, high-level representatives of the parties indicated in interviews that they focused on the concrete issues and proposals at hand and did not reflect on or discuss justice and fairness at a general or philosophical level. In the talks within the United Nations Economic Commission for Europe (UN-ECE) which led to the 1994 Second Sulphur Protocol, for example, negotiators rarely articulated their views and positions in these terms and were uncomfortable using them to analyse their experience. Concepts of justice and fairness were nevertheless strong underlying currents, as we shall see. The principles of inflicting no harm, and of differentiating obligations based on relative contribution to ecological damage, abatement costs and economic ability, became particularly influential.

14

Justice as a balanced settlement of conflicting claims

Despite the emphasis on empirical analysis, it is necessary to lay out the overarching concept of justice which has informed this study. An inquiry of this kind calls for some *a priori* notion of what it entails. Otherwise the result may be merely a description of what various persons or countries held to be just or fair on different occasions. There are usually a number of principles, and interpretations of these, which parties can invoke credibly in any one context. Their own situations and interests tend to influence their choice of principle, particularly in the initial stages of negotiations. Moreover, international negotiators are known sometimes to use ethical arguments for purely tactical purposes, and to exploit power inequalities to secure their objectives. For reasons such as these, some independent criterion is needed in order to assess what arguments are worth taking seriously.

What is the motivation for acting upon considerations of justice and fairness? Collectively, international negotiators employ such principles as a tool to reach an agreement. They are used to overcome conflicting interests and claims, and to build consensus on the nature of an acceptable outcome. In the initial phases of bargaining, the parties usually formulate their positions and proposals based on relatively narrow concepts of what would be beneficial or fair to themselves. They are naturally focused on their own interests and concerns, and may still know little about those of the other side. As the process continues they become confronted with other notions of an appropriate settlement, backed up by different principles and claims. If a positive outcome is to be achieved, each party must normally be prepared to consider and eventually endorse a more balanced set of arrangements which others can accept as reasonable and not too self-serving. It is in this phase that ideas of justice and fairness often come into play which influence the movement from original positions, the exchange of concessions, and the shape of the ultimate agreement. The motivation to take these ideas seriously recalls Barry's argument about the concern to be able to justify one's behaviour on grounds which others cannot reasonably reject.

We have noted that justice and fairness remain contested notions in current scholarly debates. The case studies which follow show that in actual international negotiations, several conflicting criteria typically exist which parties can legitimately claim to be applicable and to deserve merit. A notion of what is 'right' and 'reasonable' is therefore essential in these common situations of moral ambiguity, when competing principles and interests are invoked convincingly. The overarching concept employed in this study focuses on such situations. It is a largely procedural notion, that of justice as *the balanced settlement of conflicting claims*.

This notion recognises that the substantial meaning of justice and fairness is a complex matter, especially in real international encounters, and that it is frequently contested for good reasons. It appreciates that justice cannot be defined precisely at a general level nor be reduced to a single formula or checklist. In order to understand what 'a balanced settlement of conflicting claims' means more concretely, it is necessary to examine specific situations. We might say that fairness is achieved when this notion is applied to particular cases in a manner which takes into account the relevant contextual details.[13] These include each party's entitlement to the resource or contribution to the problem under negotiation (to the extent that this can be determined), its capacity to bear costs or forego benefits associated with a joint agreement, and any established norms for resolving conflicts in that particular issue area. What is a fair solution in one instance may be regarded as deeply unfair in another, if the normative context or the resources and contributions of the parties are different. The overarching concept here proposed consists nonetheless of certain basic ingredients. These are largely procedural principles which do not assign a particular substantial content to justice or fairness. Subsequent chapters will demonstrate that they conform well with how international negotiators themselves define and operationalise these values.

The primary ingredient is *impartiality*, which draws on Barry's theory discussed earlier. It develops the concept of impartiality by examining its many dimensions in the context of real complex negotiations, and by specifying further what makes an arrangement impossible to reject reasonably. As Barry argues, a settlement of conflicting claims which cannot be agreed freely is indeed unlikely to be just. However, voluntary agreement and the absence of coercion

---

[13] An outcome may be just in the sense of being based on a general principle, but unfair in how the principle has been applied. An agreement may also be fair to a particular group of parties, but unjust in a wider (e.g., international) sense.

are not sufficient criteria. What justice and impartiality entail more-over is *balancing different principles and interests*. Young (1994) puts forward a similar notion with respect to the allocation of public resources and burdens; for example, military duty, the siting of hazardous waste dumps, and organs for transplantation. He holds that 'equity' consists of balancing the principles of need, desert and social utility and that, as already mentioned, major theories of justice fail to capture the nuances surrounding this reality. For example, the US national formula for distributing kidneys among transplant patients balances the principles of efficiency (likelihood of a transplant succeeding), need (urgency of a transplant), compensation for dis-advantages (medical ability to accept only a small number of kidneys) and seniority (amount of time spent waiting for a transplant) (Young, 1994). In international affairs a different and wider range of circum-stances and claims, and therefore principles, must be weighed. But the basic idea is the same, that there is an important element of justice in striking a balance between these.

One reason for this is that a single criterion can rarely take account of all pertinent factors in actual international encounters. As problems become more intricate and the parties more unequal in relevant respects, a greater number of principles, reflecting a wider range of considerations, must guide any 'balanced' solution. Related to this is the fact that, as noted, there are several competing principles which can be invoked credibly in most complex international talks. Each standard will enhance justice to some party or parties in some respect, while ignoring other considerations and perspectives. The contest-ability of the relevance and interpretation of almost any principle, and its limitations if applied alone, mean that other criteria deserve merit if a balanced settlement is to result. The interests and claims of all parties should be considered, but must not necessarily be reflected to the same extent in the agreed outcome. Put differently, justice does not always consist of 'splitting the difference' or finding some midpoint compromise between various claims (when this method can be used, which is difficult in conflicts over intangible or indivisible resources). When directly relevant inequalities among parties can be established clearly – for example, in entitlement to the disputed resources or in ability to bear the costs of a joint agreement – there is usually good reason to take these into account. In negotiations over problems ranging from acid rain to free trade, the principle of differentiating obligations and benefits between rich and poorer countries, so as to address the special economic needs of the latter, has become one influential notion among others.

Subsequent case studies will show that international negotiators almost always end up balancing different principles, and thereby different claims. They associate this practice at once with justice, fairness and pragmatism: it is taken to be a reasonable way to overcome conflicting considerations and convictions, particularly when none emerges as clearly superior and salient, and as a practical way to formulate an agreement which all parties can accept as balanced and fair under the circumstances.

A third component of the notion of justice here proposed is the *obligation to honour and comply with freely negotiated agreements*. This is a well-established principle of morality and international law, although philosophical opinion and real-life regulations differ on matters such as when and how a party is entitled to break an agreement. Brian Barry argues that 'common-sense' morality upholds an obligation to comply when enough parties do so to keep the agreement effective in serving its goals, while 'utilitarianism' supports a greater obligation to comply as long as this still benefits the agreed purposes in any way (Barry, 1989b). It may in fact be justified for a party to break its commitments under a freely negotiated agreement for other reasons.[14] One example, recognised in the 1968 Nuclear Non-Proliferation Treaty (NPT), is when the basic survival or other vital interests of a signatory state are genuinely threatened.

The main point here is instead about intentional 'free-riding': if one or more parties benefit from the compliance by others, while purposefully avoiding to comply themselves in order to maximise their gains or cut costs under the agreement, the settlement of the conflicting claims is no longer balanced. In this sense, adherence to voluntary agreements is an important aspect of the notion of justice put forward here. We shall see that this conception has been very influential in some international negotiations. Another point is that the concept of justice as the balanced settlement of conflicting claims does not separate the duty to comply from the process by which an agreement was reached. It rejects the Hobbesian notion that only the post-agreement phase of implementation is subject to moral judgment, while processes of bargaining largely fall outside the domain of ethics.

The overarching concept of justice here thus involves exercising a

---

[14] This matter is further discussed in chapter 2.

measure of impartiality, balancing different principles and interests, and complying with freely negotiated agreements. It takes into account the interests of parties, but places constraints on the raw pursuit of self-interest. It may reflect some power inequalities between them, but does not simply mirror the prevailing balance of forces. Chapter 2 develops an analytical framework which fleshes out some more aspects of this concept.

Tactical uses of ethical arguments

Just as notions of justice and fairness may operate when negotiators do not express them verbally, explicit usage of the terms does not necessarily mean that such concepts are genuinely at play. Ethical arguments can be employed for purely tactical purposes. This means that a party advocates a particular principle which does not represent what it truly believes to be right, because this promises to bring greater gains. In this way statements about justice and fairness can serve as a cover legitimating demanding bargaining positions and permitting the pursuit of narrow self-interests, with minimal condemnation or other costs. A powerful party can avoid charges of exploiting its strength. A weaker one may take advantage of its feebleness and achieve a more favourable agreement by appealing to moral issues. It differs from the common situation in which a party's genuine conceptions are partly influenced by its own circumstances and thus overlap with, or at least do not contradict, some of its own interests. Such usages, while often pointed out or suspected in practice, have not been the subject of systematic empirical research.

The possibility of using arguments about justice and fairness tactically results from two basic realities. The first is the absence of consensus on one overarching standard which defines the content of such values, and the lack of consensus on priorities among recognised norms. For example, there is widespread international agreement on some core human rights. But there is no consensus on their significance relative to other norms concerning the use of force and coercion, national sovereignty and non-intervention in a state's internal affairs. Therefore, there are usually several conflicting principles on which an agreement can be based and still reasonably be considered legitimate. Good examples are recent negotiations over issues as diverse as Palestinian self-government and Israeli withdrawal from the occupied territories, European air pollution and climate change.

The second reality is that almost any principle can be interpreted and applied in different ways. Parties may agree on the general principles, but not on their precise meaning or requirements in a particular context. This has been a problematic feature of recent international trade and arms control talks, as we shall see. Factors such as precedent, any normative framework within which issues are negotiated, and their nature constrain what principles or interpretations can be judged reasonable, but some scope for tactical manoeuvring invariably remains.

When tactical uses of ethical arguments appear credible enough to be effective, this is precisely because most countries and the international community attach genuine worth and legitimacy to a variety of principles and norms and are sensitive to allegations about violations of these. If this was not the case, these arguments would lack tactical value. Moreover, tactical usage underlines once more the motivation of negotiators to be able to justify their positions and proposals on grounds which seem reasonable and not too self-serving, in order to arrive at a broadly supported agreement. Skilful negotiators know the power and appeal of behaviour which is, or at least appears, principled and always keep in mind the merits of their position.

One party's genuine fairness notion may also serve as a good defence of its interests, and another party may perceive this as merely strategic. Only access to the inside of a negotiator's mind would afford an unequivocal assessment of what ethical arguments are authentic. Without this privilege, careful observation can still go a long way to permit a sound judgment. Background knowledge from a variety of sources about the motivations of parties, the conduct of the negotiations, and the usage of language is fundamental. Specific attention must be paid to the coherence and consistency of advocated principles over time, their general credibility from an impartial standpoint, their compatibility (or not) with adopted positions and policies, and the nature of any affected self-interests. Purely tactical references to justice or fairness often appear too self-serving, and therefore fail to gain influence. The case studies on acid rain and international trade talks in subsequent chapters illustrate this particularly well. When successfully employed, however, they can certainly undermine the notion of justice as a balanced settlement of conflicting claims.

Overview of the study

We have noted that the scope of international negotiation has expanded to include new areas which raise ethical issues. What role justice and fairness play in the course of this activity, what motivation negotiators have (if any) to act upon such values, and what criteria are or are to be employed to judge processes of bargaining, are subject to lively debate in the literature. The purpose of this book is to investigate these and other related questions empirically instead, in the context of detailed case studies representing major areas of international negotiation. It employs an overarching concept of justice as the balanced settlement of conflicting claims which calls for a degree of impartiality, a balance between different principles and interests, and compliance with freely negotiated agreements. Subsequent chapters set out to demonstrate that arguments about justice and fairness in international negotiation are important and influential, and not simply a 'strife of interests masquerading as a contest of principles'.

Chapter 2 begins by developing an analytical framework which identifies the stages at which issues of justice and fairness arise in international negotiations. They relate not only to the negotiation process and outcome, but emerge already when the talks are structured and continue to do so long after a formal agreement has been concluded. The notion of justice as a balanced settlement of conflicting claims and, in fact, any serious approach to justice and fairness in international bargaining, require examining all these stages. The framework is used in subsequent case studies to recognise at what level and in what sense issues or conceptions of justice and fairness did play a role. These chapters evolve around the same basic analytical questions, while also discussing matters specific to their cases and areas.

Chapter 3 examines the rich history of negotiations within the UN-ECE aimed at reducing air pollution. Here the politically controversial issues of justice and fairness have focused on the outcome – on alternative ways of distributing the costs and other burdens of regional acid rain abatement between countries. These issues have become more influential over time, especially since the late 1980s, for reasons which will persist: scientific proof of the sources and damaging effects of air pollution, monumental abatement costs combined with unequal national resources and gains to be had from emission cuts, and previous collective experiences of using uniform percentage reductions in emissions which ignored many fairness implications. This is a case in which several conflicting principles were put forward convincingly and eventually recognised as important in providing guidelines for a solution. 'Horse-trading' among these and other concerns eventually paved the way for new important multilateral agreements, such as the 1994 Second Sulphur Protocol.

Chapter 4 moves into the global economy. It provides an analysis of the world's most significant trade talks to date: the Uruguay Round of the GATT, which lasted from 1986 to 1994 and produced agreement on greater reforms in the global trading system than any previous GATT round. Justice and fairness issues emerged at all stages, commencing already in the initial stage of agenda setting. General norms of free and fair trade guided the talks, but their exact meaning and application became subject to much controversy and intense bargaining. Disputes over the implementation of the most-favoured-nation clause and market access in the areas of agriculture and services led to stalemates which threatened the successful conclusion of the entire Uruguay Round. Broadly speaking, an emphasis on reciprocity (the reciprocation of trade-liberalising measures), balance (the consideration of the interests and concerns of all parties) and mutual gains (the design of agreements establishing a balance of benefits between countries) eventually led to an outcome which everyone could accept overall. This included preferential treatment of LDCs according to level of economic development, without which the talks could never have been successfully concluded. As mentioned the Round also witnessed a new treatment of fundamental GATT norms as negotiable items rather than automatic obligations which, according to some analysts, may undermine the international trade regime.

Chapter 5 brings us into the area of ethnic-sectarian and territorial disputes, and specifically to the Middle East. The interim talks between Israel and the Palestine Liberation Organization (PLO) under the 1993 Oslo Accords offer interesting insights into how ethical considerations can interact with sharp power inequalities. Israel's superior bargaining strength ensured that the country's security interests and notions of fairness influenced the process substantially. However, the negotiations cannot be understood merely in terms of the distribution of power between the two sides. The costs of failing to reach an agreement meant that Israeli negotiators had to concede to certain Palestinian demands and conceptions of fairness. The serious charges of injustice have emerged in the implementation phase, owing more to developments on the ground than dissatisfaction with the terms of the interim agreements *per se*. This case challenges conventional notions that there can be no role for ethical considerations when the weak confront the strong, and that parties define negotiated agreements as just irrespective of how their power relations have influenced the terms.

Chapter 6 demonstrates that issues of justice and fairness can be important even in negotiations concerned with arms control and military security. The 1995 Conference to review and extend the NPT, the world's key mechanism for controlling the spread of nuclear weapons, raised such issues at each stage of the process. The single most important one was the matter of compliance with the original terms of the NPT. It set much of the agenda, influenced bargaining positions and proposals, and caused stalemates. The prevailing conception that parties, in this case the nuclear weapons states, must honour obligations under agreements which they have entered into determined part of the final agreement, which rebalanced rights and obligations between nuclear and non-nuclear countries. The experience of the 1995 Conference and subsequent PrepComm meetings suggest that if the selective implementation of the NPT persists nonetheless, it is likely to erode this vital regime.

Chapter 7 integrates the empirical findings across the cases by returning to the questions raised in this introduction. It discusses the circumstances and factors which motivated international negotiators to take justice and fairness considerations seriously in the four cases. Notwithstanding their great diversity and differences, some conceptions were influential in more than one case. There are also similarities in terms of how such ideas affected the overall negotiation process and outcome, and how opposing notions were tackled. The notion of justice as a balanced settlement of conflicting claims corresponds well with how international negotiators themselves defined and acted upon the concept in most cases. The chapter concludes by outlining some directions which further work on this subject may usefully take.

2   Just and fair? An analytical framework

> Philologo-juridical obscurantism sits ill upon the mantle of Dame Justice and will not be permitted to besmirch the fair name of this court.[1]

We often take the importance of justice and fairness for granted, without being clear on the meaning of these values in particular contexts or how they affect our behaviour. What then concerns us exactly when we examine international negotiations? Are we merely interested in the terms of concluded agreements? Or are the conditions under which the talks take place also of concern; for example, issues of fair representation and any exploitative power relations? Do the principles which negotiators endorse, the purity of their minds, and the cleanness or not of their bargaining tactics matter? Or is justice achieved (and perceived to be so) when parties implement and comply with whatever bargain they have struck by whatever means, to their mutual advantage and consent?

In fact, all these aspects and more require attention. If we were to search in the negotiation literature, we would find largely theoretical answers focusing on outcomes. In reality, a range of justice and fairness issues arise in international negotiations and they play different roles, from the earliest phase when the talks are structured to the final phase of implementation and compliance.

This chapter presents an analytical framework which has been developed inductively from observations of negotiations and from insights based on the literature in several fields (see Albin, 1992). It identifies five categories of justice and fairness issues. These represent different points or stages in negotiations at which ethical considera-

[1] Flann O'Brien, *The Best of Myles* (1968).

24

tions arise. They concern the *structure* of the negotiations (the overall conditions and constraints under which deliberations take place; for example, issues of participation and representation, power relations, and the ordering of issues on the agenda); the negotiation *process* (the ways in which parties interact and behave as they build agreement, including the use of any deceptive or coercive tactics) and *procedures* (the mechanisms used to arrive at an agreement); the *outcome* (the principles governing the allocation of benefits and burdens in an agreement); and the *post-agreement phase* (matters of implementing and complying with commitments made, and their soundness over time with changing circumstances). As negotiations progress, the questions of justice and fairness thus change. The core issues are rarely the same prior to or during negotiations as they are after an agreement has been concluded. However, a single case will not necessarily raise important issues in each category.

The concept of justice as the balanced settlement of conflicting claims, set forth in the introductory chapter, normally requires examining negotiations along all these dimensions. At the same time, the framework can accommodate a variety of approaches to justice and is not merely an elaboration of this particular concept.

Conditions and constraints: structural issues of justice and fairness

We commonly associate justice and fairness with the results of negotiation. We may be tempted to regard an agreement as legitimate if it is based on some interpretation of a widely accepted norm such as equality and split-the-difference, or if it was concluded by the parties to their mutual advantage and consent. In a similar vein the literature on bargaining, further discussed below, tends to accept the conditions under which deliberations take place as a given. These conditions, including prevailing power relations and stated positions, provide a supposedly appropriate reference on the basis of which the nature of fair concessions and just solutions can be determined contextually inside the negotiation process. Major philosophers do not accept this approach: 'We cannot take various contingencies as known and individual preferences as given and expect to elucidate the concept of justice (or fairness) by theories of bargaining' (Rawls, 1971, pp. 134–5).

We must in fact step back and begin by examining the fundamental conditions under which negotiations occur in the first place. These can prejudice the conduct and progress of the talks and the terms of the outcome. They cannot be ignored in any serious conception of justice.

Parties to international negotiations themselves, particularly weak ones, will often question whether the overall structure of the talks could possibly yield anything just or fair. The arduous interim talks between Israel and the PLO over the implementation of the 1993 Oslo Accords, discussed in chapter 5, are a case in point. A disturbingly large segment of the Palestinian population denounces the entire Oslo peace process as coercive and unjust. This is partly because the Accords endorsed the Israeli occupation of the West Bank and Gaza as a legitimate starting point for negotiations, and because Israel used its power to continue settlement and land confiscation in these territories while talks were in progress (Khalidi, 1996).

The first cluster of justice and fairness issues thus concern the overarching structure of the negotiations, which in turn reflects the structure of the conflict and basic relations between parties. These structural components are the physical, social and issue constraints and parameters within which a bargaining process unfolds and negotiators operate. Most structural elements are determined in earlier preparatory discussions or by extraneous factors, and remain constant once formal talks have begun.

Parties

Some structural issues concern the parties to a negotiation, including any third parties: their identity and attributes (e.g., personality, culture, values, endowments), representation and relations, including power relations. Generally, offering every party a seat at the bargaining table is an important element of fairness which helps to ensure that all interests are given proper consideration (Susskind and Cruikshank, 1987). It influences public conceptions of the legitimacy of the outcome and the prospects of its implementation. An example is negotiations over the siting of unwanted facilities, such as hazardous waste treatment plants and prisons, in which much significance is attached to participation by neighbourhood residents and other groups most directly affected by the decision.

Ambiguity and disagreement over just who the legitimate parties are, however, is common. A vivid example is the controversies of recent years over whether human skeletal remains kept in museums and scientific collections should be returned for reburial to the indigenous people from whom they were taken. One argument is that whenever specific individuals or groups can be identified as direct descendants of the remains, they should be the chief party to an agreement with national authorities about appropriate usage. The view is that in this case, past injustices to indigenous people should be taken into account and that their permission be sought for any scientific usage of the human material. Some hold that when no direct descendants can be detected, by contrast, scientists serving valuable interests of the larger human community should have priority over the claims and concerns of any specific group (Jones and Harris, 1997).

On the international stage questions of who should be at the table, on what terms and why were relatively undisputed as long as matters of state security and other government affairs dominated bargaining encounters. Diplomats negotiating the end of wars and boundary disputes, the conclusion of defence or trade pacts and so forth fitted well the classic paradigm of states as the sole legitimate parties, supposedly representative and protective of all important concerns. As the use of negotiation has expanded into new areas, there is reason to re-examine the soundness of restricting formal participation to states. Many argue that large-scale negotiations over global issues, such as those conducted at the 1992 Rio 'Earth' Summit and within the UN Conference on Environment and Development (UNCED), implicate far more interests and even generations than governments can represent alone. The increased involvement of non-state actors in some areas of international decision-making suggests a *de facto* expansion of the traditional admissions criteria of statehood and sovereignty (Farer, 1995; Doherty, 1994; Albin, 1995). International organisations, multinational corporations and non-governmental organisations (NGOs) have assumed a variety of roles owing to their complementary expertise, representation of important interests, or ability to facilitate the implementation of agreements. Questions of what formal standing, if any, should be extended to such actors and particularly to NGOs, remain hotly debated.[2]

Representation raises another fairness issue, for it can prejudice the course of negotiations and prevent a balanced outcome. Every party normally claims the right freely to choose its own representatives, for

---

[2] A variety of perspectives and case studies on this subject can be found in Albin (1999).

good reasons. Until 1993 the ban on full participation by PLO members and East Jerusalem residents in peace talks with Israel served the objective, supported by Israel and the US, to keep the questions of Palestinian statehood and the sovereignty of Jerusalem off the negotiating table. A party may, of course, be unable to choose its own spokesperson. This is the case of small children in custody disputes arising from divorce, and of future generations or threatened non-human species in biodiversity negotiations. The task is then to select a representative which can credibly voice some notion of what that party's interests are or might be, independently of the control and interests of other parties to the dispute. Many analysts doubt the will or ability of national governments to represent the concerns of future generations within their territory adequately, and to ensure that issues are not settled at their expense.

Finally, unequal power relations can raise important issues. The introductory chapter pointed to different views in the philosophical and negotiation literatures on what power inequalities, if any, may be reflected in 'just' agreements. We noted that the overriding concept of justice in this study does not necessarily prohibit taking some inequalities into account. The key criteria are whether the overall arrangements are freely agreed, justifiable, reasonably balanced and so forth in the sense discussed earlier. It seems obvious, however, that if sharply unequal parties bargain, the process and its outcome may largely mirror their respective power or lack of it. They may then fail to reflect entitlements, contributions, needs, or other important considerations. Moreover, the stronger side may have acquired its bargaining strength by exploiting the other party's resources. As noted in the introductory chapter, some argue that one should not allow such past injustices and illegitimate acquisitions to be reflected in the starting positions for negotiations, in the issues being negotiated, or in the leverage and other bargaining tactics used (Gauthier, 1986). However, many international conflicts are intractable exactly because the legitimate owner of the disputed resources, the circumstances of their transfer into other hands, and any losses to be compensated are ambiguous and contestable matters. They cannot be judged with certainty even by legal or other widely accepted standards. The Israeli–Palestinian conflict, discussed in chapter 5, is a stark manifestation of this problem. A party's superiority and bargaining power may also merely reflect its own legitimate resources, but nevertheless impair the ability of the weaker side to protect its interests and to secure a balanced solution.

The presence and involvement of mediators and other third parties can influence the initial structure of negotiations. They can also change that structure once talks are underway by introducing their own interests and resources, and by supporting one side in the conflict more than the other. A powerful third party can indeed 'shift weight' and change an asymmetrical bargaining situation into a more symmetrical one, and *vice versa*. In order for the negotiation to be viewed as fair, the outside actor does not necessarily have to be neutral but is often expected to use its special relationship with any party to move it towards an agreement (Touval and Zartman, 1985). Charges of unfairness emerge if one party can lean on outside support to refuse making concessions, and to ignore the other side's need for a negotiated solution.

Issues

A second group of structural elements concern agenda-setting, and the nature and ordering of the issues to be negotiated. The importance of this activity for the success of the eventual outcome has been highlighted in some studies of pre-negotiation.[3] The influential justice and fairness issues which it can raise, however, have surprisingly been overlooked. Many international negotiations today take place within a framework of norms, principles and objectives set out in earlier multilateral agreements. This means that the agenda may already be set in broad terms prior to a particular negotiation. It also means that issues are negotiated in a normative context which is more likely to raise ethical questions. For example, the principles of 'good neighbourliness' and 'equitable utilisation of shared resources' as well as the duties to consult and exchange information are incorporated into the 1979 Convention on Long-Range Transboundary Air Pollution (LRTAP), the framework for the continuous negotiations over reducing acid rain in Europe. Reciprocity, fair competition and non-discrimination are norms incorporated into the GATT which play a central role today in negotiations within the WTO.

There is nevertheless a need to define issues and priorities on the

---

[3] See, for example, Gross Stein (1989); and *Jerusalem Journal of International Relations*, Vol. 13, No. 1, March 1991 (special issue on pre-negotiation).

bargaining table more precisely, and to decide about the order in which they will be discussed and any linkages between them. There is always scope for adding, reordering and subtracting some items. Negotiators naturally try to exploit this to create maximum coverage of the issues of most interest to themselves, and linkages which improve their own basis of bargaining and terms of trade. Linkages can thus be used to improve one side's leverage over the other side. One party can tie its readiness to move and make a deal on a particular issue to a willingness by the other to concede on another matter added to the agenda. Linkages of issues also suggest that legitimate trade-offs can be made between them. In talks over the siting of hazardous waste storage facilities, the weighing of safety and health concerns against offers of economic compensation is often seen as unethical. By contrast, some consider linkage between the protection of the global environment and issues of economic development in North–South negotiations, formally recognised since the 1972 UN Conference on the Human Environment, necessary to alleviate past injustices (Shue, 1992; Grubb *et al.*, 1993). This connection has certainly enabled LDCs to gain better terms of trade for complying with environmental regulations than would otherwise have been the case.

Agenda-setting is clearly significant for the conception of justice as a balanced settlement of conflicting claims. The major issue is the establishment of a reasonably broad and balanced agenda which includes, orders and links issues in a way which takes into account essential interests and concerns of all parties. It does not cater predominantly to one set of interests at the expense of others. This makes possible (but, of course, does not guarantee) a fair negotiation process in the sense discussed below, and an outcome which all parties can accept as balanced and worth honouring. We shall see that this conception is well supported empirically. LDCs at first opposed the inclusion of services on the agenda of the Uruguay Round of the GATT, for fear that their comparative disadvantages in this sector would reinforce North–South inequalities. There was also a general recognition that LDCs had been marginalised in the agenda-setting for earlier rounds of talks, and that industrialised states had not responded sufficiently to their concerns in areas such as agriculture and textiles. Eventually a broad agenda was constructed which balanced various competing interests, partly by making progress in talks on services conditional upon progress on issues essential to LDCs. The wide scope of the agenda permitted parties to make trade-offs across different issue areas and to formulate a package agreement considered fair and mutually beneficial overall.[4] In a different sphere, part of the international community and the Arab world consider the 1993 Israel–PLO Declaration of Principles (DoP) unfair in deferring the essential 'permanent status' issues (concerned with resources largely controlled by Israel) to the final stage of the negotiations. This view was strengthened by Israel's measures in the interim period to bolster its bargaining power over these issues even further and tilt the final talks in its favour, to the detriment of the Palestinian camp.

Rules

Rules and codes of conduct for negotiations, usually established prior to their launch, constitute another category of structural issues. Small-scale bilateral talks of limited duration may have few visible or official rules. Large-scale multilateral ones conducted over the long term, by contrast, are managed with explicit formal regulations which are often those of the forum or institution within which they take place. Rules concern voting and other methods of decision-making, the use of deadlines and procedures for communication, among many matters. Concerns about fairness arise if, for example, some parties do not have a chance to take part in the selection of the rules or are disadvantaged by them.

Voting may be open, in the name of transparency and account-ability, or it may be secret, on the grounds that this allows parties, weaker ones in particular, to voice their views freely without fear of repercussions. Decision by consensus is an established rule of pro-cedure in many international fora, which gives every party a power of veto and establishes equality between them in this sense. It reinforces the need to take all interests into account, and normally enhances the likelihood of a balanced outcome. The President of the 1995 NPT Review and Extension Conference regarded a consensus decision on extending the Treaty so vital for its moral authority and legitimacy, that he bypassed a Treaty stipulation saying that it should be decided by a majority vote. In this case, the use of consensus clearly helped to balance the competing concerns of nuclear and non-nuclear states in the final agreement.[5] However, the consensus rule may also enable a single party to hold all others 'hostage' to unreasonable demands, by threatening to block an agreement unless these are met. In the eyes of

---

[4] See chapter 4.   [5] See chapter 6.

many countries, this is what India attempted to do in the talks over a comprehensive test ban treaty within the Conference on Disarmament in the mid-1990s. They therefore considered it legitimate to bypass that forum, by submitting the final draft to the UN General Assembly for approval.

The organisational and physical features of negotiations

A final set of structural elements which may affect fairness is the organisational and physical features of the talks. These concern their location and sponsoring organisation, the provision of facilities and services, and access for audiences such as the media, NGOs and the general public. International negotiations are conducted in many different contexts but the institutional and organisational setting is often influential, as noted with respect to rules. International organisations can assume very active roles beyond their usual help with logistics, particularly in talks which continue over a long period of time. For example, selected staff can serve as chairs of the negotiations.

The site is known to influence the parties' control over physical arrangements, and their psychological mood and assertiveness (Rubin and Brown, 1975). The selection of a neutral site outside the home territory of either party and any close allies or, if the negotiations are expected to continue over a period of time, alternation between partisan sites, can therefore be important. Openness of the site and the negotiation process to public scrutiny is often seen as a fairness issue, which may affect how the outcome is eventually received and accepted (Susskind and Cruikshank, 1987). At the same time, transparency can cause inflexibility and undermine the prospects of an agreement: parties may be less willing to concede on official positions and experiment with new proposals if every move is observed and recorded in public.

Justice and fairness in the negotiation process

After years and even decades of bargaining, many international agreements are never implemented by countries whose cooperation is essential. One reason is that a few powerful states can dominate the formulation of the terms excessively, at the expense of other affected parties whose interests become marginalised. In the area of the environment, there are good examples of how the treatment of parties in the bargaining process influences the prospects of an effective outcome (Susskind, 1990). Some major powers do not even proceed to sign and ratify agreements which they have taken a lead role in negotiating themselves, to their own advantage. This was the case of the US with respect to the Law of the Sea Treaty and the Biodiversity Convention. They thereby also undermine the obligation and the incentive of other countries to honour these agreements.

The negotiation process refers to the pattern of interaction between parties as they attempt to reach an agreement. It includes the use of strategies and tactics by individual actors promoting their interests, joint problem-solving and concession-making. Processual issues of justice and fairness as here defined concern how parties relate to and treat each other in the process of negotiating, and how their ethical notions influence its dynamics.

'Fair behaviour'

This concept is elusive and resists an exact definition. The very nature of negotiation entails a measure of conflict and the use of some power, pressure and other competitive tactics. Fair behaviour concerns the degree to which rather than whether these are used – if the practice is 'fair enough'. The precise meaning of this depends on the context. There are nevertheless two matters which are essential to the concept of justice as a balanced settlement of conflicting claims. Negotiators themselves often associate fair behaviour or the lack of it with these matters, which find support in the academic literature (Earley and Lind, 1987; Lind and Tyler, 1988). The first is 'fair hearing' and 'fair input'. Does each party have an adequate chance to put forward its case and have an input into the process, from the stage when the problem is framed and options assessed to the point when the final agreement is formulated? Or is some party marginalised, possibly by a mediator or chairperson? A fair process is expected to consider as far as possible all affected interests, irrespective of the ability of the various parties to assert their concerns with force or even to be present in the negotiations.

A second related matter is 'fair play'. Are the rules of the game which the parties initially agreed upon, or subsequently changed by consensus, actually followed?[6] Do parties respect any principles intended to guide the negotiations according to previous agreement,

---

[6] The 'rules of the game' include many of the structural issues discussed earlier.

or do they compromise these to gain unilateral advantages? Does any third party involved respect its mandate? Do parties give truthful information about interests, priorities, options and their implications? There is usually some opportunity to 'bluff' about positions, alternative solutions, and the costs involved in making particular concessions. Purely tactical uses of ethical arguments, discussed in chapter 1, are an example of this. Under what conditions, if any, can the employment of such deceptive tactics be fair? Some considerations are the availability and acceptability (or not) of these tactics to all parties, the implications of everyone using them, the purposes for which they are used and access to other tactics which are less problematic ethically. In one argument, bluffing is unacceptable unless all parties know and accept that it is indeed part of the game (Lax and Sebenius, 1986). A final aspect of 'fair play' concerns whether every party is free to accept and reject proposals without being subjected to coercion and threats. According to the notion of justice as a balanced settlement of conflicting claims, stronger parties clearly need to refrain from pressurising the weak and dispossessed into accepting terms which, to most impartial observers, would appear unreasonable or even exploitative. Negotiation by its very nature cannot merely entail redistributions from the well endowed to the impoverished. But nor can it simply reflect power inequalities if it is to be considered just and fair.

The influence of justice and fairness on the negotiation dynamics

What impact do these values have on bargaining? At the level of individual actors, fairness notions influence the demands and expectations brought to the table, the formulation of bargaining positions, the evaluation of concessions and proposals, and the satisfaction with and ultimate stability of the outcome. They can be important in determining a party's 'bottom line', the minimum for which it is prepared to settle. A party will ask if the concessions which it is asked to make are justified given what is offered in return. Evaluations of the value of what is traded are rarely uniform. Yet a party will frequently view an agreement as unfair if it appears to leave others far better off than itself.

Subsequent case studies will demonstrate the many roles which ethical norms and concepts play on the collective plane. They may trigger the onset of negotiations, set the agenda, constrain the freedom of action of parties, influence the terms of the eventual agreement, enhance compliance with it, and cause uproar over violations. At the most basic level, they can affect the negotiation process in two ways: they may *guide and facilitate the deliberations* by coordinating expectations and helping parties forge an agreement; and they may complicate talks by *becoming subject to negotiation themselves*.

First, principles of justice and fairness can play an instrumental role in bargaining. This pertains to situations in which the parties from the outset have similar notions of a reasonable solution. These then help to coordinate expectations, to avoid confrontations and stalemates, and to forge timely and durable agreements in ambiguous situations with multiple alternatives. In other words, justice and fairness serve as referents guiding the negotiations and the exchange of concessions. In the research literature such shared notions are described as 'focal points' which emerge as obvious and desirable because of cultural norms, precedent, custom, analogy or other factors (Schelling, 1960). They tend to decrease competitive behaviour, speed up concession-making, and make a successful agreement more likely (Deutsch, 1973; Bartos, 1974). These effects are partly explained by the fact that a shared notion helps to reduce the inclination of each party to over-value its own concessions and underestimate those of the other side.

A common focal point is the idea of absolute equality, understood as 'split-the-difference' or equal shares. It requires, or appears to require, the same concessions from parties even when they are unequal. Let us take the example of a couple attempting to divide household chores between themselves. If they share a belief in equality, it will guide their efforts to find a workable arrangement. The task is to decide exactly what an equal distribution will entail in terms of tasks, effort, time or financial input. Will they do about 50 per cent each of all the chores (to the extent they are divisible), will they take turns doing them, or will they each take separate responsibility for about half of the chores? Or will the couple contribute equally to paying for a domestic helper?

Justice and fairness certainly play a facilitating role in some international negotiations. The absence of sharp power inequalities appears to be significant, a condition known to foster effective negotiation and mutually satisfactory agreements (Rubin and Brown, 1975). When parties perceive themselves as roughly equal, notably in their dependency on reaching an agreement and on future cooperation, they are more likely to harbour similar notions of a fair outcome. They are motivated to reciprocate concessions and search for a balanced solution. Their equality implies that attempts simply to maximise individual gains and forge some other type of agreement may cause costly delays and even fail.

Frequently, however, parties have conflicting conceptions of justice and fairness. They endorse opposing principles or interpretations of these, and disagree on the legitimacy of alternative solutions. Divergences in cultural norms, historical experience, resources, and responsibility for the problem under consideration are common contributing factors. Such opposing beliefs cannot coordinate or facilitate any deliberations. They become part of the dispute itself and can lead to violence and war (Welch, 1993). When dialogue remains possible, there are four ways in which a negotiated agreement can still be reached:

- parties may agree to conclude an agreement for reasons other than justice or fairness (that is, agree to redefine the problem and settle it based on other considerations);
- parties may resort to using a method they regard as fair to reach an agreement; for example, a random method such as flipping a coin which grants them equal chances to 'win', or 'divide-and-choose' (see the discussion below);
- the parties may agree to base the agreement largely on one side's understanding of what is reasonable, notably in situations of power asymmetry; or
- they may choose somehow to address and balance their conflicting ethical conceptions, through compromise and/or problem-solving.

Regarding the first and third ways, a party with superior bargaining power may not be motivated to contemplate, let alone act upon, others' ideas about justice. It may not experience any need to reassess its own principles, or even to be concerned with such values at all. When the weaker party has no choice but to accept what is on offer, the stronger side could secure a favourable outcome which largely reflects its own strength. In the interim talks with Israel, Palestinian negotiators were unable to infuse their notions of fairness into the bargaining over many issues. At times they were also hesitant to do so, since this could remove incentives for Israel (backed by the US) to participate. Despite rhetorical references to legal and ethical principles, Palestinian negotiating behaviour was motivated to a large extent by pragmatic considerations of what could be achieved from an acutely weak position (Sayigh, 1996; Khalidi, 1996). Deadlock or breakdown in negotiations may also result if a weak party or its constituency refuse to compromise on their understanding of justice in the name of 'realism' and 'rationality'. They may prefer to suffer any unavoidable losses instead.

The significance which parties attach to their principles means that the success of many international negotiations depends on somehow addressing and balancing conflicting ethical conceptions. This can be done by exchanging concessions and striking a compromise ('horse-trading') based on stated positions about a just and fair outcome. It may also be possible to achieve by use of a more problem-solving, integrative mode of negotiation. As mentioned in chapter 1, this refers to strategies which seek to combine and reconcile fundamental interests and needs underlying official positions in a conflict, in order to bring about more mutually beneficial and stable solutions. In such a process, new options may be created or discovered which meet the essential concerns of all parties and minimise the need for costly compromises. It stands in contrast to distributive negotiation which encourages concession-making with reference to official positions.[7]

One classic work holds that the criteria whereby negotiators evaluate what trades are equitable and what compromises are fair are but perceptions and beliefs which are 'continually modified by the bargaining process . . . it is the negotiation that develops and changes them' (Iklé, 1964:167). Genuine conceptions are not so malleable, nor can negotiation always change them. Certain problem-solving strategies can nevertheless help negotiators with opposing principles and interests to reach satisfactory agreements (Albin, 1997c; Sjöstedt and Spector, 1993). Several strategies seek to reduce the burdens involved in making a concession in order to enhance the perception of its fairness and beneficialness. As we shall see in subsequent case studies, they do so by cutting costs, providing compensation,

---

[7] While the problem and positions are already well defined by the time distributive bargaining gets under way, reconceptualisation of the issues is at the core of integrative strategies to allow new sets of possible trades and new options to emerge (Albin, 1991). Good negotiators find ways to exploit any differences between them by having each trade concessions on its less-valued items in exchange for concessions on other items it values more (Homans, 1961). Such differences may concern interests, capabilities, resources, expectations and indeed conceptions of fairness. Negotiators thereby create more mutually beneficial agreements.

expanding resources, or linking issues which are prioritised differently. Others use analogies to draw upon proposed or successful solutions to comparable cases. These strategies, while simple in concept, may encourage a reframing of the problem and greater creativity in the search for new alternatives. They are used implicitly in some international negotiations, but not as extensively or systematically as they could be.

Let us return briefly to the couple trying to divide their household chores. The man may believe in absolute equality while the woman argues that other considerations must also guide the distribution; for example, the fact that she works longer hours outside the home, brings in more income and is not much at home to enjoy the fruits of either her income being spent or the household work. A solution satisfactory to both is likely to represent some middle ground, or at least one which will allow for compensation to the party whose concerns are ill met. For example, if the woman agrees in principle to the idea of equal division, she may be able to buy herself out of some chores by hiring a domestic helper.

Many agreements in the international sphere strike a balance between different principles. For example, the 1987 Montreal Protocol on Substances that Deplete the Ozone Layer combined several norms to take account of the varied conditions and concerns of signatory states. The proportionality principle drove the Protocol's call for reductions, beginning in 1993, in chlorofluorocarbon emissions in relation to each country's emissions level in 1986. It thereby imposed a greater (unequal) cost of regulation on industrialised countries. Compensatory justice underlay the provision for financial and technical assistance to the South, and the principle of need their exemption from the stipulated emission reductions for the first ten years for purposes of economic development. Finally, the equality norm was expressed in the long-term goal of the North and the South sharing regulation costs on a basis of parity.

When conflicting notions of justice or fairness are at the heart of international bargaining and eventually result in a balanced agreement, sharp power inequalities tend to be absent. Parties refuse to forego their own principles entirely, but are nonetheless willing or compelled to recognise that standards other than their own may be valid and important. In other words every party must usually have some strength to reject unreasonable proposals and uphold its principles, if these are to be considered seriously.

Procedural issues

This category concerns the specific mechanisms used to arrive at an agreement. They may be diffuse and difficult to observe with precision, such as reciprocation. Others are clearly defined and explicit, such as voting and computer models employed in complex multilateral negotiations. All procedures could be viewed as raising a subset of process fairness issues. The essential distinction is that procedural fairness concerns the features of the mechanisms themselves, while process fairness refers to how the mechanisms are actually used (for example, if in good faith and without bluffing).[8] Negotiators can adopt and even design procedures in the bargaining process, or may establish these in advance as part of the rules of the game and overall structure of the negotiations.

Some procedures can be regarded as inherently fair in the sense of relying on impartial criteria, requiring equal concessions from parties, or giving them an equal chance to 'win'. They may nonetheless result in a very uneven allocation of benefits and burdens between parties. Scientific computer models have been welcomed in environmental negotiations by virtue of generating proposals based on ecological criteria, but often place a heavy cost burden on a few states. We will see how this problem has been handled to date in the European acid rain talks. The discussion here will now focus on procedures involving reciprocity, fair chance and fair division.

Reciprocity

Many procedures are mechanisms which govern the exchange of concessions in bargaining. One is reciprocity; that is, mutual responsiveness to each other's concessions. It is widely regarded as a principle which is intrinsically moral and impartial. It has even been labelled 'one of the universal principal components of moral codes' (Gouldner, 1960), which is instrumental in achieving cooperation in an anarchical international system (Iklé, 1964; Axelrod, 1984). Some philosophical approaches regard reciprocity as central to and indeed as a criterion of justice (Gauthier, 1986; Gibbard, 1990). Others see an element of justice in reciprocity under certain conditions; for example,

---

[8] This definition differs from that found in the literature, which uses the terms 'procedural' fairness and 'process' fairness interchangeably to refer to the negotiation process generally. Regarding game theoretical notions of the role of fairness and fair procedures in negotiations, see Brams (1990) and Prasnikar and Roth (1992).

if the baseline used to assess benefits is based on equality between the parties and is accepted freely without coercion (Rawls, 1971). Even under such conditions, Barry's theory of justice as impartiality rejects reciprocity as having the 'distasteful features of justice as mutual advantage' which excludes from ethical considerations all those who are unable to provide benefits for others (Barry, 1995, p. 50).

Academic studies of negotiation distinguish in detail different patterns of reciprocity (Cross, 1978; Walton and McKersie, 1965). They include *equal concessions*, whereby comparable concessions are exchanged in reference to initial positions; *equal sacrifices*, whereby parties make concessions causing them to suffer equally in their respective eyes; and *tit-for-tat* whereby a party responds to the other's move by matching it in substance and scope, thus responding to toughness (softness) with the same toughness (softness). *Responsiveness to trend* entails that each party makes concessions based on an evaluation of a series of moves by the other side, whereas *comparative responsiveness* means that each party acts on the basis of a comparison of its own and the other's tendencies to concede (Druckman and Bonoma, 1976). The argument is that parties will practise reciprocity when they view themselves as comparable in power, or agree on a particular outcome as fair and desirable. For example, if a split-the-difference solution is envisioned, it encourages the exchange of equal concessions (Bartos, 1974). One investigation found that 'comparative responsiveness' was the predominant pattern of concession-making in international negotiations over base rights and arms control (Druckman and Harris, 1990).[9]

Negotiation always involves the exchange of concessions. It is required to move the process forward, and to arrive at a mutually satisfactory agreement. The concept of justice as a balanced settlement of conflicting claims calls for a measure of reciprocity as well: all able parties are expected to contribute in some form, although not necessarily with concessions of the same size or kind. What sort of reciprocity is called for and from whom will, once more, depend on the relevant contextual details; for example, individual abilities, resources and entitlements. We may call this 'diffuse reciprocity', in the sense that the emphasis is on achieving arrangements which, all things considered, are reasonably balanced overall. It stands in contrast to measuring fairness by the extent to which specific conces-

---

[9] See further chapter 6.

sions are reciprocated on a bilateral (or other) basis. One reason is that this latter measuring rod may establish fairness only on the surface. It assumes that the starting positions of the parties can be accepted at face value as a reference point for determining the nature of fair concessions and a fair solution. If one party's position is far more inflated than the other's, or reflects resources and strength acquired forcefully at the expense of the other, the exchange of 'equal' concessions is unlikely to result in a balanced outcome which can be freely accepted. A second reason is that in the real world parties often value the same goods and concessions differently, and disputed resources or burdens are rarely perfectly divisible. They may not even be tangible, but largely symbolic. In this context 'specific reciprocity' – whether equal concessions, equal sacrifices, tit-for-tat or something else – may have little meaning or be nearly impossible to apply.

It is standard for international negotiators to regard reciprocity as essential to fairness, and to behave accordingly. Although the concept assumes different substantial meanings depending on the context, fairness was very rarely defined as 'specific reciprocity' in the cases examined in this book. In the Uruguay Round of the GATT, a case of negotiations over trade liberalisation in which many concessions are indeed possible to measure and compare with relative ease, the US delegation held that too many states had become free-riders and failed to shoulder the costs of the free trade system. It was determined to prevent countries from being able to gain from the liberalisation measures of others without taking adequate steps to open up their own markets. The US emphasis on reciprocity understood as the creation of an overall balance of concessions and reciprocal benefits became very influential in this round of trade talks. What appears to count most of the time is a rough sense that enough reciprocity has taken place to establish a balanced package agreement.

Procedures involving fair division, fair chance or a 'fair say'

Reciprocity seldom functions as the overriding procedure in large-scale multilateral talks, whose complexity reduces the appreciation and role of individual concessions. More manifest mechanisms are used with defined rules codifying interaction. They help to systematise and simplify decision-making, and facilitate agreement in the midst of a large number of parties, interests and issues. They do not always involve much bargaining in the sense that concessions are exchanged or divergent interests reconciled. Negotiation may be used instead to agree on the particular procedure to be used, and the outcome may involve clear winners and losers. The inherent fairness of the chosen procedure then assumes great importance.

Procedures of 'fair division' stipulate how limited resources are to be allocated. An example is *divide-and-choose*. It refers to the old custom of how to deal with two children fighting over a cake they both want. Their mother decides that one of them will cut the cake, and then the other will choose the first piece. Thus the child who cuts the cake will be induced to do so fairly, otherwise the other will choose the larger piece. A variation on divide-and-choose, which goes back to Rawls (1971), is to negotiate a division before knowing or deciding which part each will have. This has been endorsed as a procedure to promote intergenerational equality; for example, when it comes to establishing the rights and obligations of current and future generations regarding the use and protection of environmental resources (Weiss, 1989).

Divide-and-choose has on occasion contributed to the success of international talks. In the complex Law of the Sea negotiations, it was used to determine the allocation of mining sites on the deep seabed (Sebenius, 1984). It normally assumes that the parties either value the resources similarly, or that they refrain from exploiting differences in evaluations selfishly. If the divider knows the other's preferences and these are different from his own, he can often divide in a way that gives himself the larger share.

Other procedures employed in international negotiations are designed to give parties a 'fair say', or a 'fair chance' to influence the terms of an agreement or to 'win', while managing the complexity of the process. *Voting* is one. Another is the use of a *single negotiation text*. It requires parties to bargain and make concessions focusing on the same draft. A mediator or other third party usually writes and introduces the initial text, and then modifies it in several stages as parties put forward criticisms and suggestions for changes. Proposals in line with the principles of the original text are more likely to be included, so the soundness of these are important. Parties themselves can also take turns controlling the modifications of the text. A single negotiation text was successfully used in the US-mediated Camp David talks between Israel and Egypt, and in the Law of the Sea negotiations. Many multilateral environmental talks use single negotiating texts drafted by representatives of the organisation which hosts them.

Random methods such as *tossing a die*, *flipping a coin*, and arranging a *lottery* can be used as fair chance procedures. They usually assume initial equal entitlements to the resources and therefore give parties an equal chance to win. However, the odds of winning can be adjusted to reflect divergent initial rights. While perhaps appearing too simple and crude for any but the most trivial disputes, random procedures are used in significant political and social contexts. They may be employed when no outcome can be quite fair, as in the case of an indivisible resource or burden; when an agreement is needed quickly; or when the parties are unable to agree on a solution (Eckhoff, 1974). Disputants can resort to random methods when the stakes are so high that fully fledged bargaining seems inappropriate or unethical, and to avoid the ambiguity and manipulability of other instruments.

A serious case has been made for employing lotteries or tossing a coin to settle indeterminate child-custody disputes, so as to avoid the emotional harm to children of lengthy negotiation and litigation (Elster, 1989). Lotteries are actually used to allocate dangerous tasks and missions in the military in some countries. In the last years of the Vietnam War, the US military drafted young men according to their birth dates and arranged a random draw to establish the order in which they would be called to duty (Young, 1994). Finally, lottery systems have been recommended in decision-making about the siting of hazardous facilities, to determine which short-listed sites should be exempted from further consideration (Kasperson, Derr and Kates, 1983).

There are ways to reduce or eliminate unfair usages of some procedures. In the case of 'divide-and-choose', the divider's advantages can be neutralised (Young, 1994). Nonetheless, any mechanism used unwisely or dishonestly can lead to distorted outcomes which do not honour the rules of the game initially agreed upon. From the viewpoint of justice as the balanced settlement of conflicting claims, a main concern is that random mechanisms produce winner-takes-all solutions. They do not aim to take into account the parties' values, resources or other factors which would have been essential if the outcome was to appear reasonable and to secure voluntary agreement in another context. They may therefore not be durable, and may damage the long-term relations between parties. Yet, when all other avenues to an agreement have failed, randomisation can be used to establish ownership and subsequent negotiation may then reduce some negative side effects.

Issues of outcome fairness and justice

The outcome of a negotiation may take a variety of forms. It may be a specific agreement, a general framework for continued talks on particular arrangements, or deadlock and failure to reach a joint outcome (with possible agreement to re-attempt negotiation at a later stage). In international multilateral decision-making, it is common practice first to negotiate a framework convention which defines shared principles, goals and institutional arrangements for continued talks over the long term. Under such a convention, specific protocols are then drafted over a period of time.

Another category of justice and fairness issues concerns what principle(s) should guide the allocation of benefits and burdens in an agreement. While addressed in the negotiation process, they pertain to the outcome. Among the important questions which negotiators ask are: what terms will be balanced enough to secure widespread approval and support? What kind of agreement can be justified on grounds that everyone can accept as legitimate? What is, and what will be seen as, the appropriateness of taking these considerations into account and applying these criteria over others? Different principles can yield drastically different distributions. A single principle rarely emerges as sufficiently authoritative on its own. This explains in part why issues of outcome fairness and justice can be so prominent and disputed in international negotiations.

As discussed in the introductory chapter, there are three basic types of standards which may be used: internal, external, and impartial. We shall see that in contrast to what the literature proposes, negotiators usually employ these in combination to determine the nature of a balanced agreement.

Internal (contextual) criteria

These define the meaning of justice or fairness inside the negotiation process without reference to any external guidelines. A widespread notion is that the mere fact that something has been negotiated and agreed is a strong indication that it is legitimate. Negotiation is a form of decision-making which takes place when the parties to a problem prefer a joint solution. Even a weak party is allegedly empowered to veto an outcome which it views as unfair by breaking off the talks (Zartman, 1991). Just agreements are then, in this notion, based on terms which the parties themselves have established and voluntarily agreed to honour. These must be mutually beneficial. There is no place for justice or rationality outside the context of mutually beneficial cooperation, since parties strive to maximise their own gains. A 'just' and rational agreement must, it is argued, leave every party better off than it would have been without it. These contextual notions normally accept prevailing power relations as given, and do not require the negotiation process to fulfil any particular requirements. Many agreements will naturally reflect relative bargaining strength as measured by each party's BATNA, and yet be taken as perfectly just and fair.

External criteria

A second approach holds that just outcomes are to be based on well-recognised distributive principles whose general content is external to particular bargaining situations. These include equality, proportionality, compensatory justice and need.[10] A main task of negotiation is to reach consensus on what standard is to be applied.

As noted in the previous chapter the principle of *equality*, advocating the allocation of identical or comparable rewards and burdens to parties, can be interpreted in a number of different ways. International negotiators frequently endorse the notion of equal resource distributions. It converges with intuitive, popular ideas about intrinsic or impartial justice ('all countries should be treated the same') and enjoys wide acceptability as a basis for concession-making which supposedly produces fair agreements. In this interpretation the equality principle is relatively simple and unambiguous in both concept and application. It can be justified to important constituencies. Forging some other type of agreement often requires more time, information and justification (Schelling, 1960). Intrinsic and popular appeal, legitimising power, simplicity, and explicitness are indeed valuable advantages in any complex international negotiation. In coming chapters, we will see negotiators apply the equality principle to issues as diverse as acid rain emission reductions and arms control measures when operating in a difficult political or scientific context.

A drawback is that international negotiators frequently resort to the norm without taking account of whether countries, while equal in their legal status as sovereign states, are indeed equal in relevant respects. Much emphasis has been placed on uniform treatment as an

---

[10] See chapter 1 for a conceptual discussion of these.

intrinsic value in itself, in isolation from other pertinent differences among parties. Therefore the principle has often served to establish justice and fairness only in a limited sense. When European states were asked to reduce their different acid rain emission levels by the same percentage, the actual result was that poor East European countries were required to undertake some of the greatest and most costly measures to the benefit of richer countries.

International negotiators frequently apply the *proportionality* principle as well, as subsequent chapters will show, particularly when they recognise themselves as unequal. Unlike the equality norm (as commonly interpreted), this standard seeks to establish justice and fairness by taking account of pertinent differences among parties in their assets and contributions, broadly defined. A shortcoming is that the proportionality principle leaves ample scope for controversy: what justifies unequal treatment? What are the relevant 'inputs' and their worth? What is the proper ratio of inputs to rewards? Furthermore, variations such as 'equal sacrifices' and 'equal excess' require negotiators to agree on ways to measure and compare different experiences of loss and gain, and reveal any tactically distorted portrayals of these.

The principles of *compensatory justice* and *need* are applied less frequently in international affairs, and usually in combination with other principles. In international trade negotiations under the GATT and in the WTO, differential and preferential treatment of LDCs in view of their special development and economic needs is one established principle among several others. It has influenced many environmental negotiations as well, resulting in privileges such as exemptions and extended deadlines for LDCs. Compensatory justice and need nonetheless pose many challenges, particularly in an international context. As for the first principle, the relation of the compensation to the damages suffered is often more decisive than its amount. The more directly the compensation can address the costs suffered or the benefits lost by unjust treatment, the more likely it is to be accepted.[11] However, among the requirements are to specify the

---

[11] An example from domestic affairs is affirmative action in university admissions to compensate for equal opportunities earlier denied, as opposed to financial compensation for discriminatory hiring practices. Foa and Foa (1975) argue that the more intangible (or personal) a resource is – for example, status as opposed to money – the more intangible (or personal) the good should be for which it is replaced. This reciprocation-in-kind rule reduces, and can even eliminate, the perceived costs of both delivering and accepting compensation.

nature of the inflicted harm, find resources that can serve as adequate compensation, identify the parties who should supply the compensation and those who should receive it, and motivate the former to provide the remedy.[12] For instance, while many countries have surely suffered injustices from colonialism, who is to compensate whom today for what harms and how? Many conflicts with an ethnic component involve resources and issues which are perceived as irreplaceable, partly for symbolic reasons. A case in point is the Israeli–Palestinian struggle for Jerusalem.

Impartial criteria

These indicate features which a negotiation process and outcome ought to have. The first chapter showed that the specific requirements vary across approaches which endorse a notion of impartiality. They vary particularly with the assumptions made about the motivation to behave justly. However, they all agree that negotiations which take place in a coercive or manipulative context are unacceptable. When successfully used, threats and coercion may deprive a party of resources or benefits without regard for its needs or entitlements, and undermine cooperation in the long term. They also agree that impartiality entails constraining the role of narrow self-interests and the use of power. In the words of one analyst:

> Justice is about not squeezing people for everything one can get out of them, especially when they are already much worse off than oneself . . . a willingness to choose to . . . accept only agreements that are fair to others as well as to oneself. Justice prevents negotiations from being the kind of rational bargaining that maximises self-interest no matter what the consequences are for others. There are some bargains too favourable for a just person to accept. Justice means sometimes granting what the other party is in no position to insist upon. (Shue, 1992)

Subsequent chapters will show that this kind of looser notion of impartiality corresponds well with those of international negotiators faced with concrete and complex issues. The blind pursuit of self-interest without regard for others, the exploitation of weak parties, coercion and involuntary agreement are all matters which they associate with injustice and unacceptability.

---

[12] O'Neill (1986, 1991) discusses problems of determining rights to compensation in an international context.

Choosing and combining criteria

There has been no systematic examination of what factors determine the choice of criterion in international negotiations, or of how parties in fact balance and combine different types of standards. Social-psychological research findings suggest that perceptions of justice and the choice of principle in interpersonal negotiations are influenced by age, status, gender, culture and the nature of the relationship between parties and their goals (Piaget, 1948; Sampson, 1975). For example, need appears as a predominant standard when individual welfare is a common goal. Equality is fundamental when good long-term relations or solidarity are valued. Proportional distribution takes precedence when economic productivity is the primary concern (Deutsch, 1975). Different cultures certainly have different understandings of justice. One would expect these to play more of a role when a small number of parties negotiate for a brief time period. Processes involving numerous parties over the long term are prone to diminish the role of national cultures, possibly in favour of transnational 'professional cultures' (see Lang, 1995). In the cases examined in this study, the normative context of the talks was a prime factor influencing the choice of criteria.

International negotiators frequently use a combination of principles to weigh all pertinent factors and to forge an agreement. The combined criteria are internal, external and impartial. Among the internal ones, the mere fact that something has been debated and agreed is commonly perceived as a strong indication of fairness. Moreover, many high-level negotiators interviewed for this study indicated that one aspect of fairness is that agreements must deliver benefits to all parties, although the benefits should be 'balanced'. The external principles used come from the normative framework within which the talks are conducted. Some are particular to certain issue areas (e.g., the 'polluter pays' principle), while others are found across issue areas (e.g., differentiated obligations based on economic ability). Absence of coercion and voluntary agreement are impartial standards which negotiators clearly endorse.

Impartial procedural standards are at the core of the notion of justice as the balanced settlement of conflicting claims. It does not endorse any particular external substantial principles, but the emphasis on balancing different interests and standards clearly calls for their use as well. Reliance on internal criteria alone is inadequate especially in a situation of sharp power inequalities. In such a context negotiation is unlikely to produce legitimate outcomes unless certain requirements are fulfilled, or else justice is simply defined in terms of the prevailing balance of forces.

Justice and fairness after the agreement

Once an agreement has been signed, justice and fairness involve two essential matters: the extent to which its principles and distribution of benefits or burdens remain sound over time; and actual implementation and compliance with it. Renewed talks may be needed to combat free-riders and ensure that all parties honour their part of the bargain, or to adjust the original terms in light of new developments. In subsequent chapters the 1995 NPT Extension and Review Conference, the Israel–PLO interim talks and the Uruguay Round of the GATT all provide poignant examples of how decisive these issues can be. The role of justice, fairness and negotiation in this stage, which often determines whether an agreement on paper will result in an effective outcome, has hitherto been uncharted territory. It stands in sharp contrast to the extensive knowledge accumulated on processes of formal bargaining and pre-negotiation.

A range of factors can erode the legitimacy of an agreement over time. First, the issues may be such that they cannot be resolved conclusively in negotiations. Scientific knowledge about the nature of a problem, the possible remedies and the effects of these may still be evolving. Important new information may come to light after an arrangement has been made which reveals deficiencies in the original provisions. The surrounding political and even moral environment may change and cast doubts on hitherto accepted practices. This last factor has certainly played a role in a case mentioned earlier: it helps to explain the recognition of indigenous groups as a party to new agreements on the uses of historic human remains, and the return of such material to many affected aboriginal communities or the placement of limitations on scientific uses of them.

Secondly, one or more parties may not proceed with implementing an agreement, or may delay doing so for years at the expense of other compliant parties. In respect of the environment, extensive post-agreement negotiations both between and within countries are often required to resolve complex technical, legal and political questions surrounding the ratification, monitoring and enforcement of treaties

(Spector, 1992a, 1992b). Domestic stakeholders not directly involved in formulating the terms of international agreements, such as industry, business, political parties, and grass-roots organisations, can also play a role. They may see their own interests too adversely affected by national implementation of the provisions, and succeed in blocking or delaying it. Reluctance to concede sovereign rights, a perceived lack of urgency, and insufficient incentives to comply can pose even more fundamental difficulties (Susskind, 1994; Weissbrodt, 1982). States can sometimes avoid honouring an agreement and yet enjoy many of the same benefits as participating countries; that is, gain unfairly from the compliance by others. If it transpires that the costs of an agreement are in fact paid by a few to the benefit of others, its durability is likely to depend on reducing or eliminating such free-riding.

Thirdly, countries which have not taken part in negotiating an agreement can impede its goals and impose losses not only on signatory parties but the entire international community. Future agreements on greenhouse gas emission reductions, for example, will almost certainly be ineffective without the participation and colla-boration of highly populous states such as China, India and Brazil. The failure of former Israeli Prime Minister Netanyahu to honour the spirit of the 1993 Oslo Accords on several issues contributed to a deep sense of injustice and growing support among ordinary Palesti-nians for Hamas, the Islamic resistance movement which rejects the peace process. In early 1996 and early 1997, Hamas succeeded in bringing the Israel–PLO negotiations and interim agreements to the brink of collapse by staging suicide bombings inside Israel. PLO leader Arafat's inability to prevent this violence and the loss of Jewish lives in turn led Netanyahu to place new conditions on the continuation of the talks, and even to consider terminating them altogether.

The introductory chapter argued that honouring freely negotiated agreements is essential in the notion of justice as a balanced settlement of conflicting claims. We here recognise that agreements can some-times become unjust and unacceptable over time, for different reasons. New talks may be required to restore their legitimacy. The process may have to include new actors and conditions, adjust the allocation of benefits and burdens, or build more flexibility into the provisions to maintain fairness over time with changing conditions. This may necessitate a reinterpretation of the principles underlying the original arrangements, or entirely new ones.

Conclusion

This chapter has developed a framework which identifies the major points at which ethical issues arise in international negotiations. They relate to the structure, process, procedures, outcome and the post-agreement phase. The framework highlights an important argument of this study, that it is not enough solely to examine the distributive principles and terms underlying negotiated agreements. Issues arise already when the talks and the agenda are arranged, and continue to do so long after the formal agreement has been signed. A notion of justice as the balanced settlement of conflicting claims, and indeed any serious approach to justice and fairness in international bargaining, require examining all these five dimensions.

They are, of course, closely interrelated both in concept and in practice. Structural issues of justice impact upon the fairness of the negotiation process and the terms and acceptability of its outcome. Notions of a fair solution often influence the choice of procedures. This includes situations in which there is so much conflict over the substance of a solution that parties resort to using a mechanism which all can accept to determine the outcome. The duty to implement and honour an agreement cannot be separated entirely from its terms and principles, nor from the process by which it was formulated. If either is seen as illegitimate, the risk of non-compliance is considerable.

Justice and fairness issues do not always arise, and are rarely equally important, at all five levels in one and the same case. If the negotiation structure, process and procedures are already well established and accepted, the focus is likely to fall more on the question of what principles should guide the terms of an agreement. The chapter on the European air pollution negotiations provides an example of this. In other instances, the very nature of the issues (e.g., the prevention of global climate change and the preservation of biological diversity) makes it difficult to measure and calculate with certainty the benefits and costs associated with alternative outcomes. The negotiation structure and process, including the representation of all affected interests, may then be subjected to greater scrutiny. Disputes in which no outcome can be fair, possibly because the good or burden is indivisible and nothing else can serve as adequate compensation, may highlight the importance of procedures used to settle the problem. Finally, the judgment that some party has not honoured its part of an agreement, while benefiting from others' compliance with it, can provoke deep resentment. It may overshadow all other issues, including any earlier reservations about the terms of the agreement itself. This was the case during the 1995 NPT Review and Extension Conference and in the aftermath of the negotiation of the Israel–PLO interim accords.

We must beware of single-factor models and explanations, which characterise the traditional literature on bargaining. International negotiations are certainly not driven by considerations of justice and fairness alone. In order to win acceptance agreements must also be mutually beneficial, politically feasible, verifiable, and so forth. The coming chapters will pay close attention to how the role and influence of ethical conceptions are affected by factors such as the political, institutional and normative setting; power relations; scientific knowledge (or lack of it); national domestic politics and interests; assessments of the requirements for reaching a successful negotiated agreement; and the exercise of leadership.

In analysing complex cases of international negotiation, the framework elaborated here provides direction and guidelines. It is flexible enough to allow us to do so from many different perspectives, and to tease out at what level and in what sense issues of justice or fairness did play a role in a specific instance. It makes few *a priori* assumptions about any particular negotiation, and permits us to learn from a wealth of empirical data about a subject which remains disputed and little understood among scholars and practitioners alike.

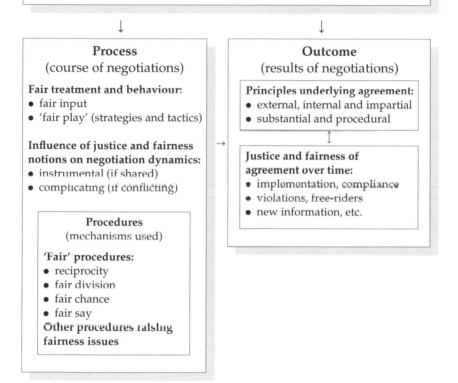

Structure
(conditions and constraints)

Context and forum of negotiations:
- any guiding principles or norms
- sponsor (e.g., institution or organisation)
- site (e.g., if open, neutral)
- access to information, other support

Parties and participants:
(direct and any third parties)
- standing and role
- representation
- power relations

Rules
(e.g., of decision-making)

Agenda-setting:
- who establishes the agenda
- issues included and excluded
- order and linkages of issues

↓   ↓

Process
(course of negotiations)

Fair treatment and behaviour:
- fair input
- 'fair play' (strategies and tactics)

Influence of justice and fairness notions on negotiation dynamics:
- instrumental (if shared)
- complicating (if conflicting)

→

Outcome
(results of negotiations)

Principles underlying agreement:
- external, internal and impartial
- substantial and procedural

↕

Justice and fairness of agreement over time:
- implementation, compliance
- violations, free-riders
- new information, etc.

Procedures
(mechanisms used)

'Fair' procedures:
- reciprocity
- fair division
- fair chance
- fair say
Other procedures raising fairness issues

Note: Entries are illustrative and do not constitute a 'complete list'.

Figure 1   Issues of justice and fairness in negotiation:
an analytical framework.

3   Negotiating the environment: justice
      and fairness in the battle against
      acid rain

The key question driving the negotiations has been, 'What would be
an acceptable agreement?' Equity figures into this, because no one
can force you to sign an agreement.[1]

Bargaining over the environment: the centrality
of justice and fairness

In recent years, environmental negotiations have assumed a prominent place in international affairs. The first concerted international
effort to address environmental issues was the UN Conference on the
Human Environment held in Stockholm in 1972, which also recognised their connection to questions of economic development. This
landmark conference was followed by multilateral talks over marine
and air pollution, ozone depletion, hazardous wastes and North–
South trade and aid, among other matters. Until the fall of the Berlin
Wall and the end of the Cold War, however, such negotiations, being
unrelated to the superpower competition, remained in the diplomatic
backwaters. The relatively low priority and limited attention they
attracted from the major powers, and the prevailing East–West
hostilities, made negotiations outside the areas of 'high politics' ill
equipped to produce breakthroughs.

The phenomenal increase in the number and range of environmental talks in the last decade stems partly from the improvement in
East–West relations, and the expanded notions of national interests
and international security which this change has stimulated. One

---

[1] Ambassador Lars Björkbom, Chair of the acid rain negotiations within the UN
Economic Commission for Europe (UN-ECE) (personal interview, 1997).

54

aspect of this redefinition is the recognition that the protection of many environmental resources is integral to national and international welfare, and requires transboundary cooperation at unprecedented levels.[2] The result of another hallmark event, the 1992 UN Conference on Environment and Development (UNCED) in Rio de Janeiro, was the development of principles, goals and procedures for both new and continued negotiations over threats such as ozone layer depletion, climate change, air and water pollution, the loss of biodiversity, desertification, deforestation and hazardous wastes.[3]

Conducted at the global, regional and bilateral levels, environmental talks have certain features which set them apart from other negotiations (Faure and Rubin, 1993; Albin, 1995). These characteristics help to explain why international environmental decision-making tends to be so complex and protracted, despite the urgency of measures being undertaken in many areas. Among the attributes are the significance of scientific knowledge and evidence to the progress of negotiations; the limitations of conventional instruments of power and state control; and the involvement of non-state actors such as scientists, engineers, representatives of international agencies, and lobbies defending ecological as well as business interests. Environmental talks are often conducted in the shadow of general principles, legal or ethical, pertaining to the problem at hand. These may be enshrined in multilateral framework agreements, which then provide a broad normative context within which specific measures are negotiated over a period of time. The 1979 Convention on Long-Range Transboundary Air Pollution (LRTAP), under which several protocols on acid rain emission controls have been drafted, is founded on principles such as 'good neighbourliness' and 'no harm', 'polluter pays', the equitable utilisation of shared resources, and the duties of cooperation, exchange of information and consultation.

---

[2] There is now a considerable literature discussing the concept of 'environmental security'. See, for example, J. Tuchman Mathews, 'Redefining Security'. *Foreign Affairs*, Spring 1989; R. H. Ullman, 'Redefining Security'. *International Affairs*, Summer 1983; *Our Global Neighbourhood*. The Report of the Commission on Global Governance (Oxford, 1995); T. F. Homer-Dixon, 'Environmental Scarcities and Violent Conflict'. *International Security*, Summer 1994; and I. Rowlands, 'The Security Challenges of Global Environmental Change'. *Washington Quarterly*, Winter 1991.

[3] Analyses of the Rio Conference and the broader UNCED process can be found in Grubb *et al* (1993) and Spector, Sjöstedt and Zartman (1994). Susskind (1994) assesses the achievements and shortcomings of global environmental treaties both within and outside the UNCED process.

Another feature of environmental negotiations is the presence of dual and conflicting time frames. In the long term they promise significant benefits, particularly to future generations. In the shorter term, however, they are often of a 'win–lose' nature as they must distribute financial and other burdens among countries whose gains from environmental protection can vary considerably. Negotiations over new or unallocated environmental resources which promise near-term benefits, such as those over the Law of the Sea and Antarctica, are increasingly rare.[4]

A major hurdle in reducing transboundary environmental threats is how to tackle fundamental questions of justice and fairness. These concern the exploitation and preservation of scarce or finite environmental resources which are essential to human well-being, the international allocation of the high costs of protective measures coupled with inequalities between countries and, many would argue, obligations of present generations to future ones. Poor states hold that they should not have to compromise on their own welfare or economic development in order to bear the cost of resolving environmental problems, especially those caused mainly by rich industrialised nations such as climate change and ozone depletion. They maintain furthermore that all countries, regardless of their financial or technological assets, should have equal access to the 'global commons' (resources considered to be held in common by or affecting the international community as a whole).

These arguments have influenced negotiations over several issues including transboundary air pollution, ozone depletion, the protection of the world's seas and oceans, and international trade in toxic wastes. For example, many industrialised countries exporting their hazardous wastes to poor countries for cheap disposal once sought global regulations based on the principle of 'prior informed consent'. This would permit trade if the recipient agreed to import the waste before it was sent. Developing countries, by contrast, viewed any regulation as the legalisation of an unjust practice and insisted on an outright ban of the practice (Clapp, 1994). The 1988 Basel Convention adopted the principle of 'prior informed consent' with additional conditions, but by 1994 the UN Environment Programme had established a global

---

[4] This and other obstacles in international environmental negotiations are discussed in 'Developments in the Law. International Environmental Law'. *Harvard Law Review*, Vol. 104, 1991.

ban on international trade in toxic wastes. Negotiations over climate change and biodiversity are still in a too early stage to suggest how the justice issues which they raise, and which are recognised in the Biodiversity and Climate Change Conventions, will be handled.

The European acid rain talks provide a fascinating case study of how justice and fairness issues can influence international negotiations, and how they interact with factors such as political 'pragmatism', domestic politics and interests, and scientific considerations. Like climate change and many other environmental issues, it raises clear-cut questions about obligations and cost-sharing because of differences in responsibility between polluting and victim countries, in sensitivity to the problem and gains to be had from regulatory agreements, and in economic and technological ability to implement protective measures. As further discussed below prevailing economic and environmental efficiency criteria tend to require poor European countries with few resources to undertake the greatest and most costly measures, to the benefit of rich countries which often have more to gain from abatement. Unlike the climate change case there is now a solid record of the acid rain talks conducted for more than two decades under the LRTAP Convention within the UN-ECE, which serve as the focus of this chapter.[5] They have resulted in decisive emission reductions over time, and in the development of effective mechanisms to monitor and tackle air pollution which may be used in other threatened regions such as South Asia. While European acid rain abatement clearly could not have succeeded as well as it has without addressing some justice and fairness issues, questions about the distribution of the cost burden remain.

The European acid rain negotiations: an overview

The basic distributive issues in negotiations over air pollution concern who should undertake emission cuts (given inequalities in past, current and future projected emission levels) and at whose cost (given differences in resources, responsibility for the problem, and in gains to be had from regulations), and by how much emissions should be reduced and by when (given at once the high costs of abatement and the devastating effects of pollution on some countries). How then

[5] Another important forum for negotiations over European acid rain is the EU (previously the EC).

have governments handled these issues? What notions of justice and fairness have actually influenced the process to date and why? How have conflicting conceptions been tackled? Do issues of justice and fairness appear to have had a bearing on the results and the success of the negotiations?

We will discover that the European acid rain talks have raised difficult issues of justice and fairness ever since their inception in the mid-1970s. The parties accepted early on the overall structure, process and procedures of the talks under the UN-ECE, which are well-established. The controversial issues have largely concerned the outcome – the distribution of the burdens and benefits arising from acid rain abatement.[6] We will see that the political and scientific context of the negotiations has influenced the extent to which equity considerations have been taken into account. For a long time, East–West hostilities and mistrust, along with scientific uncertainty and conflicting arguments about the benefits to be had from costly abatement measures, pervaded the discussions and left little room for ethical concerns. As one negotiator recalls: 'In the past, we had to work one against the other, at least that was the feeling' (Kakebeeke, 1997). The end of the Cold War, coupled with improved scientific evidence of the causes and harmful effects of transboundary air pollution, changed this situation. Starting with the deliberations over a second sulphur protocol in 1991, the talks have become less political and more 'problem-solving' in nature. They have also been grounded in agreed scientific and environmental criteria, allowing certain conceptions of justice and fairness to play a greater role.

A fundamental basis and engine of negotiations over acid rain and other environmental problems is the principle of 'no harm'. It holds that states must avoid harming the environment of other countries and, when they fail to do so, remedy the damage caused. Improved scientific evidence has strengthened the role played by this principle over time (that is, the claims to a right to remedy advanced by

[6] There have been disagreements over other matters. Eastern European states did not recognise the EC as a separate negotiating party when the acid rain talks first got started within the UN-ECE. More recently, some countries have argued that a fair process requires greater openness and transparency in the scientific modelling work supporting the negotiations. The data and values used to calculate optimal abatement strategies with integrated computer assessment models, such as the RAINS model discussed below, should be exposed to greater scrutiny (Williams, 1997). However, unlike climate change and several other environmental cases, such disputes over rules of procedures and parties have not marked the UN-ECE acid rain talks significantly.

countries suffering unprovoked harm from transboundary air pollution), and has helped to drive forward the process of reaching agreement on emission controls. Apart from this norm, however, arguments about justice and fairness were generally not taken seriously and had no real impact on the UN-ECE acid rain talks during the first decade. We will note that political, tactical and scientific considerations explain the heavy reliance on the principle of equal percentage reductions during this time, when the first sulphur protocol was negotiated. By contrast, from the latter part of the 1980s and onwards several, partly conflicting notions of outcome fairness and justice, and 'horse-trading' among these and other concerns, guided the talks.

The differentiation of obligations, given inequalities in circumstances and resources among countries, has been an influential principle in the acid rain talks, as in those over ozone depletion (reflected in the 1987 Montreal Protocol on the Depletion of the Ozone Layer) and climate change (reflected in the 1992 Climate Change Convention). We will see that it was expressed in the second sulphur protocol (the Oslo Protocol) of 1994 which, in allocating targets and deadlines for fulfilling emission cuts, took into account environmental impact according to the 'critical loads' criterion. This is a measurement of susceptibility to ecological damage from acid rain. 'Critical loads' refers to deposition levels for sulphur as well as nitrogen below which significant harmful effects on specified sensitive elements of the environment (including forests, freshwater and fish) do not occur according to present knowledge. The use of this criterion alleviated bitter conflicts over how to credit countries which had already undertaken abatement measures and faced more costly options for further emission cuts. The LRTAP Convention states that acid rain abatement policies should take into account efforts already made at the national, as well as international, levels (Article 3). Another important feature of the Oslo Protocol is the differentiation of emission targets and deadlines with a view to economic ability. Taking account of divergences among countries has been critical to the progress in acid rain abatement since the end of the 1980s. Indeed, negotiators have come to view responsiveness to such considerations as vital to effective cooperation on environmental protection.

One major fairness issue, which arose especially in the drafting of the Oslo Protocol, remains unresolved: the most environmentally effective and cost-efficient abatement measures tend to impose heavy burdens on poor polluting states, with relatively few resources and gains to be had from combating acid rain. Calls for financial and technological transfers to these states have not been acted upon in the official talks to date. By contrast, such resource transfers have been an important part of other environmental agreements and their success, including the 1987 Montreal Protocol. It is too early to assess whether this will have a major impact on the fulfilment of commitments made under the second sulphur protocol. Without such 'cost-sharing' in the future, however, the need to continue to compromise on environmentally required acid rain emission targets in order to accommodate poorer countries appears unavoidable.

Getting talks underway: the role of scientific evidence and the principle of 'no harm'

'Acid rain' has come to refer to transboundary air pollution generally. Several kinds of air pollutants can travel over long distances in the atmosphere, before they are deposited on the earth's surface. The chief ones are sulphur dioxide (SO_2), nitrogen oxides (NO_x), volatile organic compounds (VOCs), and ammonia (NH_3). Scientific understanding has deepened dramatically about such emissions: their sources (notably coal- and oil-fired power and heating stations, combustion plants, machines, and road and off-road vehicles), their transport across national boundaries, and their damage to forests, freshwater, agricultural crops, ecosystems and buildings.

Acid rain remains a serious environmental problem today. One issue is the steady deterioration in the condition of European forests. A survey in 1994 showed that between 20 per cent and 60 per cent of the sample trees in eighteen European countries, and over 26 per cent of the total sample, were defoliated or discoloured. The most severely affected areas are found in Central and Eastern Europe, but defoliation is also high in parts of northern and south-eastern Europe.[7] Scandinavian lakes and fish populations continue to suffer considerable damage. There is at present no consensus among scientists on what linkages, if any, exist between air pollution levels and human

---

[7] 'The State of Transboundary Air Pollution'. Report prepared within the framework of the Convention on Long-Range Transboundary Air Pollution. Air Pollution Studies, No. 12. Economic Commission for Europe, United Nations, Geneva, 1996 (ECE/EB.AIR/47). It should be noted that air pollution is one of several probable causes of the observed damage to forests.

diseases or deaths. Different research studies have yielded different conclusions and interpretations. A major UK study published in 1997 established a temporal, but not a causal, relationship between increases in air pollution levels caused by road traffic fumes and increases in heart attacks (Poloniecki *et al.*, 1997; Poloniecki, 2000). In Bulgaria, SO_2, NO_x and VOCs emissions have been reported to have adverse effects in parts of the country which are inhabited by over 40 per cent of its population.[8]

The commencement of negotiations over European air pollution was triggered by Scandinavian countries, particularly Sweden which argued that foreign sources of SO_2 emissions were responsible for the acidification of its lakes. The 1972 UN Conference on the Human Environment greeted these Swedish assertions with scepticism, but adopted unanimously the principle of 'no harm' among other norms. An investigation by the Organization for Economic Cooperation and Development (OECD) verified soon thereafter that imported sulphur was indeed causing the numerous problems reported in Scandinavia, including forest decline, acidification of lakes, and reduction in fish populations. Another turning point was the 1975 Helsinki Conference on Security and Co-operation, at which the Soviet Union proposed the environment as a relatively apolitical area for pursuing the East–West dialogue (Sokolovsky, 1997). Sweden and Norway managed to secure air pollution as the focus of these discussions (McCormick, 1989). The OECD lacked the appropriate membership, as well as legal mechanisms for ensuring the implementation of agreements. The UN-ECE, representing Western and Eastern Europe as well as North America, therefore became the organiser and forum of the talks that got underway in 1977.

The first achievement in the negotiations was the UN-ECE Convention on Long-Range Transboundary Air Pollution. Signed by thirty-four countries and the European Community (EC) in 1979, it entered into force in 1983. It contained none of the commitments to actual reductions in SO_2 or NO_x emissions on which Sweden and Norway had insisted. The opposition was too fierce from a coalition of acid rain exporters, led by the United Kingdom (UK) and the Federal Republic of Germany (FRG) which relied on coal-fired power stations.

---

[8] 'Strategies and Policies for Air Pollution Abatement'. 1994 major review prepared under the Convention on Long-Range Transboundary Air Pollution. Economic Commission for Europe, United Nations, Geneva, July 1995 (ECE/EB.AIR/44).

The Convention established vague obligations to limit and, 'as far as possible', gradually reduce and prevent transboundary air pollution. Yet, together with EC environmental legislation, it has provided the main institutional frameworks and principles for subsequent negotiations over specific emission cuts. The UN-ECE was given the administrative and secretarial responsibilities for implementing the Convention (Article 11). The organisation has also become influential in the actual bargaining process. It has several of its senior advisors on the Executive Body, the Convention's main organ, and plays a role in working groups and meetings in which protocols are drafted. While *ad hoc* working groups previously negotiated protocols under the LRTAP Convention, the Executive Body created in November 1991 a permanent body, the Working Group on Strategies, responsible to itself. This group is now in charge of negotiating and implementing new protocols.

Eight protocols relating to the Convention had been concluded by early 2000. The first five were the 1984 Protocol on financing the European Programme for Monitoring and Evaluation of Transboundary Air Pollution, the 1985 Helsinki Protocol on the reduction of SO_2 emissions, the 1988 Sofia Protocol on the control of NO_x emissions, the 1991 Geneva Protocol on the control of VOC emissions, and the 1994 Oslo Protocol on further SO_2 emission reductions. They were followed by the adoption of the 1998 Protocols on Heavy Metals and Persistent Organic Pollutants, and the 1999 Protocol to Abate Acidification, Eutrophication and Ground-Level Ozone.[9] We will focus on examining the talks leading to the Helsinki Protocol, the Sofia Protocol, and the Oslo Protocol.[10]

[9] The texts of the LRTAP Convention and most of the protocols to date can be found in *1979 Convention on Long-Range Transboundary Air Pollution and its Protocols*. Economic Commission for Europe, United Nations, Geneva, October 1996 (ECE/EB.AIR/50). The 1998 Protocols on Heavy Metals and Persistent Organic Pollutants were published in ECE/EB.AIR/66, and the 1999 Protocol to Abate Acidification, Eutrophication and Ground-Level Ozone was still being prepared for publication in early 2000. Lars Björkbom, a key participant in all the talks under the LRTAP Convention to date, points out that the drafting of the protocols was perceived and presented as an extension of the LRTAP Convention. In fact, however, they are free-standing in the sense that the Convention does not foresee the negotiation of protocols or other specific instruments on acid rain abatement (Björkbom, 1997b).

[10] Overviews of the problem and politics of European acid rain can be found in Park (1987); T. Schneider, ed., *Acidification Research: Evaluation and Policy Applications* (proceedings of an international conference, Maastricht, The Netherlands, 14–18 October 1991); J. Alcamo, R. Shaw and L. Hordijk, eds, *The RAINS Model of*

The early days: equal percentage reductions as a facilitating principle

Soon after the signing of the LRTAP Convention, the Scandinavian countries, still bitter victims of transboundary air pollution, continued their efforts to secure actual cuts in SO_2 emissions. They won an unexpected powerful ally in 1982 at the Stockholm Conference on the Acidification of the Environment. The FRG, until then a major exporter of SO_2 emissions opposed to reductions, on this occasion turned into a vigorous proponent of abatement. The possible risk of getting the German Green Party into a pivotal position in Bonn after the 1982 election, and the discovery that acid rain was damaging German forests extensively, triggered the sudden change of heart.

At the first session of the Executive Body of the LRTAP Convention in June 1983, two blocs of countries confronted each other. Sweden, Norway, Denmark and Finland proposed a 30 per cent equal percentage reduction in the SO_2 emission levels of 1980 by 1993, with one important exception: credit would be given to those countries which had recently reduced their SO_2 emissions. The FRG, Switzerland and Austria, while endorsing this plan along with Canada and Denmark, added that the best available technology (BAT) which was economically feasible should be used to achieve these cuts. This stricter proposal also targeted SO_2 emissions from mobile and smaller sources, and referred to the possibility of NO_x emission reductions (Chossudovsky, 1988). The US, the UK, France, the Soviet Union and several Eastern European countries formed a second bloc which objected to any substantial emission cuts. The UK and the US for their part argued that more research was first needed to increase scientific understanding of the causal relationship between domestic SO_2 emissions and acid deposition abroad. This strong opposition meant that once again only a vague agreement was reached on the need to decrease SO_2 emissions 'effectively' (Lammers, 1991).

Disappointed by the inaction, the ministers of nine Western European states and Canada assembled in Ottawa in March 1984 and formed the '30 Per Cent Club'. They thereby committed themselves to

Acidification. Science and Strategies in Europe (Kluwer Academic Publishers, Dordrecht, The Netherlands, 1990); Boehmer-Christiansen and Skea (1991); J. Carroll, ed., *International Environmental Diplomacy* (Cambridge University Press, 1988); and Fraenkel (1989). Chossudovsky (1988) provides a more detailed account of the negotiations leading to the Helsinki Protocol than is possible to include in this chapter.

unilateral cuts of at least 30 per cent in their 1980 levels of SO_2 emissions over a ten-year period. Another eight Western and Eastern European states joined the Club at an environmental conference in Munich three months later. The influence of the Soviet Union secured the inclusion also of the Central and Eastern European countries. This was significant given the nature of the acid rain problem, and the requirement of at least sixteen ratifications for the protocol to enter into force. The creation and expansion of the 30 Per Cent Club put pressure on other countries to follow suit, and set the stage for the talks leading to the 1985 Helsinki Protocol.

Across-the-board 30 per cent cuts in SO_2 emissions (by 1993 based on 1980 emission levels) emerged once again as the formula acceptable to most participating countries in these talks.[11] Scientific knowledge was most advanced about ways to combat air pollution caused by SO_2 emissions, and the parties therefore agreed to focus on this pollutant. The majority of states also endorsed the choice of 1980 as the baseline year, which had been widely accepted for some time. Most national emission levels had peaked around this time, and monitoring and data concerning emissions prior to 1980 were unsatisfactory. However, a dispute arose over the arguments of the US and the UK that an earlier base year be selected, so as to credit them for SO_2 emission reductions undertaken in the 1970s. The two countries held that the choice of 1980 was unfair, placing a heavier burden on them by disregarding earlier reductions and requesting them to undertake the same percentage cuts as other states (Nitze, 1997). Initially the Dutch delegation made a similar argument about being entitled to credit for pre-1980 reductions. It then accepted the proposal of a 30 per cent cut in 1980 emission levels, having calculated that the Netherlands would be able to honour it (Kakebeeke, 1997). Other parties considered the UK and US abatement measures prior to 1980 insufficient and rejected their request for an earlier base year, which would have required insignificant or no further reductions of them.

Eastern European negotiators objected to the suggested uniform obligations, and attempted unsuccessfully to promote a multi-tiered protocol. Under this proposal, countries not yet able to undertake a 30 per cent reduction by a fixed date would be offered the alternative of a

[11] 'Positions and Strategies of the Different Contracting Parties to the Convention on Long-Range Transboundary Air Pollution Concerning the Reduction of Sulphur Emissions or their Transboundary Fluxes'. Economic Commission for Europe, United Nations, Geneva, 6 August 1985 (ECE/EB. AIR/7).

lower reduction target, a freeze in SO_2 emissions, or an extended deadline (Levy, 1993). Having eventually accepted the equal percentage approach, the Soviet Union pressured other Eastern bloc states also to agree to a 30 per cent emission cut. Among those which did officially, knowing that they lacked the necessary national abatement programmes to achieve the goal, were Czechoslovakia, East Germany, Bulgaria and Hungary (Zurek, 1997). The Soviet delegation pointed out that national emissions which were unharmful to other countries did not violate any international norm, and fell outside the scope of the LRTAP Convention which targets transboundary air pollution only. It was therefore 'unfair' to regulate such national emissions. Moscow then managed to secure the inclusion of the option to reduce transboundary fluxes. This permitted the country to fulfil its own obligations under the protocol quite cheaply: the Soviet Union moved its emission sources eastward and thereby reduced transboundary fluxes. The concession was essential to secure Soviet adherence to the Helsinki Protocol.

The final terms of the protocol required member states to reduce national annual SO_2 emissions or their transboundary fluxes by at least 30 per cent compared to emission levels in 1980, as soon as possible and no later than 1993. Parties were also urged to consider further cuts beyond this requirement 'when environmental conditions warrant'.[12] Twenty-one states signed the protocol in Helsinki in July 1985, including polluters such as France, Italy and the Soviet Union which had previously rejected emission controls. It entered into force in September 1987. Nine of the thirty parties to the LRTAP Convention chose not to adhere, most of them for reasons involving arguments about justice or fairness. Poland, which had never accepted the equal percentage approach, held that it lacked the abatement technology and financial resources necessary to achieve a 30 per cent reduction. Poland did not sign the protocol despite Soviet pressures to do so (Zurek, 1997). Four relatively poor countries (Spain, Greece, Portugal and Ireland) had already been permitted under an EC provision to increase their SO_2 emissions, so that their economic development would not suffer.

Most notable was the failure of the UK, Western Europe's greatest SO_2 emitter, and the US, the world's greatest SO_2 emitter, to sign. Both

---

[12] The Helsinki Protocol of 8 July 1985, Article 3, in *1979 Convention on Long-Range Transboundary Air Pollution and its Protocols*, Economic Commission for Europe, United Nations, Geneva, October 1996 (ECE/EB.AIR/50).

countries held once again that the terms of the protocol were arbitrary, and that existing scientific evidence was insufficient to justify the costs involved. The US insisted that the substantial emission cuts which it had undertaken prior to 1980 should be taken into account. The UK Minister of State at the Department of the Environment stressed that the 30 per cent reduction and the chosen baseline year had no particular legitimacy over other, at least equally justifiable standards. If the protocol had demanded a 40 per cent reduction based on the year of peak emissions, for example, the UK would already have fulfilled its obligations.[13]

By the target year of 1993, all parties to the Helsinki Protocol had reduced their national SO_2 emissions by at least 30 per cent. Taken together they had reduced the 1980 levels of SO_2 emissions by 48 per cent. Eastern European countries reached their targets largely because of their severe economic situation in the early 1990s. Twelve parties to the protocol had achieved cuts of at least 50 per cent.[14] Having resisted a formal commitment to the 30 per cent goal, the UK and Poland reported that their emissions too had in fact decreased by at least this percentage. Decline in domestic economic activity was an important reason behind the Polish achievement. The UK government ceased denying in 1986 that SO_2 emissions, including from UK power stations, were causing transboundary damage and that scientific knowledge about the damage justified substantial abatement measures. This new recognition diminished the relevance of UK arguments about credit for pre-1980 emission cuts. Nonetheless, the UK, like the US and Poland, among the greatest producers of SO_2 emissions, did not become parties to the protocol.

Explaining the Helsinki Protocol negotiations

Matters involving controversial justice and fairness issues triggered the most difficult phases in the talks leading to the Helsinki Protocol. These disputes over specific emission limits, choice of baseline year, and time for implementation ultimately concerned the question of

[13] Speech by William Waldgrave, UK Minister of State at the Department of Environment, to the German Foreign Policy Society, Hamburg, 1985, quoted in Lammers (1991).

[14] 'Strategies and Policies for Air Pollution Abatement'. 1994 major review prepared under the Convention on Long-Range Transboundary Air Pollution (quoted above), Tables 1 (p. 4) and 17 (p. 137).

whether abatement requirements should take account of differences among countries, such as divergences in past clean-up efforts, access to modern abatement technology, and capacity to afford protective measures. The negotiations never resolved these disagreements satisfactorily in the eyes of several polluting countries, which eventually chose not to sign the protocol. The US and the UK certainly used fairness arguments tactically to serve domestic interests and to justify their positions, but genuine perceptions of unfair treatment also contributed to their decision not to sign (Björkbom, 1997b; Nitze, 1997).

The principle of uniform reductions clearly influenced the course and outcome of the talks significantly, and an alternative approach was never seriously considered. At first it may seem to have played such a pivotal role as a standard of justice. The principle of equality is rooted in Western political thought and is applied frequently in international negotiations, understood as equality in benefits, burdens or obligations regardless of differences in resources, contributions or other circumstances. It appears to have had some intrinsic appeal also in this case. Relying on this notion 'would at least give the impression that all [countries] had to make the same effort at the same time' and accept the same burden (Kakebeeke, 1997). In the European acid rain talks, however, the widespread use of equal percentage cuts had little to do with the parties' ideas about fairness. In fact, several countries, among them the Soviet Union, Poland and other Central and Eastern European states, made clear that they considered the approach an unfair, inadequate and unscientific way of tackling the acid rain problem: it failed to reflect the real inequalities among countries in emission levels, in contributions to transboundary ecological damage, and in economic resources (Sokolovsky, 1997; Zurek, 1997).

Why then did so many countries accept a sulphur protocol based on this approach? How did the 30 per cent figure become such a significant standard for evaluating national abatement efforts? Importers of acid rain, notably Sweden, Finland, Norway and Canada, proposed equal percentage cuts as early as in the mid-1970s. When the LRTAP Convention came into force in 1983, the Scandinavian countries proposed the negotiation of a protocol calling for at least 30 per cent cuts in SO_2 emissions. The 30 per cent figure was introduced on a trial basis, 'to start the ball rolling towards a target, which hopefully could be defined and defended on scientific grounds later on' (Björkbom, 1997c). In the Helsinki Protocol talks specifically, it was expected to facilitate substantial emission cuts at a time when pollution levels were alarmingly high and the Convention had yet to result in any actual reductions. This figure was judged to entail the strongest possible measures which states would not find too demanding economically or otherwise, and which they therefore could support. For example, existing abatement technology in a number of key countries was estimated to make a 30 per cent reduction feasible (Klaassen, 1996). The clarity of the concept and application of uniform obligations was also a significant advantage given existing scientific uncertainties and the tense Cold War climate. These calculations proved their value with the creation of the 30 Per Cent Club in 1984. The normative pressure which the Club and the 30 per cent norm could exercise on reluctant states secured a rapid growth in its membership.

The high degree of scientific uncertainty at the time also explains the broad acceptance of uniform obligations in the Helsinki Protocol talks. Very little was known about critical loads, the relative contribution of a given country's emissions to acid deposition in other states, and the depth of emission cuts which would be required (and from whom and by when) to reach particular environmental goals. While also exploiting this insufficient knowledge as an excuse for inaction, the US and the UK were thus right to claim in the negotiations that the principle of uniform cuts and a 30 per cent reduction lacked scientific justification and that the environmental benefits of undertaking the costly measures were unclear. However, an agreement based on differentiated obligations (larger cuts and burdens for some states, and lighter or no burdens for others) would have called even more for a precise and solid justification, probably involving scientific evidence which was not readily available (Churchill, 1997). Uniform reductions thus emerged once again as the politically most realistic and, under the circumstances, reasonable approach to the majority of participating countries. It was a means to secure a common basis for action without the need for prolonged discussions about scientific data or past abatement efforts.

Although Soviet President Brezhnev sought to make the environment an area of successful East–West cooperation, Cold War tensions and mistrust prevailed throughout the Helsinki Protocol talks. Eastern European countries did not share data on their emissions when this could disclose information about sensitive activities, and the West did not accept some statistics released by the Eastern bloc (McCormick, 1989). The politicised climate helps to explain the positions and behaviour of many parties, and the narrow scope for discussing arguments about fairness and environmentally based approaches seriously. The East–West division may also have played a role in the rejection of Poland's request that a sulphur protocol accommodate countries not yet able to undertake a 30 per cent reduction by a certain date, and of Soviet suggestions for exchange of advanced technologies (Sokolovsky, 1997). Soviet pressures certainly pushed many Eastern European countries to sign the Helsinki Protocol. These states may in fact never have intended to implement it, and may in any event not have been able to do so in the absence of the economic recession which later occurred (Kakebeeke, 1997). In sum, the talks took place in a competitive environment which favoured a simple approach such as uniform reductions to ensure some progress.

As in other international negotiations, the political and economic interests of countries influenced the Helsinki Protocol talks significantly. While cost–benefit calculations led most to accept 30 per cent reductions, they also caused a few states to refuse to sign the protocol. The US had under its 1970 Clean Air Act (amended in 1977) already committed itself to SO_2 emission cuts which enjoyed a domestic political consensus and was not prepared to move further (Nitze, 1997; Park, 1987). Moreover, it was far more engaged in the dispute over air pollution with Canada. Therefore, the US may not have signed the Helsinki Protocol even if it had approved of its terms. The UK, an exporter of acid rain with relatively little to gain from the protocol, was also reluctant to commit itself to new measures for domestic reasons. At the time it was considering privatising the electricity sector, and the country's future energy requirements were uncertain.[15] By contrast, among victims such as the Scandinavian countries and the FRG, domestic pressures for effective action were strong and influential. Apart from the promise of a healthier environment, Sweden and the FRG were keen to develop a lucrative export industry of clean technology These economic interests stood in sharp contrast to those of Central and Eastern European countries, which depended on imported technology to meet new emission reduction requirements. In sum, however, most states saw the protocol as either

---

[15] Speech by William Waldgrave, UK Minister of State at the Department of Environment, to the German Foreign Policy Society, Hamburg, 1985, quoted in Lammers (1991).

compatible with their existing national abatement plans, or as well within their capacity to honour (Björkbom, 1997b).

These political, scientific and tactical considerations explain how the principle of equal percentage cuts came to influence an important international negotiation extensively, all while ignoring and in some cases violating certain conceptions of fairness. Many countries easily met and outperformed their Helsinki Protocol obligations because of already existing national abatement plans. Some analysts therefore argue that the SO_2 emission cuts achieved from 1985 and onwards would have occurred even without this international agreement. However, it is clear that the protocol put legal constraints on the future emission levels of signatory states, strengthened the LRTAP Convention considerably, and stimulated continued negotiations on further air pollution regulation. Experience would soon vindicate the proposition that 'once the first step in a regulated and managed process of multilateral co-operation is taken, the inner logic of the need to go further tends to assert itself inexorably' (Chossudovsky, 1988).

The 30 per cent reduction standard succeeded in maintaining the momentum in the talks and in facilitating agreement by virtue of its simplicity. But in due course its drawbacks became all too apparent with respect to fairness, environmental effectiveness and economic efficiency. There are in fact no objective criteria for selecting a required percentage reduction, a reference year on the basis of which cuts or ceilings will be calculated, or a target year by which requirements are to be achieved (Haigh, 1989). Any such percentages, years and ceilings are bound to be arbitrary, notably in how past reductions and present emission levels are treated.

More generally, the equal percentage approach cannot recognise differences in responsibility for the acid rain problem, in resources available to reduce it, and in gains to be had from abatement measures.[16] The actual distribution of the collective costs and benefits resulting from reducing national emission levels by an identical

---

[16] Under national reduction plans of the early 1990s, rich countries with very low SO_2 emission levels, such as Switzerland (62 kton in 1990) and Norway (54 kton in 1990), would be able to undertake cuts of about 50 per cent by 2000 compared to 1980, at the cost of merely 0.01 per cent and 0.09 per cent of their GDPs, respectively. By contrast, Poland would undertake a 37 per cent reduction of its SO_2 emissions (3,210 kton in 1990) at the cost of 0.31 per cent of its GDP annually, and Ukraine a 56 per cent reduction in its SO_2 emissions (2,782 kton in 1990) for 0.44 per cent of its GDP, by the year 2000 compared to 1980 (Klaassen, Amann and Schöpp, 1992).

percentage will therefore be very unequal across countries. Many heavily polluting states required to undertake the greatest cuts in real terms are least able to afford abatement strategies, such as the development of alternative energy sources and 'add-on' technologies (e.g., the use of low sulphur fuels and desulphurisation of fuels). In addition, they often prioritise other more imminent needs. Such factors reduce the number of states willing to accept agreements based on uniform obligations, as in the case of the Helsinki Protocol. This approach also ignores differences in the sensitivity of various ecosystems, and imposes limits on the total level of national emissions without targeting transboundary emissions specifically. It does not distribute reduction requirements among countries in such a way as to attack the pollution problem most effectively on a regional scale.

Searching for greater effectiveness and fairness: the Sofia Protocol negotiations

Negotiators learnt from these early experiences, and used more sophisticated formulas in producing the next generation of protocols on acid rain (Jagusiewicz, 1997a). The question became not whether but how to take account of the circumstances of countries so as to bolster their ability and will to comply with international regulations. This new approach thus recognised the fairness issues which had been raised but not resolved in connection with the Helsinki Protocol, and their importance to the effectiveness of agreements on acid rain abatement. It surfaced in the talks leading to the 1988 Sofia Protocol on NO_x emissions, although these still came to resemble the Helsinki experience in several respects. Already in discussing the terms of the first sulphur protocol, several delegations had stressed the need to secure international agreement on other major air pollutants. Targeting NO_x emissions became a priority given their contribution to both acidification and the formation of ground-level ozone. The Executive Body for the LRTAP Convention established a Working Group 'to prepare the necessary substantiation' for agreed reductions in NO_x emissions or their transboundary fluxes, which began to meet in the autumn of 1985.[17]

---

[17] 'International Strategies to Combat Air Pollution Reviewed by the Executive Body at its Third Session, Helsinki, 8–12 July'. Press Release, 12 July 1985. Economic Commission for Europe, United Nations, Geneva (ECE/ENV/7).

The technological and scientific context was far more complex now than it had been in the work on the sulphur protocol. The need to control NO_x emissions from not only stationary sources (power plants) but also mobile ones demanded difficult national policy-making on the use of road vehicles. There were scientific uncertainties and disputes about the magnitude of the problems caused by NO_x emissions and the benefits of alternative abatement strategies. Insufficient knowledge about what measures were actually required, and by whom, to protect Europe's ecosystems meant that ecological and scientific criteria could not be used. The Soviet Union argued for long that NO_x emissions caused no transboundary damage and therefore were not a matter for negotiation or regulation under the LRTAP Convention. Western scientists presented evidence which eventually made this position untenable (Björkbom, 1997c; Kakebeeke, 1997). Once the Soviet Union and Eastern European states had accepted the evidence and ceased their overt resistance to NO_x emission controls, the mandate of the Working Group on NO_x was expanded in November 1986 to include the drafting of a new protocol within a year.

The arduous negotiations which eventually resulted in the adoption of the Sofia Protocol came in fact to last for two more years. There were profound differences from the outset over the appropriate way forward. Sweden, the Netherlands, Austria, Switzerland and the FRG insisted on a uniform 30 per cent reduction in the NO_x emission levels of 1985 by 1994. The FRG had comparative advantage in producing abatement technologies, and the relatively large engine size of German cars reduced the costs of fitting catalytic converters to reduce emissions. Moreover, the German auto industry generally accepted that NO_x emissions would have to be reduced (Levy, 1993). While now prepared to support a protocol, the Soviet Union and Eastern Europe opposed actual emission cuts. They objected to a 30 per cent reduction specifically, citing its failure to take account of 'scientific, technological and economical aspects' (Sokolovsky, 1997). Eastern European specialists had concluded that NO_x emission cuts would be impossible to achieve for the foreseeable future, in the absence of financial and technology transfers from the West. At the time their countries experienced a rapid increase in the production and use of cars, which lacked adequate pollution control technology. Still other countries favoured a protocol calling for emission freezes. Among these were the UK and France, where the domestic auto industries lobbied vigorously against stricter emission standards for cars.

Major difficulties and deadlocks in the talks arose from the position of the world's biggest producer of NO_x and other air pollutants, the US.[18] As in the Helsinki Protocol talks, the US delegation insisted on being given credit for emission cuts undertaken prior to the suggested reference year of 1985. It argued that countries should be allowed to select their own reference year, and that 1978 would be a less arbitrary baseline year for the US. Washington held moreover that equal percentage cuts were ineffective and unfair, as they ignored ecological requirements and past abatement efforts. Canada, for its part, feared further environmental damage at home if US NO_x emissions were allowed to increase.

The general concern about securing US adherence to a protocol on NO_x ensured responsiveness to the US arguments. This responsiveness, however, eventually eroded the initial goal to lower existing NO_x emission levels. A new proposal for a mere freeze in the 1987 emission levels was tabled in April 1988, which the US agreed to consider. Countries seeking more substantial measures promised not to leave the talks until Washington had responded. For several months the US showed no sign of accepting the plan. It finally won US acceptance, once adjusted to incorporate the US request that countries be permitted to select their own baseline year at which emissions would be frozen. Washington alleviated the Canadian concerns with two concessions. the US would undertake by 1996 small cuts in those NO_x emissions most responsible for environmental damage in Canada, and its average emission levels or transboundary fluxes would not exceed the 1987 levels (Fraenkel, 1989).

As in previous talks Eastern European states, particularly Poland and the Soviet Union, presented the issue of complimentary or subsidised technology transfers from the West as a matter of justice and fairness. They said that they could not afford or would suffer unreasonably from undertaking emission cuts without access to Western clean technology. Given the inequities in wealth between East

---

[18] In the latter part of the 1980s, the US emitted on average over 20,000,000 tonnes of NO_x and over 20,000,000 tonnes of SO_2 per year. By 1994, US NO_x emissions had increased to 21,423,000 tonnes. 'The State of Transboundary Air Pollution'. Report prepared within the framework of the Convention on Long-Range Transboundary Air Pollution. Air Pollution Studies, No. 12. Economic Commission for Europe, United Nations, Geneva, 1996 (ECE/EB.AIR/47).

and West, these countries argued that there ought to be resource transfers or else they had more to lose than to gain from abatement. There was no perception of a right to or need for technology transfers among most Western states, which held that such transactions should be made in the free market based on mutual benefit (Björkbom, 1997b). On a Polish initiative, the final version of the Sofia Protocol included vague provisions for promoting exchange of technology.[19] These reflected Western preferences for commercial exchanges, but Eastern European countries accepted them as a potentially important commitment which might help to eliminate the 'technological barrier between East and West Europe' (Zurek, 1997).

The NO_x Protocol was adopted in October 1988 in Sofia (Bulgaria) and signed by twenty-five members to the LRTAP Convention. Among these were the US, Canada, the UK, the Soviet Union, Poland and some other Eastern European countries.[20] It entered into force in February 1991. The protocol required parties to control or reduce their annual national levels of NO_x emissions or transboundary fluxes so that these, by the end of 1994, would not exceed their levels in 1987 or any previous selected year. 1987 was the year for which most countries had reliable data available on their NO_x emissions, and it was therefore accepted as the general reference. In case a country chose a year prior to 1987 as its baseline year, as the US did to receive credit for its earlier abatement efforts, the annual national emission levels between 1987 and 1996 should on average not exceed the 1987 level. Furthermore, parties were required to control emissions from major existing stationary sources, and to apply national emission standards to major new and modified stationary sources as well as to new mobile sources, using the best available technologies which were

[19] Article 3 in 'Protocol to the 1979 Convention on Long-Range Transboundary Air Pollution concerning the control of emissions of nitrogen oxides or their trans-boundary fluxes'. First revised edition. Economic Commission for Europe, United Nations, Geneva, May 1995 (ECE/EB.AIR/21/Rev.1).

[20] While signing the Sofia Protocol in late 1988, Poland never followed up with ratification and therefore did not become a party to it. A member of the Polish delegation at the time points to the sudden and profound political changes of 1989 in Eastern Europe. Poland was experiencing a rise in its NO_x emissions as a result of new imports of Western cars and new domestic automobile production, and doubted its ability to meet the demands of the Sofia Protocol. Moreover, in the years that followed the changes of 1989, the environment was not a government priority in Poland or elsewhere in the region (Jagusiewicz, 1997b). The EC acceded to the Sofia Protocol in December 1993, and Greece ratified it in 1998. By early 2000 Belgium, like Poland, had still not done so.

economically feasible. In doing so countries should take into account a 'Technical Annex' on the performance and costs of alternative NO_x abatement strategies, which was attached to the protocol. The Technical Annex initially focused on road vehicles, but was amended in November 1996 to include abatement strategies also for aircraft, ships and other off-road vehicles and machines.[21]

The protocol presented these obligations as a first step. As a second step, the parties should negotiate measures and a timetable (commencing by January 1996) to achieve actual NO_x emission cuts based on internationally agreed critical loads. There was nonetheless disappointment that three years of painstaking talks had resulted merely in an agreement to freeze emissions. Twelve Western European countries thus made a declaration parallel to the Sofia Protocol, pledging to undertake unilateral 30 per cent cuts in their NO_x emissions by 1998. They had not all supported the inclusion of a 30 per cent reduction in the protocol, but this pledge allowed more time for implementation and the freedom to choose a baseline year between 1980 and 1986.

In the years following the adoption of the Sofia Protocol, NO_x emission levels were in fact stabilised and slightly reduced. Roughly speaking, the total emissions of the twenty-five parties to the protocol in 1993 were reduced by 4 per cent compared to 1987. Eighteen of these countries had fulfilled their obligations under the protocol by 1993 and five had, in addition, reduced their NO_x emissions by more than 25 per cent. While NO_x emission levels in Southern Europe increased, the total emissions for all parties to the LRTAP Convention were stabilised at the 1987 level by 1990 and reduced by 4 per cent by 1993.[22] To the disappointment of the Eastern bloc, the protocol's

---

[21] Article 2 in 'Protocol to the 1979 Convention on Long-Range Transboundary Air Pollution concerning the control of emissions of nitrogen oxides or their transboundary fluxes' (the November 1996 amendments to the Technical Annex are contained in document EB.AIR./WG.6/R.25/Rev.1); records of UN-ECE Senior Advisers on Environmental and Water Problems, Working Party on Air Pollution Problems, 19th and 20th Sessions, Geneva, 10 April 1990–22 May 1991 (ENVWA/WP.1/R.23&24 and Add.1; 25–32); 'Tackling Air Pollution from Lawnmowers to Jumbo Jets'. UN-ECE Press Release, 28 November 1996, by Lars Nordberg, Deputy Director, Environment and Human Settlements Division, Economic Commission for Europe, United Nations, Geneva.

[22] 'Strategies and Policies for Air Pollution Abatement', p. 63. 1994 major review prepared under the Convention on Long-Range Transboundary Air Pollution. Economic Commission for Europe, United Nations, Geneva, July 1995 (ECE/EB.AIR/44).

provisions for exchanging technology to reduce emissions were not implemented and have not had any practical effect. Western advanced technology is largely privately owned and traded on a bilateral basis, and the scope for action by the UN-ECE or the parties to the protocol in this area is limited (Jagusiewicz, 1997a).

The Sofia Protocol as a turning point

The talks leading to the protocol on NO_x evolved extensively around conflicting positions on acceptable abatement strategies. As in past negotiations, there was considerable overlap between countries' arguments about fairness and their own perceived interests. The various conceptions of fairness were also genuinely held, however, and not put forward merely to gain advantage. The US, for example, certainly sought to achieve the best possible deal for itself by resorting to the language of fairness among other tactics. At the same time, it truly felt that a baseline year ignoring all US NO_x emission cuts prior to 1987 would be grossly unfair.

Disputes over the wisdom and scope of equal percentage cuts and the choice of baseline year were, as in the Helsinki Protocol talks, largely questions of whether requirements should take account of countries' past emission reductions or their technological and financial resources. Unlike the Helsinki experience, however, the Sofia talks sought to address and strike a compromise between opposing notions of fairness and acceptability, as a means to enhance the effectiveness of the outcome. Some high-level negotiators involved describe this process as 'horse-trading' and 'incremental concession-making' so typical of international bargaining (Kakebeeke, 1997; Nitze, 1997; Björkbom, 1997b). While it undermined the initial objective of achieving actual NO_x emission cuts rather than mere emission freezes, key polluting countries were thus induced to adhere to the protocol.

Two examples are the compromises reached between the US and Canada, and between Western countries requesting substantial NO_x emission cuts and the Eastern bloc seeking resource transfers to implement such cuts. The responsiveness to the US argument about credit for pre-1987 abatement measures on the one hand steered the talks away from the goal of substantial reductions. On the other hand, it brought the world's biggest producer of NO_x to enter, for the first time, into a binding agreement to reduce emissions and to limit acid rain affecting Canada (McCormick, 1989). The Eastern bloc's demand for transfers resulted in an agreement to facilitate technological exchange which has not been implemented. However, the flexible terms of the Sofia Protocol helped to ensure that some Eastern European states did sign and implement it. This flexibility enabled parties to get credit for pre-1987 NO_x emission cuts, whether resulting from control measures or from economic decline, and to select a baseline year prior to 1987 in which annual national emissions were higher than in 1987. They could thereby be allowed to increase emissions, as long as average national levels from 1987 to 1996 did not exceed the 1987 level. In fact, the economic recession in Eastern Europe eventually 'helped' countries in this region to meet their obligations under the Sofia Protocol.

The principle of uniform obligations, irrespective of individual circumstances, remained influential in this case: in the process leading to the adoption of the Sofia Protocol, with the proposals for equal percentage cuts, and in the outcome, with the protocol's requirement of flat-rate emission freezes and the additional pledge of twelve countries to unilateral 30 per cent reductions. The reasons for the continued support for uniform measures were similar to those in the Helsinki Protocol talks: they were largely political, tactical and scientific, and had little, if anything, to do with the parties' conceptions of justice or fairness. This approach was judged to have the best prospects of achieving any NO_x emission controls. An agreement on differentiated obligations appeared unrealistic, given the limited scientific evidence available to justify them and the tense East West political climate. Moreover, most countries calculated that the equal percentage cuts or freezes required were either compatible with their national abatement plans or well within their capacity or interest to implement (Levy, 1995). Victims of transboundary air pollution advocated the greatest reductions. The commitment of numerous Western countries to 30 per cent cuts, made in parallel to the Sofia Protocol, was a political declaration designed to express dissatisfaction with that agreement and to pressurise other states to go further (Kakebeeke, 1997). It is reminiscent of the purposes behind the formation of the 30 Per Cent Club in the earlier talks to reduce SO_2 emissions.

The Sofia experience was nevertheless distinct in marking a turn towards differentiating obligations. The NO_x Protocol's flexibility regarding choice of baseline year already allowed for some differentiation and thereby bolstered its fairness in the eyes of certain parties. It also ruled that future negotiations should establish new targets for combating air pollution based on critical loads and BAT. The first-mentioned criterion allocates abatement obligations in relation to the vulnerability of each country's ecosystem(s) to acid deposition, in order to maximise their environmental impact and value on a regional scale. It was the first time that this scientific criterion was incorporated into an international agreement. The Soviet Union endorsed the use of critical loads over equal percentage cuts already in the talks leading to the Helsinki Protocol, but most countries then regarded it as too difficult to employ given scientific uncertainties (Sokolovsky, 1997). In the Sofia Protocol, the parties agreed to undertake research and cooperate to develop a critical loads approach to acid rain abatement.[23] It reflected the reality that uniform reductions had become viewed as ineffective and unfair in both financial and environmental terms.

It has been argued that the countries signing the Sofia Protocol agreed only to measures which were already part of their domestic abatement plans and that the protocol therefore did not bring about the subsequent NO_x emission freezes (Levy, 1995). It is true that several states had abatement schemes in place which naturally influenced their positions in the negotiation of the protocol. There were also Southern, Eastern and Central European countries which did not. The Polish government, for example, adopted a national abatement programme only in 1989 after having signed the Sofia Protocol (Zurek, 1997).

The essential contributions of the Sofia Protocol are more long term. It provided impetus for continued talks to tackle acid rain under the LRTAP Convention. Most importantly, it paved the way for the use of new criteria of effectiveness and fairness in future talks. Apart from the critical loads criterion, two additional principles were adopted in subsequent discussions within the UN-ECE as the basis for new protocols on SO_2 and NO_x: the relative costs of reducing emissions in different countries, and the relative contribution of a country's emissions to acid deposition in other countries ('source–receptor relationships').[24] Negotiators came to rely extensively on these criteria in subsequent work.

---

[23] Articles 2(3) and 6 in 'Protocol to the 1979 Convention on Long-Range Transboundary Air Pollution concerning the control of emissions of nitrogen oxides or their transboundary fluxes'.

[24] 'The Critical Load Concept and the Role of Best Available Technology and Other Approaches'. Report of the Working Group on Abatement Strategies, September

Other developments: the 1988 EC Large Combustion Plant Directive

The EC, now the European Union (EU), provides the other major forum for tackling European acid rain. Talks within it have often influenced, and themselves been influenced by, negotiations within the UN-ECE. The regulations adopted in the form of EC/EU Directives now form a substantial part of the overall regime governing European transboundary air pollution. It is not possible to discuss these here.[25] However, a brief examination of the negotiation of one EC Directive, namely the Large Combustion Plant Directive of 1988, provides another interesting illustration of the turn towards differentiated obligations as a means to achieve more effective and fairer agreements on acid rain.

The initial drafts of the Directive were modelled on German legislation, and called for limits on SO_2 and NO_x emissions based on BAT (Haigh, 1989). Such limits won the support of environmentally activist countries for removing the unfair conditions of competition, and unfair allocation of abatement costs, resulting from their own higher levels of environmental protection (Boehmer-Christiansen and Skea, 1991). However, the formal EC Commission proposal of 1983 over which talks began called for equal percentage cuts by all member states. It stipulated a 60 per cent reduction in SO_2 emissions, and a 40 per cent reduction in emissions from NO_x and particulate matter, from large combustion plants by 1995 based on emission levels in 1980. The UK, supported by less industrialised states such as Spain and Ireland, found this proposal one-sided. The UK argued that it failed to consider abatement measures undertaken in the 1970s, emission cuts from smaller plants, and the steep costs involved for countries dependent on the coal industry.

The resulting stalemate was partly overcome by an elaborate proposal in early 1986 from the Netherlands (then holding the Presidency of the Council of Environment Ministers) that countries undertake different percentage cuts. The proposal was put forward as an alternative to the EC Commission's plan of 1983 for uniform

---

1991. Economic Commission for Europe, United Nations, Geneva (EB.AIR/WG.5/ R.24/Rev.l).

[25] Regulations and negotiations concerning acid rain within the EC are discussed in Magraw (1991) and Boehmer-Christiansen and Skea (1991).

reductions. According to the Dutch plan, SO_2 emissions would be reduced first by 45 per cent and then by 60 per cent in the EC *as a whole* no later than 1995 and 2005, respectively. The emission cuts required of individual states to achieve the initial 45 per cent target varied widely, and were calculated using multiple criteria. These included impact of emission limits on a country's industrialisation, its ability to pay for clean technologies as measured by gross domestic product (GDP) per capita, past and current emission levels, per capita energy use and thermal power plant use, and current national abatement policies (Boehmer-Christiansen and Skea, 1991). This particular plan failed, but its sophisticated approach to differentiated obligations was well reflected in the Large Combustion Plant Directive.

The final version of the Directive ruled that all new power plants must be fitted with the best available abatement technology (thus reducing emissions as far as technically feasible). Generally, NO_x emissions were to be reduced first by 20 per cent and then by 40 per cent no later than 1993 and 1998 respectively, with adjustments made for certain states. The UK was to reduce its SO_2 emissions in two stages, to reach a 60 per cent target by 2003. A number of exceptions were made to cut the costs of the agreement for less industrialised countries and the UK. For example, the emission limits could be renegotiated or surpassed for a transitional period in cases of excessive abatement costs, technological problems with plants, difficulties with the use of indigenous or essential sources of fuel, and unforeseen and substantial changes in the supply of certain fuels or in energy demand. Spain was permitted to build an additional coal-fired electricity generating capacity with laxer controls until the year 2000.[26]

The success of these difficult talks is largely explained by the adoption of a formula which balanced numerous concerns, and bridged divergent positions and conflicting notions of fairness. Although domestic factors (notably in Germany) and foreign policy considerations (especially UK concern about German assistance in the Single European Act debate) were influential, this formula based on a mix of norms was decisive in reconciling the opposing UK and German positions which had dominated the negotiations. The Directive was a clear endorsement of countries undertaking comparable

---

[26] 'Council directive on the limitation of certain pollutants into the air from large combustion plants'. Commission of the European Communities (7 December 1988), 88/609/EEC. Brussels: *Official Journal of the European Communities*, L336.

reduction efforts in view of their differing situations and resources, rather than equal emission cuts. It demonstrated that even in cases of deeply opposing positions, effective agreements could be reached over lowest-common-denominator compromises. In this case it was achieved partly by cutting the economic and other costs for some countries to agree to certain stipulations. The measure enhanced the acceptability and beneficialness of the agreement in the eyes of these parties, and secured their compliance.

After the conclusion of the 1988 Sofia Protocol, negotiations continued within the UN-ECE on an instrument to control VOC emissions, the second major air pollutant after NO_x responsible for ground level ozone. In 1991 twenty-one parties signed the Geneva Protocol concerning the Control of Emissions of Volatile Organic Compounds or their Transboundary Fluxes. Like the Sofia Protocol, it allowed for a measure of differentiated obligations by permitting countries to choose among three alternative targets: a 30 per cent reduction in VOC emissions by 1999 using a baseline year between 1984 and 1990 (the option selected by most signatories); a 30 per cent reduction within a so-called Tropospheric Ozone Management Area and a cap on total national emissions so that these by 1999 would not exceed 1988 levels; or, in countries in which 1988 pollution levels did not exceed certain levels, a stabilisation of emissions at those levels by 1999. The Protocol on VOC emissions also called for exchange of technology, and presented itself as a step towards later regulations based on critical levels.[27] Some analysts describe this protocol as the first under the LRTAP Convention to go beyond and improve existing national abatement plans (Levy, 1995). An even more important achievement in the history of European acid rain abatement was made about three years later, with the signing of a second sulphur protocol.

Negotiating a second sulphur protocol

The 1985 Helsinki Protocol and its shortcomings triggered in due course renewed talks on the reduction of SO_2 emissions. It stipulated no further action after the achievement of the 30 per cent emission

---

[27] The 1991 Geneva Protocol Concerning the Control of Emissions of Volatile Organic Compounds or their Transboundary Fluxes, in *1979 Convention on Long-Range Transboundary Air Pollution and its Protocols*. Economic Commission for Europe, United Nations, Geneva, October 1996 (ECE/EB.AIR/50).

cuts by 1993, and despite these measures European emission levels remained too high to avoid environmental damage. In due course the Working Group on Abatement Strategies convinced the Executive Body about the merits of using a critical loads approach. In 1991 the Executive Body asked this Group to formulate provisions for a new sulphur protocol, based on a scientifically sound and politically fair approach (Churchill, Kütting and Warren, 1995). The overriding objective was to achieve new truly effective emission cuts. Specialised working groups and task forces had by then done extensive preparatory work in two important areas: the use of the critical loads criterion in formal negotiations, and the possible inclusion of a 'burden-sharing' scheme in the new protocol.

The parties to the Sofia Protocol had already in 1988 agreed on the importance of developing and eventually applying an approach based on critical loads. Collaborative research resulted in data and maps defining critical loads for sulphur, and in information on emission sources. Integrated assessment models were then developed to link information about long-range atmospheric transport and deposition, their effects on sensitive elements of the environment, energy use, and costs and impacts of emission control strategies. These models were used as tools to generate alternative abatement strategies designed to achieve maximum environmental protection, and eventually critical loads, at the lowest possible cost for the region as a whole.[28] It was agreed that a second sulphur protocol should be based on the use of such scientific models incorporating the critical loads criterion. The overwhelming view among parties was that agreements would then be less arbitrary in requiring emission cuts based on empirical knowledge about environmental harm (Kakebeeke, 1997; Williams, 1997). Competing models yielded different results and recommendations, and at times appeared to threaten rather than facilitate the talks. Eventually there was a virtual consensus that the Regional Acidification Information and Simulation (RAINS) model developed at the International Institute for Applied Systems Analysis in Austria should be used as the base model (Björkbom, 1998b).

Recommendations resulting from models such as RAINS tend to

[28] 'The Critical Loads and Levels Approach and Its Application in Preparation of the New Sulfur Protocol'. Report by the Bureau of the Working Group on Effects for a Special Session in Oslo, 13–14 June 1994. Executive Body for the Convention on Long-Range Transboundary Air Pollution, Economic Commission for Europe, United Nations, Geneva, 3 May 1994 (EB.AIR/R.85).

require poor states to undertake some of the greatest abatement measures, to the benefit of richer countries which are net importers of acid rain. This is not only because poor countries are among the worst polluters. The emphasis on cost-effectiveness in the RAINS model requires reduction measures to be taken where they are the cheapest, namely in predominantly poor countries in the UN-ECE region. Some Central and Eastern European countries might therefore have to spend up to 5 per cent of their gross national product (GNP) on abatement costs without generally making any comparable gains, environmental or other, on a national scale.[29] In preparations for the formal talks on a second sulphur protocol, concerns about reducing this negative impact and maximising participation in new abatement plans induced discussions about possible cost-sharing schemes. The Dutch first raised the idea in 1989 on behalf of the poorer European countries (Klaassen, 1997). They became a strong supporter of cost-sharing, along with Russia and Poland.

The UN-ECE Task Force on Economic Aspects of Abatement Strategies then studied at length various cost-sharing mechanisms including the establishment of an acidification fund, a tradable emission permits system, and joint implementation of emission cuts by two or more countries. Much time was spent considering different principles for allocating financial support which a cost-sharing fund might use, and institutional requirements to operate it. Under one proposal countries would contribute to or receive monies from a fund based on GDP, GDP per capita, national abatement costs, and/or relative gains from participation in the venture.[30] The Task Force

---

[29] The 5 per cent figure comes from Sliggers (1997). In one scenario using the RAINS model, the objective was to reduce sulphur deposition to the 50 percentile critical sulphur deposition levels at a minimal cost to Europe as a whole. About 3 per cent of the European ecosystems would then be exposed to deposition above the critical sulphur deposition values when taking account of current national reduction plans, compared to 18 per cent with the latter alone. Some countries would have to cut their emissions by over 90 per cent compared to levels in 1980, and would experience a multifold increase in abatement costs (e.g., an increase by 560 per cent for Poland). Other countries would have no or a negligible cost increase, or could even increase their emissions (Klaassen, Amann and Schöpp, 1992; and Amann *et al.*, 1992).

[30] 'Economic Principles for Allocating the Costs of Reducing Sulphur Emissions in Europe'. Report submitted by the delegation of the Netherlands to the Group of Economic Experts on Air Pollution, Executive Body for the Convention on Long-Range Transboundary Air Pollution, for the 5th Session, 26–28 June 1989. Economic Commission for Europe, United Nations, Geneva (EB.AIR/GE.2/R.26, 19 May 1989). See also Sliggers and Klaassen (1992) and Bergman, Cesar and Klaassen (1992).

established that the relevant basis for any allocation rule was incremental cost; that is, the amount by which a country's cost of achieving multilateral targets exceeded the cost of its national abatement plans.[31]

The Central and Eastern European countries were conciliatory or even passive in the discussions of cost-sharing, despite being the main potential beneficiaries of it. In the preparatory as in the formal talks, they never demanded that a new sulphur protocol include a burden-sharing plan. In the substantive negotiations which began within the Working Group on Strategies in August 1991, there was hardly any discussion of cost-sharing schemes other than joint implementation of emission cuts. The Chair steered the talks away from the matter, convinced that any Eastern European insistence on direct financial or technological compensation would result in confrontation with Western states and make a new protocol impossible. Western European governments accepted that some burden-sharing was necessary, but argued that existing voluntary aid channels and bilateral agreements should be used rather than a formal obligatory scheme (Björkbom, 1997b). One stated reason was that Central and Eastern European abatement costs could be smaller than the estimates of the RAINS model (Keiser, 1997).

The official negotiations developed in two overlapping phases. The first consisted of discussions on collective environmental goals for the UN-ECE region as a whole that a new protocol should promote or achieve, based on the RAINS model criteria (e.g., critical loads, source–receptor relationships and relative abatement costs). The second stage involved bargaining over the different SO_2 emission cuts and deadlines required of individual countries to meet these regional objectives, taking into account also technological capacities, economic costs, equity concerns and social factors not included in the RAINS model. At the outset, the RAINS and other computer models were used to generate information about different scenarios according to the desired level of environmental protection and financial cost. Parties recognised that the critical loads concept would be used only as a guideline, and that the actual achievement of critical loads was a long-term objective. They agreed that, in a second stage, they had to

[31] 'Progress Report by the Chairman of the Task Force on Economic Aspects of Abatement Strategies' of 9 January 1997 to the Working Group on Strategies, section IV on 'burden sharing' (EB.AIR/WG.5/R.70).

negotiate 'target loads' which also account for other factors. It was accepted that critical loads could not be achieved at that time, even if BAT was used (Wuester, 1997c). A level of acid deposition causing no damage to any part of Europe's ecosystems would moreover have required prohibitive financial expenditures, which would fall unevenly on states in the absence of a cost-sharing scheme.

The actual negotiations on a second sulphur protocol therefore came to focus, first, on establishing an acceptable degree of 'gap closure' between the critical loads level and existing rates of sulphur deposition. It was agreed that critical loads would be calculated to protect all but the most vulnerable 5 per cent of Europe's ecosystems. This measurement of critical loads was seen as an inevitable compromise, given that protection of the most sensitive 5 per cent of the ecosystems would entail exceptionally high costs. According to calculations using the RAINS model, it would cost the same to protect the 96th through to the 98th percentiles as the entire first 95 percentiles. The last 2 per cent could not be protected at any cost.[32] In the talks during 1993, most parties felt that new emission targets should reduce by 60 per cent the gap between critical loads (calculated to protect 95 per cent of the ecosystems) and the 1990 emission levels. In early 1994, as various states started to object to the reduction requirements or deadlines they had been allocated, the collective goal shifted to a 50 per cent gap closure. Agreement was eventually reached on the goal of a 60 per cent gap closure and incorporated into the new protocol.[33]

The most protracted talks concerned what specific SO_2 emission cuts and deadlines would be required of individual states, to reach the target gap closure at the regional level. Indeed, disagreement over reductions and deadlines for implementation meant that the new protocol could not be completed by late 1993 as originally intended. Sweden, Germany, the Netherlands and Austria favoured high reduction targets with early deadlines. Southern European countries (Greece, Italy, Spain and Portugal) and Ireland, all spared from significant problems with acid rain, were concerned about the costs of abatement. The Central and Eastern European countries, also preoccupied with economic considerations but much affected by acid deposition, were willing to support reductions. The UK insisted on a later deadline for itself (the year 2010 instead of 2005 or 2000). The UK

---

[32] *Energy Economist*, November 1993, referred to in Levy (1995).
[33] *Acid News*, No 4, October 1993; *Acid News*, No. 1, February 1994.

delegation argued that its abatement measures would otherwise be too costly and even wasteful, in requiring new pollution control technology on plants scheduled to be closed in due course (Murlis, 1995). The US and Canada occupied an ambiguous position in the talks. They fell outside the geographical scope and mandate of the European Programme for Monitoring and Evaluation of Trans-boundary Air Pollution (covering Europe from the Atlantic to the Urals) on which regional models such as RAINS are based. While supporting sulphur emission controls in principle, they were already bound by their own bilateral acid rain agreement and reluctant to accept further commitments.[34]

There was a consensus in the first part of 1993 that Western countries should reach their reduction targets to bring about a 60 per cent gap closure by 2000, while Eastern European states would have until 2005 to do so. However, in August 1993 it became clear that the proposed measures of all states would not achieve the 60 per cent gap closure. A review of the suggested national emission cuts followed. In the next month several countries objected to the requirements and deadlines which had been allocated to them. A group of countries seeking lower targets (the UK, Belgium, Denmark, France, Ireland and Spain) confronted a coalition of other states advocating higher targets (including Sweden, Norway, Germany, the Netherlands and Austria). Eventually nine states committed themselves to greater emission cuts than demanded by their domestic plans. Ten states agreed to measures already set out in their domestic abatement plans and two, Portugal and Greece, would do less than they had originally foreseen (Klaassen, 1996). Disappointed by the outcome, Executive Body Chairman Jan Thompson noted at a session in December 1993 that a 60 per cent gap closure was unlikely to be met before 2015.

Another point of dispute concerned BAT standards. In the early stages of the negotiations, some countries fiercely opposed the intro-duction of compulsory BAT standards for new stationary emission sources. Two of these, Norway and the UK, cited too high costs and may have sought to avoid similar expensive requirements in future protocols. More difficult to resolve was the question of whether mandatory BAT standards should apply to new as well as existing

---

[34] *Acid News*, No. 4, October 1993. It may also be noted that while European policy had now come to focus on environmental effectiveness, US policy was said to be based on human health-related effects of pollutants.

emission sources. Germany, France, Switzerland, Austria and the Netherlands made a joint proposal invoking EC emission limits for new and existing plants. They argued that emission targets could not be met without BAT and that the 'precautionary principle' should apply.[35] This principle holds that lack of full scientific certainty should not be a reason for postponing measures to tackle serious environmental problems. The argument is that some environmental damage may be irreversible by the time full scientific evidence becomes available, and that definite proof is not even possible to obtain in some cases.

As a leading producer of abatement technology, Germany had much to gain from promoting an ambitious application of BAT standards. Other states rejected this proposal on the grounds that it was not cost-effective. The objections of Norway and the UK to mandatory BAT requirements eventually receded. The strong opposition from the US and Canada resulted in these countries being exempt from such requirements, with reference to their own North America Air Quality Agreement. The BAT controversy was resolved in the new sulphur protocol mainly by following EU legislation: EC standards which had already been adopted became binding, while stricter standards would serve only as guidelines (Wuester, 1997b).

The possible inclusion in the protocol of a provision for joint implementation of abatement obligations was also debated. It would allow parties to reach their own targets by paying for emission cuts in another country with lower abatement costs. Although possible to view as a form of cost-sharing, the idea was raised and discussed in the talks as a potential means to improve cost-effectiveness on a regional scale. The agreed emission ceilings had already been calculated based on cost-effectiveness, using the RAINS model, and on knowledge available in 1991. The main purpose of joint implementation would therefore be to enhance the economic efficiency of reduction allocations among countries in the event the RAINS estimates were incorrect (not optimal), or new technologies shifted cost advantages (Wuester, 1997e). States which had implemented substantial controls in the past might find that further measures would be easier technologically and financially to undertake elsewhere, such as in the Central and Eastern European countries. In other words, they

[35] *Acid News*, No. 2, April 1993, p. 2; and *Acid News*, No. 1, February 1994, p. 12.

might be able to reduce emissions to the same extent at much lower cost in countries with few abatement measures already in place.

However, the idea raised serious concerns about environmental effectiveness and fairness. These became a focus of the talks and influenced the outcome extensively. First, joint implementation deals could undermine the effectiveness of emission cuts and the new protocol's environmental objectives for Europe, especially the achievement of critical loads. A change in the location of acid rain emission reductions as a result of such arrangements would affect the location and depth of their environmental impact, due to the varying sensitivities of different ecosystems. The range of factors harmed by acid rain (e.g., ecosystems, human health and buildings) also makes it technically difficult to compare the effects of sulphur emissions and emissions cuts from different sources (Bailey *et al.*, 1996). Secondly, if two parties with different abatement costs are allowed to implement their obligations jointly to their mutual benefit, it may have negative environmental effects on third parties.

Disagreement thus emerged in the negotiations over whether joint implementation schemes should be permitted and, if so, on what conditions. Norway's Ministry of Finance initially raised and then pushed strongly for the idea. Being dependent on oil for its energy needs, Norway foresaw difficulties in fulfilling its obligations under a new sulphur protocol without such schemes. Through joint implementation, the government could avoid taxing the oil industry and maintain its abundant oil supply. The majority of countries, by contrast, were critical. The Netherlands argued that the RAINS model had already optimised cost-effectiveness. Germany held that joint implementation conflicted with the BAT concept that states should do all they can technologically to cut emissions, and almost blocked the inclusion of such a provision in the protocol (Sliggers, 1997). France insisted on strict conditions. For example, joint implementation could be restricted to neighbouring countries to prevent major changes in the location and impact of emission cuts, and only a fraction of emissions reduced in this manner could be credited. Knowing that the new protocol would not enter into force until after some years, the parties eventually decided that the issue required more work before a detailed agreement could be reached. This decision secured Norway's signature.

The Protocol on Further Reduction of Sulphur Emissions, replacing the 1985 Helsinki Protocol, was adopted in Oslo in June 1994 and signed by twenty-eight parties. Canada received special provisions as a signatory state. The US never signed it, viewing the critical loads criterion as being in conflict with its 1990 Clean Air Act.[36] The new protocol did nonetheless bring several new countries into the process of multilateral abatement. It entered into force in June 1998, when the sixteen ratifications needed for this purpose had been acquired.

The Oslo Protocol aims to reduce the gap between critical loads and the 1990 levels of SO_2 emissions by 60 per cent, using three target years (2000, 2005 and 2010). This is designed as a first step towards reaching critical loads. The individual emission cuts required vary enormously. Wealthier states such as the Scandinavian countries, Germany, Austria, France and the Netherlands must reduce their 1980 emission levels by between 74 per cent and 83 per cent by the year 2000 (the UK by 50 per cent by 2000 and by 80 per cent by 2010). Poor states may implement smaller reductions and also take more time. Hungary, Bulgaria, Croatia and the Russian Federation, for example, are expected to cut their emissions by between 22 per cent and 60 per cent by 2010.[37] Greece and Portugal are allowed to increase emissions until the year 2000, at which point they should stabilise and then start to decline. The national targets agreed in some cases did not follow the 60 per cent gap closure scenarios. The protocol also contains requirements and provisions with respect to emission limits for major power plants (all new and certain existing ones), the sulphur content of gas oil, the exchange of technology and, as discussed earlier, the use of BAT. There are no stipulations for crediting cuts in transboundary fluxes. The precautionary principle was incorporated into the protocol, with the addition that precautionary measures should be cost-effective. A novelty compared to past protocols is the creation of a relatively strong implementation regime, although it lacks the capacity to guarantee or enforce compliance. The tasks of an eight-party Implementation Committee are to monitor compliance, review regularly the parties' original targets in view of the long-term goal of reaching critical loads and, when necessary, renegotiate these.

The process of ratifying the 1994 Oslo Protocol has been slow,

---

[36] *Acid News*, No. 1, February 1994, p. 13.

[37] Annex II to 'Protocol to the 1979 Convention on Long-Range Transboundary Air Pollution on Further Reduction of Sulphur Emissions and Decision on the Structure and Functions of the Implementation Committee, as well as Procedures for its Review of Compliance'. Economic Commission for Europe, United Nations, Geneva, 1994 (ECE/EB.AIR/40).

especially among the Central and Eastern European countries. By the end of 1997 eleven of the signatory parties had proceeded with ratification of which only one, the Czech Republic, was a Central and Eastern European country.[38] By February 2000, twenty-two states had ratified the protocol including Croatia, Slovakia and Slovenia. Six of the signatory parties still had to ratify it and five of these were Central and Eastern European countries, namely Bulgaria, Hungary, Poland, the Russian Federation, and Ukraine.

The protocol made no provisions for cost-sharing. Poor countries could of course receive loans and grants for abatement measures through regular European and international aid channels, including the European Bank for Reconstruction and Development and the World Bank and through bilateral agreements on technology or financial transfers. Any such assistance was not linked formally to the protocol. The Task Force on Economic Aspects of Abatement Strategies continued work on possible cost-sharing mechanisms after the adoption of the protocol, but in 1997 the issue ceased to be part of its mandate. By early 2000 government delegates had still not acted upon the final paper which the Task Force produced, arguably because its proposals for cost-sharing were not 'practical' enough to settle a question which is as political as it is technical and financial.

The Oslo Protocol stated that reduction requirements may be implemented jointly, with the agreement of the parties to the protocol and in accordance with rules and conditions to be adopted by the Executive Body. After the signing of the protocol, work was undertaken to further define the concept and possible consequences of joint implementation. It focused on the development of a scheme which would avoid erosion of environmental effectiveness (critical loads) and negative effects on third parties, and on ways of processing proposals for joint implementation from individual countries. In 1996 government delegates accepted a set of provisions in this area, according to which any joint implementation project must not change the national deposition levels of third parties expected under the protocol's original scheme. Countries would be required to submit to the UN-ECE Secretariat, at their own cost, the proposed agreement detailing its environmental and economic effects. All parties to the protocol would then consider this information at an Executive Body

---

[38] The eleven countries were Canada, the Czech Republic, Denmark, France, Liechtenstein, Luxembourg, the Netherlands, Norway, Spain, Sweden and the UK.

session and, if acceptable, adopt the proposal by consensus. Every arrangement for joint implementation would be monitored, and terminated if any party failed to comply with its terms.[39] Negotiations on the matter continued within the Working Group on Strategies. There, and later in the Executive Body, it was eventually agreed that any deviation from the regionally optimised distribution of emission reductions must be marginal and largely insignificant. The 1997 decision of the Executive Body on methods and criteria for joint implementation also ruled that any resulting change in a third party's deposition would require the agreement of all parties to the Oslo Protocol (Wuester, 2000).

The Oslo Protocol represented a new breed of international environmental agreement. It broke new ground by establishing emission targets based on critical loads, emphasising the importance of equitable distribution of abatement costs, and by introducing relatively strong compliance provisions. In all these respects it served as a model for the 1999 Protocol to Abate Acidification, Eutrophication and Ground-Level Ozone. This protocol, as do the 1998 Protocols on Heavy Metals and Persistent Organic Pollutants, have the same principal compliance regime as the one designed for the Oslo Protocol. The Executive Body also decided that this regime should be used for the earlier substantial protocols on SO_2, NO_x and VOCs adopted in the 1980s and early 1990s (Björkbom, 2000).

Explaining the 1994 Oslo Protocol: concerns about effectiveness and fairness

The political context surrounding the drafting of the second sulphur protocol was dramatically different from that of previous talks, and far more favourable. The end of the Cold War, the improvement in East–West relations, and the greater scientific knowledge now available about environmental harm and needs allowed the negotiations to become more 'problem-solving' in nature than had hitherto been the case. Although the economic decline and transition process in Eastern

---

[39] 'Joint Implementation under the Oslo Protocol'. Report by the Chairman of the open-ended group of experts (meeting in Oslo, 9–10 November 1995) to the Working Group on Strategies (16th session, 19–23 February 1996). Economic Commission for Europe, United Nations, Geneva, 23 November 1995 (EB.AIR/WG.5/R.57). In late November 1996, the Executive Body approved an amendment to the 1994 Oslo Protocol regarding by-products (EB.AIR/WG.6/R.34).

Europe raised sensitive issues of burden-sharing and financial help from the very start, the Western countries and the Central and Eastern European countries cooperated well in moving the process of air pollution abatement forward. Former Eastern bloc countries were eager to integrate into the rest of Europe. The Chair of the talks emphasises that these states sought to use their participation in a second sulphur protocol and in international environmental negotiations generally to gain accession to the EU, and that this was an important factor making the 1994 Oslo Protocol possible (Björkbom, 1997b).

This new context also permitted sharper focus on the issues at hand, and left more scope for justice and fairness to play a role. High-level negotiators point out that such considerations were at the heart of the process and more important in the negotiation of the Oslo Protocol than had previously been the case (Kakebeeke, 1997). They concerned the use of the RAINS model, burden-sharing, differentiation of obligations based on economic ability, and joint implementation of emission cuts. In all areas except burden-sharing, concepts of justice or fairness influenced the talks and the outcome significantly.

The parties held that the RAINS model would improve the scientific basis and effectiveness of the new protocol. Allocating emission cuts based on criteria such as what the environment can endure (critical loads), and countries' relative contributions to ecological harm and relative abatement costs, was also regarded as far less arbitrary than earlier approaches (Zurek, 1997; Williams, 1997). The RAINS model naturally tends to require greater reductions of heavily polluting states, to save states with high abatement costs from having to undertake extensive emission cuts, and to reward control measures undertaken previously. It yields long-lasting requirements rather than time-limited uniform cuts or ceilings on emissions. While using them primarily on scientific grounds, the parties thus believed simultaneously that the critical loads concept and the RAINS model incorporated important principles of fairness.

In differentiating obligations based on scientific and economic efficiency criteria, the RAINS model simultaneously raised another question. In practice it places a particularly heavy burden on poor polluting states with relatively little to gain from acid rain abatement. This situation prompted the debate on the burden-sharing issue which, according to the Secretary to the Working Group on Strategies, raised the most essential issues of justice and fairness in the process leading to the Oslo Protocol (Wuester, 1997e). The Netherlands held that a form of cost-sharing or financial aid to help poor states required to make large cuts in SO_2 emissions was a matter of fairness as well as necessity. This contradicted the otherwise generally accepted 'polluter pays' principle, according to which those responsible for environmentally harmful activities should pay for the damage through compensation and clean-up efforts or the adoption of abatement measures.[40] The Dutch argued that assistance was justified when the countries concerned were unable to meet their obligation to pay themselves. This would help to ensure their participation in new ambitious abatement plans to the benefit of all. But the majority of Western countries, which would be the financial donors, opposed the idea. One key argument in line with the 'polluter pays' concept was that Western countries have no duty to finance reductions in acid deposition which originates within Central and Eastern European countries. The fact that a formal cost-sharing scheme was never discussed seriously in the formal talks or included in the protocol reflects, in yet other eyes, a marginalisation of poor countries in the negotiation process (Levy, 1995).

Eastern European countries, especially Russia, asked in the negotiations for Western financial and technological aid with abatement and presented it clearly as a matter of justice and fairness. But they never insisted on the adoption of a formal burden-sharing scheme. Nor did they attempt to link their cooperation or compliance to the receipt of assistance. These states were very accommodating on the issue, despite being faced with difficult economic and political conditions at home and with costly requirements under a new protocol. This behaviour is probably best explained by their eagerness to demonstrate environmental responsibility and financial independence in efforts to gain entry into the EU, and a realisation that most Western countries would never accept formal cost-sharing (Sprinz, 1997). There was also a lack of clarity about the benefits of cost-sharing for one sole pollutant, and technical difficulties with designing a viable scheme.

The abandonment of the idea of formal cost-sharing paved the way

---

[40] 'Progress Report by the Chairman of the Task Force on Economic Aspects of Abatement Strategies' of 9 January 1997 to the Working Group on Strategies, section IV on 'burden sharing' (EB.AIR/WG.5/R.70). The OECD has noted an exception to the 'polluter pays' principle when the polluters concerned are economies in transition to a new form of organisation, such as a market economy.

for another conception of justice to influence the negotiations considerably: that of differentiating obligations, such as the depth of emission cuts and deadlines, with a view to economic ability rather than the RAINS criteria alone. One negotiator holds that the parties agreed to this principle early on without dispute, exactly because they considered it to be a justice and fairness issue (Keiser, 1997). Later deadlines for fulfilling reduction obligations and, in some cases, lower targets were granted to Central and Eastern European countries in transition and other poorer states, at their request. Only when a few well-to-do countries such as the UK, France and Belgium requested favourable differentiation for themselves to save costs did a debate occur. Although compromising the RAINS recommendations, this approach was deemed to be a more feasible way to compensate for inequalities in resources and abatement costs than formal burden-sharing. It could be seen as an informal cost-sharing device which struck a balance between several conflicting principles which had arisen in the talks, including 'no harm', 'polluter pays', formal burden-sharing based on economic ability and need, and those underlying the RAINS model.

It is very difficult to assess the implications of the absence of a formal burden-sharing scheme. Agreement on such a mechanism is certainly likely to have reduced the need to renegotiate and relax the original targets and deadlines based strictly on ecological requirements and cost-effectiveness (Sliggers and Klaassen, 1994). Existing aid channels may not be as effective, as they tie much financial help to conditions of the donor agencies or countries. But it is also worth recalling the argument of the Chair of the talks that the Central and Eastern European countries' 'flexibility' on the issue of formal burden-sharing made the successful conclusion of the Oslo Protocol possible.

With regard to the delays in ratification, there are several possible reasons. The Oslo Protocol is a complex legal text which, compared to earlier protocols, requires more demanding measures of many countries than they had previously planned, including changes in energy policies. Additional time is therefore required to adapt domestic policies to the new commitments. While the EU accession process would compel Central and Eastern European countries to comply with the Oslo Protocol, many of these face uncertainties regarding their actual chances of becoming EU members. Expert assessments vary as to whether the absence of a formal cost-sharing scheme has played a considerable role. Several negotiators involved, including from the Czech Republic and Poland, have argued that economic factors would not be most decisive (Jilek and Sochor, 1997; Zurek, 1997). Other observers hold that the issues relating to burden-sharing were never truly resolved in the drafting of the protocol, and that this might help to explain the slow pace of ratification among Central and Eastern European countries (Sokolovksy, 1997). Few of the parties themselves have provided explanations. Russia and Bulgaria have, however, pointed to their desperate economic situations and high abatement costs. In the case of such countries, greater technical and financial assistance could certainly have speeded up ratification (Wuester, 2000).

Ethical considerations played a key role in the talks over joint implementation. The domestic interests of various countries first pulled the matter in different directions, but the provisions on which government delegates agreed in 1996 reflected important principles of procedural and substantial justice.[41] The rules for joint implementation eventually adopted by the Executive Body, although not quite as stringent, were based on critical loads and the principles of no harm to third parties and strong protection of third party interests. No joint implementation project had yet been proposed by early 2000. The Chair of the negotiations stated that he did not expect any such project to be implemented under the Oslo Protocol (Björkbom, 2000). It should be noted that the protocol's emission targets were already calculated to minimise costs and thus leave little scope for further savings, and any joint implementation with the potential to cut expenses substantially would tend to have large third party effects (Wuester, 2000).

There are several similarities between the talks leading to the second sulphur protocol and previous acid rain negotiations. The domestic politics and perceived self-interest of many countries influenced their bargaining positions and alignments, including on controversial issues such as the depth of emission cuts, BAT, formal cost-sharing and joint implementation. Political 'pragmatism' and practical necessity were influential if not decisive factors when parties agreed to act upon particular conceptions of justice or fairness (such as granting later deadlines and lower emission targets to economically

---

[41] 'Joint Implementation under the Oslo Protocol'. Report by the Chairman of the open-ended group of experts (meeting in Oslo, 9–10 November 1995) to the Working Group on Strategies (16th session, 19–23 February 1996). Economic Commission for Europe, United Nations, Geneva, 23 November 1995 (EB.AIR/WG.5/R.57).

weak countries), and when they neglected others (such as formal cost-sharing and the 'polluter pays' principle). Several, partly conflicting conceptions were nonetheless influential. These help to explain why the RAINS recommendations, which ignored the reality of unequal abatement capacities and cost distributions on a national level, had to be renegotiated and why the Oslo Protocol could not simply endorse environmentally or economically 'optimal' abatement strategies. This protocol was the first to call for an improvement in calculations of internationally optimised allocations of emission cuts, taking into account an equitable distribution of abatement costs (Article 6).

Conclusion

The question 'What would be a just and fair solution?' has not primarily driven the acid rain talks. The overarching concern has been to improve European environmental conditions, at an acceptable cost to the region as a whole and to individual parties. As in other international negotiations, the principal factors driving the behaviour of participating states have been perceived national interests (economic and other) and domestic considerations (e.g., energy and transportation policy, damage from acid deposition and access to clean technology). Such self-interests and individual circumstances have in turn influenced what countries, for both genuine and tactical reasons, have taken and argued to be reasonable, and what ethical conceptions they have acted upon. While the parties have invoked principles serving their own interests in the talks, their arguments have at the same time often been seen as legitimate from a more impartial viewpoint. Moreover, the goal of improving environmental protection at acceptable cost has required countries to be responsive to ethical issues and conceptions other than their own.

The European acid rain case illustrates well that the engine running international negotiations does not consist solely of the promotion of individual interests and the maximisation of individual gains in a narrow sense. First, the principle of 'no harm' has provided the foundation for negotiations over transboundary air pollution from the outset. Secondly, the shared concern about protecting Europe's ecosystems has raised influential questions concerning the allocation of the benefits and financial burdens of acid rain abatement. In response, as the previous discussion shows, governments have modified their positions in order to accommodate certain ethical issues. Clearly, pragmatic considerations of how to move the negotiations to a successful outcome often determined whether a particular issue or conception of justice was taken seriously. For example, it is doubtful that the Oslo Protocol could ever have materialised without resort to the principle of differentiated obligations. There are also examples of arguments about justice or fairness being ignored at the price of losing important signatures and eroding effectiveness (as in the talks leading to the Helsinki Protocol), and of ethical issues influencing the negotiations because of their perceived moral weight (as in the talks on rules for joint implementation of abatement obligations).

Shared norms, such as those of 'no harm' and differentiated obligations based on economic and ecological considerations, have facilitated the process of achieving new collective abatement measures. Opposing notions of justice and fairness have, however, been as common and caused arduous episodes in the European acid rain talks. This does not merely reflect countries' different interests, which undoubtedly inform their choice of principle. It is also an expression of the fact that, as discussed in the introductory chapter, many negotiating situations are plagued by moral ambiguity. There are frequently several conflicting principles recognised as important in providing guidelines for a solution; in this case, those of 'no harm', 'polluter pays' and critical loads versus burden-sharing and differentiated obligations based on economic ability. The effects-based approach using RAINS illustrates well that what may be reasonable and effective at one level can be seen as grossly unfair in other respects. As a result parties usually make competing ethical claims, all of which may merit consideration. On occasion agreement was still possible to reach despite (or, some would argue, because of) the subjugation of some notions of fairness. What more often permitted a successful outcome, however, was the recognition that conflicting ideas about justice or fairness had to be balanced and reconciled in order to win the acceptance of those concerned. Such 'horse-trading' is a reflection of the moral complexity surrounding international negotiations, as well as an exercise in political pragmatism.

Disagreement persists over the significance of resource transfers to poor polluting countries. Some observers argue that burden-sharing remains an unresolved issue which has slowed down progress in European acid rain abatement (Keiser, 1997; Klaassen, 1997). Others hold that it is now largely irrelevant: both Western and Eastern European countries will have to undertake costly emission cuts under new protocols, and the transition process of Central and Eastern European economies has reached an advanced stage (Björkbom, 2000). There are moreover informal, bilateral and multilateral channels of aid (Wuester, 2000). Many factors influence whether countries choose to adhere to an environmental agreement, and the financial cost of implementation and its perceived fairness is only one of these. Yet without cost-sharing there appears to be no escape from the need – for reasons of justice, fairness and pragmatism – to renegotiate and relax scientifically established emission targets and deadlines for poorer countries. A burden-sharing mechanism, possibly based on costs to achieve collective targets above national abatement expenditures or 'incremental costs', might have avoided this. The talks leading to the 1999 Protocol to Abate Acidification, Eutrophication and Ground-Level Ozone sought to increase effectiveness by discussing multiple pollutants simultaneously, and recognising that different pollutants affect each other and that more than one pollutant usually causes a particular environmental problem. They used optimised scenarios, permitting different countries to reduce the pollutants involved in different mixes which would maximise cost-effectiveness on a re-gional scale. Once more, however, the final provisions departed considerably from the ideal, most cost-effective scenario: Russia and Poland raised the matter of cost-sharing, but instead negotiators extended less demanding reduction requirements than prescribed by this scenario to Central and Eastern European countries (Björkbom, 2000).

It is clear that conceptions of justice and fairness have become more influential in the European acid rain negotiations over time. The circumstances behind this development will subsist. Among them are scientific evidence concerning the emitters and damaging effects of air pollution, monumental abatement costs coupled with inequalities in national resources and in gains to be had from emission cuts, contra-dictions between the nature of effective measures at the regional and national levels, the diffusion of power between many countries, and the early experiences of ignoring ethical issues by use of uniform obligations.

In the review of existing protocols and in the search for agreement on new measures over the years to come, the demands both for fairness in the distribution of the cost burden and for cost-effective-ness will undoubtedly persist. Formulas balancing environmental, economic and technological considerations with ethical concerns will be essential. In the future battle against air pollution in regions as diverse as Europe, North America and Southeast Asia, and indeed environmental degradation in other areas, two decades of acid rain negotiations within the UN-ECE have much to say and much to teach about the unavoidability of justice.

4 Managing the global economy: disputes over freer and fairer trade in the Uruguay Round of the GATT

> All parties [eventually] accepted the agreement, because they all thought that the concessions exchanged were fair and that the balance of rights and obligations was right.[1]

The management of the global economy has become a central area of international relations. Since the fall of the Bretton Woods institutions in 1973 and the emergence of a less orderly economic world, the significance of collective regulation for domestic and international politics and security has become all too obvious. Governments now regard good economic performance at home and engagement in economic governance on the international stage as essential to the welfare of their populations and to their own political survival. Growing transborder flows of trade, financial capital and investment have integrated national economies. People today purchase foreign goods, invest in overseas markets and run businesses across state boundaries on a hitherto unprecedented scale. Since the early 1980s transborder trade in shares and currencies has increased ten times as rapidly as the world's GDP, foreign direct investment has augmented three times as fast, and trade in goods and services has grown twice as fast.[2]

The five decades of lively commercial exchange which preceded the First World War remind us that economic 'globalisation' is not a new phenomenon. But there are new developments suggesting that the economic integration of our age will proceed at a steady pace.

---

[1] Ambassador B. K. Zutshi, chief negotiator for India in the Uruguay Round of the GATT and Chair of the Contracting Parties to the GATT in 1993 (personal interview, 1998).

[2] *The Economist*, 18 October 1997, p. 135, chart 2.

Advances in technology and communications, the advent of powerful multinational corporations and new financial tools, and the institutionalisation of the free trade regime among others fuel globalisation in ways which are difficult to halt. While such forces will continue to encourage growth of the world economy as a whole, the concern of governments to 'manage' it cooperatively is likely to persist.

The practice of negotiation lies at the heart of all efforts to manage the global economy.[3] It has been crucial in maintaining stability in the world economic system and in adapting it to changing conditions, and will continue to be so. Today international economic talks, multilateral and bilateral, are very wide in scope and diverse in nature. They vary from institutionalised, continuous talks between states over free trade at the global and regional levels and negotiations between international financial institutions and indebted poor countries over repayments and interest rates, to talks between governments or private firms over the sale of products and joint ventures. Negotiations across this range share nonetheless the objective of creating economic gains or growth.

A stark manifestation of the globalisation of the world economy and the increased significance of international negotiation are found in the area of trade. The fact that international commerce has expanded much faster than the world economy is an indication of greater economic integration. From 1948 to 1998 the world's merchandise trade grew by an average of 6 per cent annually, while merchandise output grew by 4.2 per cent and GDP per capita by 1.9 per cent. In 1998, countries traded about US$5.3 trillion worth of goods (an increase of US$2 trillion compared to a decade earlier) and US$1.3 trillion worth of commercial services.[4] This spectacular growth in international trade results to a large extent from negotiated agreements on worldwide reductions in trade barriers. Falling transportation costs and the opening of new markets such as China and Mexico are other explanations.

---

[3] Works specifically on international economic negotiations include J. Odell, *Negotiating the World Economy* (Cornell University Press, 2000); 'International Economic Negotiations', special issue of *International Negotiation*, Vol. 5, No. 1, 2000, edited by Alice Landau; and V. Kremenyuk and G. Sjöstedt, *International Economic Negotiation: Model Versus Reality* (Edward Elgar Publishing, forthcoming).

[4] The figures are taken from 'Some Facts and Figures: Stats for Seattle', the 3rd WTO Ministerial Conference, 30 November–3 December 1999 (available at the WTO website at http://www.wto.org/wto).

Trade negotiations are no longer limited to the elimination of conventional obstacles such as tariffs and import quotas for goods. The Uruguay Round under the GATT made greater advances in liberalising trade than any previous global agreement, including with respect to services and non-tariff barriers. The growing membership of the GATT and its successor, the WTO, partly reflects the importance which more and more countries attach to this process. Free trade is widely regarded as an engine of economic growth which uses world resources efficiently to raise productivity and overall living standards. However, the benefits and costs of that growth are not necessarily distributed evenly at the global, regional or local levels. Within countries suppliers facing foreign competition must find ways to cut costs and improve productivity in order to survive. On the international stage poor countries are asked to liberalise and to compete with states at a far more advanced economic and technological stage which, in addition, retain protectionist barriers in some of their own markets. A number of factors in recent years have challenged the prospect of further trade liberalisation at the global level. We shall see that many of these were present already in the Uruguay Round, and evoked powerful resentments about unfairness.

One factor has been the persistent conflict between established GATT norms on the one hand and, on the other, certain conceptions of fairness which challenge those norms. In the Uruguay Round of talks on services, the US stressed the importance of creating an overall balance of reciprocal benefits from an agreement. It held that unconditional commitments to the most-favoured-nation (MFN) clause, further discussed below, had encouraged 'free-riding', undermined the objective of trade liberalisation and created asymmetries. The US delegation thus opposed an obligation to MFN without corresponding commitments to national treatment and market access (Self, 2000a). It was a means to deal with the problem of parties who benefited unfairly from other states' removal of trade barriers by failing to open up their own markets adequately. Many other countries regarded the MFN norm as a cornerstone of liberalisation and were critical of the US position. It was nonetheless reflected in the ultimate agreement (Ahnlid, 1996). In the agricultural talks, opposing interests and fairness notions were at the heart of the dispute between the US and the EC. The US delegation attacked the EC's Common Agricultural Policy (CAP) for distorting competition among the world's farmers through export subsidies and other market tools. The EC, by contrast, defended the CAP as a cornerstone of European unity which sought to ensure equality in prices and a decent living standard for the farmers of its member countries. Their protracted argument over compensatory payments to farmers eventually ended through a bilateral deal involving exemption for both sides. It was another instance of automatic, across-the-board application of GATT norms being questioned and indeed rejected.

This chapter examines the influence of concepts and norms relating to justice and fairness in the Uruguay Round of the GATT, which lasted from September 1986 until December 1993.[5] Although the voluminous research literature which exists on the GATT and the Uruguay Round covers the nature and functions of norms (Rhodes, 1993; Qureshi, 1996), no work to date has explored in depth the roles of concepts of justice and fairness in this essential area of international negotiation. After a brief overview of norms of free trade and the Uruguay Round, we will focus on the talks in two key sectors which constitute a large part of the world economy: agriculture and services.

Free trade, fair trade: principles and norms

The global trading system is founded on a number of principles and norms.[6] These have influenced all negotiations to date under the GATT and, more recently, the WTO. The principles are those of economic liberalism and are embodied in the GATT treaties. A pillar stone is David Ricardo's doctrine of 'comparative advantage' on which classic international trade theory is built. It holds that the

---

[5] There are many debates among scholars and policy-makers over the morality or justice of international trade practice which go beyond the scope of this chapter. One issue is the patterns of specialisation and the terms of exchange which free trade establishes or promotes, and their implications for developing countries as exporters of primary goods. Another concerns the use of international trade to further certain values and goals including human rights, labour standards (e.g., abolition of child labour), environmental protection and animal welfare. Questions of whether such values can ever be universally accepted or applicable across cultures and countries, and of who chooses the values to be promoted, have made the use of sanctions and other trade barriers against 'violators' deeply controversial.

[6] 'Principles' are often defined as a set of general beliefs of fact and causation (a fundamental doctrine). From these are derived 'norms' which are referred to as more specific standards of behaviour defined in terms of rights and obligations (Brown, 1997). Principles and norms may be explicit (e.g., expressed in writing) or implicit (understood informally).

comparative production costs for different goods will virtually always vary among countries. This means that even if a country can make several goods more cheaply than another, it should specialise in the good which it can manufacture *most* efficiently and allow the other country to produce the other commodities. The same holds for an inefficient country which cannot produce any good more cheaply than another. If nations follow this rule and engage in trade, they will all acquire more goods and maximise their own economic welfare as well as that of the world as a whole (Ricardo, 1819). A number of other principles follow from this proposition. Free market forces should regulate international commerce as far as possible. Governments should remove barriers to trade and keep any necessary interference to a minimum. As countries then specialise in the products in which they have comparative advantage, all people will enjoy a higher living standard. Furthermore, international trade should not be based on economic power alone nor be hampered by arbitrary measures. Norms of acceptable behaviour, and rules on protectionist measures permitted in exceptional circumstances, should guide them and be enshrined in agreements with legal status. This will create order, fairness, and predictability in international trade relations and thereby promote free commerce (Josling *et al.*, 1996).

The GATT treaties specify a set of norms derived from these principles which lie at the heart of the well-established international trade regime.[7] They are found in the main treaty texts and portrayed as general and enduring obligations, while individual countries' commitments to market access and rules for specific sectors are detailed in annexes and are subject to negotiation. The norms have persisted well over time, but the exact meaning and emphasis attached to them have evolved through bargaining. Their ultimate objective is trade liberalisation as a means to promote global economic growth and prosperity. They embody numerous considerations of fairness and economic policy deemed essential to that goal. Among these are fair competition, non-discrimination and reciprocity. The quasi-legal system created by the GATT treaties and the legacy of decades of bargaining within it help to explain the strength of these norms (Sjöstedt, 1998). They are used to assess and, when necessary,

---

[7] The concept of 'regime' is defined in chapter 1, footnote 11, p. 7 above. The expectations of countries do tend to converge in the area of trade, which highlights their widespread acceptance of norms concerning free and fair trade.

discipline the behaviour of member states on trade matters. In negotiations parties typically perceive it as imperative, or at least as advantageous, to base their positions and claims on some interpretation of GATT norms concerning free and fair trade. Credible arguments based on these have proven difficult to override.

A cardinal norm around which the free trade regime was built is the *most-favoured-nation (MFN) clause*, expressed in Article 1 of the GATT Treaty of 1947. It holds that countries must treat their trading partners equally, without discrimination. Any special trade concession or favour given to one country must be extended automatically to all other GATT (WTO) members, so that imports are treated in the same manner at state borders irrespective of their origin. If a government lowers customs duties for one country's products, it is generally obliged to ensure that all other member states are 'most-favoured' in the same way for the same goods. Some exceptions are permitted. For example, regional free trade areas and customs unions which have been agreed voluntarily including the European Union, the European Free Trade Association and the North American Free Trade Area are sanctioned. Industrialised states are allowed to discriminate in favour of LDCs. Barriers may be raised against countries which trade certain products 'unfairly'.[8] We shall see that the MFN norm became much debated in the Uruguay Round of talks which led to the General Agreement on Trade in Services (GATS) and the Agreement on Trade-Related Aspects of Intellectual Property Rights. A related norm found in the three main GATT/WTO agreements is that of *national treatment*. It prohibits states from modifying the conditions of competition to the advantage of domestic goods, services or providers. As long as these conditions are equal for foreign products once they have entered the local market, host countries may treat them either in the same way as or differently from their own domestic equivalents.[9] MFN and national treatment are meant to ensure *non-discrimination* of member countries when it comes to market access, competition and pricing. The norm of *transparency*, which also figured prominently in the Uruguay Round, seeks to ensure that instruments of trade reform do not hide any protectionist measures.

Another pillar of the international trade system is *reciprocity*, that is,

[8] The General Agreement on Tariffs and Trade (opened for signature on 30 October 1947).

[9] This norm is expressed in Article 3 of the GATT, Article 17 of the GATS, and Article 3 of the Agreement on Trade-Related Aspects of Intellectual Property Rights.

mutual responsiveness to each other's concessions (discussed in chapter 2). The goal of creating reciprocal and mutually beneficial trading relationships is established in the GATT's preamble, and applied to various issues in subsequent Articles. Although based on the notion of comparative advantage, trade talks have come to define a 'concession' as a country's agreement to let in more imports by reducing its own import duties or other trade barriers.[10] Furthermore, reciprocity has come to mean foremost a 'fair balance' of concessions in the sense that each country should be compensated for its import-liberalising measures and increased imports with foreign trade barrier reductions of comparable value. For domestic political reasons, governments often resist lowering trade barriers unless other countries respond in kind.

Part 4 of the GATT grants LDCs special treatment in the form of privileges and exemptions from some norms and rules. For example, LDCs are supposedly not expected to reciprocate the reductions in trade barriers which developed states extend to them (Article 36(8)). The rationale is to bolster their economic development and living standards through preferential access to foreign markets, reasonable and stabilised prices for their exports, and increased export earnings. Any country is entitled to violate its GATT obligations temporarily, in order to retaliate against (reciprocate) specific instances of unfair trade practices. Negotiators continue to debate and to disagree over whether this provision enhances open competition and reduces free-riding, or rather encourages protectionism and trade wars.

Nonetheless, the GATT treaties remain explicit on the subject. For example, member states may use countervailing duties to neutralise competitive advantages which some countries derive from subsidising their exports. A tariff is a sanctioned means to combat dumping, defined as a state selling goods abroad more cheaply than the cost of comparable products in its home market. If this practice hurts domestic industry in the recipient country by distorting its actual competitive edge, the government may undertake antidumping measures designed to protect that industry against price discrimination. The Uruguay Round revealed deep mistrust and disagreement among countries concerning the adequacy and uses of the 1979 Antidumping Code, which was modified as a result (Stewart *et al.*,

---

[10] See, for example, the General Agreement on Tariffs and Trade, Part I: II. Schedules of Concessions.

1993a). The 'safeguards' provision of the GATT (Article 19) permits member states in certain circumstances to restrict imports. Its distinct objective is to protect domestic industry from serious harm rather than to combat unfair trade practices. The Uruguay Round resulted in agreement on, among other matters, new criteria for assessing when safeguards are justified and procedures specifying requirements regarding their use (Stewart *et al.*, 1993b). It was prompted by concern over growing resort to such measures without GATT authorisation.

The GATT, the Uruguay Round and fairness: an overview

The GATT was born in 1947 when twenty-three countries signed the Treaty in Geneva, and it entered into force the following year. It was negotiated at a time when war, discriminatory protectionism in trade and economic depression had shattered the world economy. As a recipe for recovery and the promotion of international peace, the GATT aimed to foster economic growth and development by reducing trade barriers such as customs duties and import quotas on a multilateral basis. The US, having emerged as the world's greatest economic power, had much to gain from these objectives. US leadership and influence were a key driving force not only in the creation of the GATT, but also in many subsequent rounds of trade talks. From 1947 to early 2000, there were eight rounds. The first six of these resulted in substantial reductions in tariffs on imported industrial goods and expanded the GATT membership. They were clearly successful in spurring the post-war economic recovery which occurred in the industrialised world. Thereafter, from 1973 to 1979, the Tokyo Round engaged nearly 100 countries in talks which led to tariff cuts on manufactured goods. It also initiated discussions over a wide range of non-tariff trade barriers, and placed them on the agenda for future negotiations.

A prolonged and conflictive pre-negotiation process spanning over seven years, from 1979 to 1986, preceded the Uruguay Round. The previous rounds had to a large extent been a continuation of past GATT talks, which reduced the need for extensive preparations prior to the official negotiations. The main controversies concerned the necessity of another round of talks, reform in the sensitive sectors of agriculture and textiles, and the inclusion of new sectors on the agenda which hitherto had not been covered by the GATT nor framed

107

as international trade issues. These included services, intellectual property rights and foreign direct investments. Influenced by its own economic interests, the US assumed a decisive role in securing the start of new talks and the inclusion of the new issues.

The adoption of a Ministerial Declaration in Punta del Este, Uruguay, on 20 September 1986 marked the official start of the Uruguay Round with nearly 100 participating countries. Its proclaimed objectives were to further liberalise and expand world trade, to strengthen the multilateral trading system, and to promote economic growth and development. This should be achieved in accordance with the rules and obligations set out in the GATT and to the benefit of all countries, especially less-developed countries in need of financial resources. The Declaration provided various guidelines to be followed in the negotiations. It emphasised the importance of 'balanced concessions', meaning that a country's removal of trade barriers should be reciprocated with foreign liberalising measures and expanded export opportunities of comparable value. Such concessions should be sought within subject areas to avoid cross-sectorial demands.

The Ministerial Declaration also stressed the importance of differential and favourable treatment of LDCs. They would have to reciprocate trade liberalisation measures undertaken by the industrialised world only if and to the extent that this was consistent with their 'individual trade, development or financial needs'.[11] Once their economic situation and capacity to reciprocate had improved, LDCs would be expected to carry out GATT obligations on a basis of greater equality with other states. The results of the talks would be evaluated with the interests of LDCs in mind before being finalised. The Declaration set out the negotiating agenda, and detailed the structures and bodies to be established for the new round of talks. It provided for the formation of a Group of Negotiations on Goods, charged with creating issue-specific negotiating teams as required. Two decision-making councils were also set up for cross-sectional issues, including services.

Disputes involving fairness and justice issues arose throughout the Uruguay Round and help to explain why it took seven years, almost twice the original schedule, to complete. These concerned the struc-

---

[11] 'Ministerial Declaration on the Uruguay Round', 20 September 1986, p. 3, section B(v) (GATT Doc. No. MIN.DEC).

ture of the talks (especially the issues and their order on the negotiating agenda), the process and procedures (such as the reciprocation of concessions and the linkage of trade-offs or agreements across issue areas) and the outcome (the distribution of the costs and benefits of free trade, compliance, and free-riders). The early stage of the talks on trade in services, for example, stumbled over the question of what services sectors they should include. Deep-seated disagreements over what special treatment and exemptions were justified for LDCs plagued the deliberations in this and other areas. The US and the EC among others made their removal of barriers to trade in tropical products conditional upon LDCs also undertaking liberalisation measures, in the same area or with respect to agricultural goods. Many of these countries protested that they could not be expected to reciprocate fully, given the critical dependency of their economies on the exports of such products (Fennell *et al.*, 1993). In the talks over intellectual property rights, LDCs first opposed increased protection on the grounds that it would hamper their access to modern technology. Subsequently they stressed their particular economic, developmental and other needs in seeking favourable treatment with regards to time for implementing new measures, enforcement measures, and harmonisation of pertinent legislation (Ross and Wasserman, 1993).

In the talks on textiles, both the industrialised world and LDCs denounced the existing system of quotas and restrictions under the Multifiber Arrangement as discriminatory.[12] Blaming each other for the situation and disputing how or how fast the textiles trade should be liberalised, they also made ample references to justice and fairness. There was persistent disagreement over linking these talks to other areas in the Uruguay Round. The EC argued that the outcome of the talks on textiles depended on the successful conclusion of the negotiations over tariffs, non-tariff measures, subsidies and other matters. Many LDCs rejected this linkage as lacking foundation in the Punta del Este Declaration. At the same time they reportedly refused to move forward in other areas until progress was secured in the textile talks. The Indian delegation maintained that the success of the entire

---

[12] The Multifiber Arrangement, officially known as Arrangement Regarding International Trade in Textiles (GATT Doc. No. TEX.NG/1), was negotiated between developed and developing countries in the 1960s and entered into force in January 1974.

Uruguay Round depended on resolving the issue of textiles (Hurewitz, 1993).

Arduous negotiations continued until the signing on 15 April 1994 of the Uruguay Round agreements, the 'Final Act', which addressed almost all the areas identified by the original Punta del Este Declaration. They entered into force on 1 January 1995, and were scheduled to be fully implemented in 2002. Although no agreement could be reached on several issues, this outcome went further than any previous GATT deal in reforming the world's trading system. The new provisions included freer trade in agriculture and services, and the removal of some non-tariff barriers to trade. They established the WTO whose new stricter mechanisms for ensuring compliance and resolving trade disputes strengthened the international trade regime considerably (Weaver and Abellard, 1993). Member countries failing to honour their obligations could now face sanctions.[13] In the process which eventually led to the Final Act, the talks concerned with liberalising commerce in agricultural products and services were among the most difficult. In fact, they prevented the Uruguay Round from being concluded successfully in 1990 as originally foreseen. We will now turn to a more detailed analysis of the talks in these two sectors.

Negotiating the intractable: reforming agricultural trade

Despite earlier efforts to liberalise trade in agricultural goods, this sector remained largely exempt from the usual rules and norms of international commerce when the Uruguay Round got underway. At the time of its foundation in 1947, the GATT defined agriculture as a special case and made stipulations which conformed with the domestic agricultural regulations of the major signatories (Hathaway, 1987). This permitted many industrialised countries and regional trading blocs to pursue elaborate protectionist policies without restraint for several decades. The justifications and goals were generally to secure price stability and a 'fair' level of income for farmers, adequate food supplies at reasonable prices for consumers, and a

---

[13] 'The Final Act Embodying the Results of the Uruguay Round of Multilateral Trade Negotiations'. Signed by ministers in Marrakesh on 15 April 1994. GATT, Geneva, 1995 (GATT 94/4).

sustained or increased volume of exports. Major trading states such as the US, Canada, Japan and EU member countries are cases in point where governments had relied on export subsidies, import quotas, licensing requirements, voluntary export restrictions and other devices to influence prices and the volume of imports and exports in the agricultural sector. At the core of the EC's agricultural policy was import duties and export subsidies ('export restitution payments') designed to ensure equality in commodity prices among member states, and equal revenue from the sale of the same products whether done outside of or within the Community's borders (Breen, 1993).

While successful in supporting the agricultural sector of the industrialised world, this protectionism had been very costly in other respects. It had instilled resentment and conflict in trade relations. Policies pursued in the name of fairness in a local or national context and, in the case of the EC, at the regional level resulted in distorted terms of trade and perceptions of gross injustices on the international stage. Those trading with the EC lost a share of the world market because of the latter's protectionist agricultural policy. Agricultural protectionism also entailed massive government expenditures in industrialised nations, financed by their consumers and taxpayers. In the early 1990s, the CAP accounted for over half of the EC's overall expenditure.

In the years leading up to the Uruguay Round, a consensus developed on the need to place agricultural trade under effective GATT regulations. The 1986 Punta del Este Declaration, which marked the official launch of the new Round, signalled a firm commitment to end the long-held special status of the sector. It called upon countries to negotiate cuts in import barriers, subsidies and other distortive measures, and to minimise the adverse impact of sanitary regulations on agricultural trade, especially for LDCs.[14] The subsequent talks, conducted within the Negotiating Group on Agriculture, became nonetheless complex and protracted. Many disputes surfaced over how the global agricultural trade system ought to be transformed: the desirable types and levels of reductions in trade barriers and the best ways to measure them, reform of the EC's CAP and any compensation to European farmers for cuts in export subsidies, and what special consideration and treatment LDCs and

---

[14] 'Ministerial Declaration on the Uruguay Round'. 20 September 1986 (GATT Doc. No. MIN.DEC).

countries highly dependent on imports for their food security may deserve.

The most prominent dispute developed between, on the one hand, the EC and, on the other, the US which enjoyed the general support of the Cairns Group, a coalition of agricultural exporting countries.[15] It caused other parties to express resentment in due course over slow progress and lesser attention given to other issues in the talks. The US administration sought to eliminate protectionism as far as possible in favour of a market-driven trading system. It wanted stricter regulations concerning the use of export subsidies, stronger dispute resolution and enforcement mechanisms, improved market access, and a gradual removal of all trade-distorting domestic subsidies and import barriers over ten years. The last-mentioned item, known as the 'zero-option', was included in the initial US proposal. According to its Trade Representative at the time, the US did not truly hope to achieve a total phase-out: the request was meant to draw international attention to the US resolve to secure far-reaching reforms (Yeutter, 1998). As a means to tackle trade distortions caused by government support of the agricultural sector and by production surpluses, the US advocated 'decoupling' all domestic support and their effects from production. In November 1988, a US framework proposal was put forward which called for the conversion of all non-tariff trade barriers into more visible and measurable tariffs ('tariffication'), which would be reduced and eventually eliminated through negotiation (Hillman, 1994). The chief target of these demands was the EC's CAP, which the US and the Cairns Group held responsible for many dilemmas in agricultural trade. The US was particularly concerned about liberalising trade in cereals and oilseeds.

By contrast the EC, on whose behalf the EC Commission negotiated, favoured a market-managed trading system involving partial liberalisation which could raise world agricultural prices (de Zeeuw, 1998). A fundamental longer-term objective was to reduce the steep costs of supporting farmers' income. EC delegates refused to phase out the CAP, which they described as a cornerstone of European unity, but admitted that the policy had to be reformed and agreed to consider 'decoupling'. They accepted limited tariffication, but insisted on

---

[15] The Cairns Group included Argentina, Australia, Brazil, Canada, Chile, Columbia, Fiji, Hungary, Indonesia, Malaysia, New Zealand, the Philippines, Thailand and Uruguay.

'rebalancing' rather than reducing market access barriers as a means to preserve the CAP. In other words, they wanted to be able to reduce export subsidies and other aid extended to their most protected agricultural goods, and in exchange give more support to other poorly sheltered products (e.g., oilseeds). To this effect, the Community further suggested the use of an aggregate measure of support calculating the total domestic assistance to agriculture across all programmes. Countries would thereby retain the flexibility to decide what subsidies they wanted to change and to what degree. The US and other major exporters rejected both these proposals as contrary to the central purpose of the negotiations. EC representatives stressed throughout the talks that the CAP was an internal matter to be negotiated only within the Community, not in an international context like the Uruguay Round. Those advocating reform of the CAP added that the EC was the only forum in which protectionist forces would concede to liberalising measures (Hellström, 1998).

The agricultural talks had made little progress by December 1988, and the parties were unable to conclude a mid-term agreement as planned. In April 1989 a broad framework agreement was finally reached in Geneva. It confirmed the goal of a substantial reduction in trade-distorting agricultural support without specifying the types of measures necessary to achieve this. It held that LDCs were entitled to 'special and differential treatment' and that the final arrangements had to take account of their needs. The accord lent some legitimacy to concerns about food security by stating that any negative impact of reforms on agricultural importing countries should be given special attention.[16] Nevertheless, another five years of protracted negotiations took place before the Uruguay Round could be concluded. The EC–US dispute again caused deadlock in the agricultural talks in the late spring of 1990, this time over the question of reductions in farm subsidies. In an attempt to break the stalemate, the Chairman of the Negotiating Group on Agriculture issued a draft text to serve as the basis for further discussion. The EC delegation responded negatively, because the text proposed faster cuts in export subsidies than in other forms of support. In July the US and the EC agreed to shift the focus to more technical matters, so as to prevent a collapse of the talks (Breen, 1993).

The intractability of the EC–US dispute re-emerged all too soon,

---

[16] 'Mid-Term Meeting'. 21 April 1989 (GATT Doc. No. MTN.TNC/11).

however. In preparation for a ministerial meeting scheduled for December 1990 in Brussels, the Secretary-General of the GATT asked all parties to detail their final offers on what liberalising measures they were prepared to accept. The US demanded over ten years a 90 per cent cut in most export subsidies, a 75 per cent reduction in the most trade-distorting domestic support measures, and a 30 per cent cut in the less distorting ones. It requested tariffication and a 75 per cent reduction with respect to border protection. The US thereby abandoned the 'zero option' officially, and also agreed to measure all deductions in assistance using the Aggregate Measure of Support. The EC offered a 30 per cent cut in domestic support over ten years, and insisted on a provision for 'rebalancing' as a condition for accepting partial tariffication. There was no promise of a specific reduction in export subsidies. The EC delegates argued that given the operation of the CAP, a general commitment to reduce domestic support using the Aggregate Measure of Support would result in proper cuts in border protection and export assistance. They also wanted reductions in levels of support to be calculated based on average reference prices between 1984 and 1986, thus giving the EC credit for reductions made during the Uruguay Round. The US and the Cairns Group rejected these terms, fearing that they would enable the EC to evade reduction requirements (Ingersent *et al.*, 1994). On another front, Japan protested that the US plan for tariffication would leave its vital rice market too vulnerable (Hemmi, 1994).

The 1990 Ministerial Meeting in Brussels was meant to produce the final agreements. Only the Negotiating Group on Sanitary and Phytosanitary Measures succeeded in producing a draft text in time for this encounter. The LDCs had expressed concern about the standards for such measures which, they feared, discriminated against the products of poorer countries. Industrialised states thus proposed harmonisation of standards based on scientific evidence, which was agreed. But the EC–US disputes stalled the negotiations in all areas. The Chair of the agricultural talks, Sweden's Agriculture Minister Mats Hellström, attempted to break the stalemate by presenting a compromise plan. The EC rejected this because it used 1988 as a base year for measuring subsidy cuts and omitted the option of 'rebalancing' reductions. The Community delegates held that a base year after 1986 would be unfair in failing to take account of liberalisation measures undertaken since the launch of the Round. Hearing the EC's response the US and the

Cairns Group, which had accepted the Swedish plan, walked out of the talks.

A factor contributing to the failure of the Brussels meeting concerned net food-importing nations such as Japan and Korea with highly protected agricultural markets. They rejected the provisions for minimum market access in the Hellström compromise and later in the Dunkel Draft, for failing to recognise the concept of food security adequately. Throughout the Round these countries stressed the importance of considering their special conditions; namely, the vital importance to them of self-sufficiency and the land and climatic constraints on their agriculture. They held that food security was a reasonable justification for protective border measures like import quotas, especially for their staple food, rice. Japan pointed to how weather conditions could cause large fluctuations in world supplies and prices of rice, and stated that liberalising the rice trade could threaten its population and cause political unrest (Hemmi, 1994). Jamaica and some other food-importing LDCs claimed that they ought to be compensated for likely increases in food prices. The underlying argument was that agricultural goods differed from industrial goods and that non-economic factors such as food security, and environmental and cultural concerns, must be taken into account in making rules about trade in them (Akao, 1998). The Japanese delegates insisted that the GATT rules be revised to permit border measures which could sustain a secure level of domestic food production. They pointed to the inequality of gains that would otherwise result from liberalisation: while countries such as the US had nothing to lose, Japan had nothing to gain.

The US and the Cairns Group argued by contrast that self-sufficiency is ineffective, expensive and damaging to other countries, and no excuse for undertaking trade-distorting policies (Breen, 1993). The US delegation held that the argument about food security might lock a permanent distortion into world trade, and refused to accept it. Compensation could simply not be given every time a measure of liberalisation disadvantaged some country in the short term (Yeutter, 1998). The US Trade Representative condemned the Japanese position in moral terms: 'If the second largest industrialised market in the world, a market spreading the rest of the world with manufactured goods, is insisting on maintaining the surplus of manufactured goods, but refusing to take the agricultural output of poor nations that have nothing else to sell, you can be sure that the poor nations will not stay at the bargaining table' (Rapkin and George, 1993, p. 83).

After several top level efforts to end the deadlock the Director-General of the GATT, Arthur Dunkel, issued in December 1991 the first draft of a legal agreement addressing all areas of the talks. It included points of agreement which had been reached, compromise solutions where disputes remained as in the agricultural sphere, and a four-track approach for completing the Round.[17] The US and most members of the Cairns Group accepted the draft. The EC objected on several grounds, including that it used a volume-based method for measuring export subsidy cuts and failed to sanction EC compensatory payments to farmers. The prospects of progress turned brighter when the EC member states in May 1992 agreed to reform the CAP substantially. The plan, based on cuts in the support prices for cereals, beef and dairy products, brought the US and other countries back to the bargaining table. But EC–US disputes on several issues, especially the matter of oilseed subsidies, persisted and continued to threaten a successful outcome of the Round. They were not settled until the signing in November 1992 of the so-called Blair House Accord, which changed certain key elements of the Dunkel Draft (Schott and Buurman, 1994). French farmers protested furiously against this agreement, which France refused to ratify. In the following year, a breakthrough on market access at the Group of Seven meeting in Tokyo paved the way for a conclusion of the Uruguay Round. The Blair House Accord was revised again in December 1993, when the talks finally ended after seven years. During subsequent months, the parties were able to examine each other's proposed schedules for implementing commitments and to make adjustments.

Trade ministers from 123 countries and the EU signed the 'Final Act' in Marrakesh, Morocco, on 15 April 1994 and thereby made their commitments legally binding. The agreements affecting agricultural trade entailed substantial liberalisation, including almost full tariffication, and were seen as steps in a process to establish a fair and market-oriented trading system with special concern for LDCs. They strengthened the rules governing this trade and thus improved its stability and predictability to the benefit of both importers and exporters. First, the agreements placed ceilings on and stopped the escalation of

---

[17] 'Draft Final Act Embodying the Results of the Uruguay Round of Multilateral Trade Negotiations'. 20 December 1991 (GATT Doc. No. MTN.TNC/W/FA).

export subsidies. Developed countries and the EC/EU were required to reduce the value of such subsidies by 36 per cent and their quantity by 21 per cent below the 1986–90 base period over six years from January 1995. Developing countries were to undertake reductions which are two-thirds of those of developed states over ten years. No requirements applied to the least-developed nations. Secondly, the provisions for market access converted virtually all non-tariff barriers into tariffs and bound all tariffs on imported goods.[18] They established minimum access tariff quotas and opened up the long-closed markets of numerous countries, including Japan's and Korea's rice markets. Industrialised countries were to reduce tariffs by an average of 36 per cent over six years, and LDCs by 24 per cent over ten years. No tariff cuts were required of the least-developed countries. Thirdly, the provisions placed ceilings on the total domestic subsidies provided to farmers, using the Aggregate Measure of Support. They must be reduced during the implementation period by 20 per cent in developed states and by 13.3 per cent in LDCs (no requirements for the least-developed). Some measures were exempted, notably direct income support payments (e.g., payments 'decoupled' from production) and policies with a minimal trade-distorting impact (so-called 'green box' policies). Fourthly, the agreement on sanitary and phytosanitary measures specified when the use of import restrictions is legitimate. Basically, countries would be entitled to take such measures when necessary to protect human, animal and plant life or health if they are based on scientific standards and do not arbitrarily or unjustifiably discriminate between states where similar conditions prevail. Countries could use their own standards but if these are stricter, they must be applied consistently and be justified by science or a non-discriminatory level of acceptable risk which does not target imports.

The negotiations over services

Another much protected area which had escaped GATT regulations until the launch of the Uruguay Round was services. The term refers to a wide range of sectors including communications, transport,

---

[18] 'Bound' tariffs or other commitments mean that they can be modified or withdrawn only after negotiations with affected countries, which may require compensatory payments. 'Unbinding' is difficult in practice, and the commitments are therefore virtually guaranteed and secure.

banking, health, legal and financial services, advertising, retail, tourism and engineering. Historically, these areas of economic activity had been regarded as matters of domestic commerce to be regulated by individual countries. For four decades therefore, multilateral negotiations over trade liberalisation focused almost exclusively on goods. There were several reasons behind the final decision to include services in the GATT. Their necessity to the efficient production and exchange of goods appeared obvious. Since the 1970s, international trade in services had grown far more rapidly than trade in goods and had become vital to the economies of many countries. At the same time national regulations restricting market access, currency movements and so forth prevented full expansion of this lucrative area of commerce.

Several industrialised countries with the US in the lead began attempts in the early 1980s to include services, of which they are large exporters, on the agenda of multilateral trade talks. While having much to gain from reduced protectionism they held that it was essential to economic growth and well-being in all GATT member states, including poorer ones. Studies commissioned by the GATT subsequently supported the proposition that discriminatory bilateral and regional regulations would expand if multilateral rules were not developed for trade in services. The US, the world's largest exporter of services with an economy crucially dependent on this sector, felt particularly strongly about the issue. It threatened to leave the GATT unless services were placed on the negotiating table. The matter evolved into a major dispute, as others were not convinced. EC member states initially resisted the inclusion of services: like many others, they were unclear about the impact which trade liberalisation would have on their interests in this area and more generally (Tran, 1998). The greatest opposition came from LDCs, which held that they needed and were entitled to more time to develop their own services sectors before exposing them to outside competition. Moreover, they considered progress on liberalising trade in agriculture and textiles a far more pressing matter.

The eventual outcome of this dispute was a compromise, reflected in Part II of the 1986 Punta del Este Declaration. The decision was that services would indeed be negotiated, in tandem with goods and with GATT rules and procedures as the guidelines. However, the concerns of poorer countries were addressed in three major ways. The talks would be conducted in a separate forum formally outside the GATT system, and be overseen by a Group of Negotiations on Services. A Trade Negotiations Committee, chaired by the Director-General of the GATT, would coordinate this track with the talks over goods. The Declaration recognised that the process must respect national regulations in the services area and consider the LDCs' needs (e.g., for expanded export opportunities, technology transfers, and time for adjustment) if they were to benefit fully from a liberalisation of the services trade (Reyna, 1993).

The official talks over services became difficult and protracted. In the period from the Punta del Este Declaration to a mid-term review in Montreal in 1988, the parties sought with limited success to establish the parameters for a new agreement on trade in services. The agenda was set out in a report by the Chair of the Group of Negotiations on Services, Felipe Jaramillo of Columbia. It soon emerged that the issues it raised were contentious and complex, partly because of the lack of agreement on basic definitions and poor data. One question concerned whether such an agreement should cover all or only certain service sectors. The US delegation among others were pressurised domestically to exclude particular sectors, including aviation and maritime transportation, on grounds including national security. The majority of parties, by contrast, considered coverage of all sectors a necessary means to balance the diverse interests of countries. Another issue was whether the existing GATT structure and norms could apply to an agreement on services given how they differed from trade in goods. India and Brazil argued that a good case had yet to be made for applying these rules to services (Colt, 1988).

The mid-term review meeting in Montreal in December 1988 produced little progress. The Trade Negotiations Committee then issued a report which detailed the basis for further negotiations.[19] It reiterated that the coverage of sectors should balance the concerns of all parties and address the export interests of LDCs. The GATS should also include a provision on the MFN clause and non-discrimination. The report urged parties to begin discussions on how GATT norms would actually be applied to services, sector by sector. These got underway in late spring 1989. By September of that year, largely all

[19] 'Mid-Term Meeting'. Report on the results adopted by the Trade Negotiations Committee at its mid-term review held in Montreal on 5–9 December 1988 and in Geneva on 5–8 April 1989. 21 April 1989 (GATT Doc. No. MTN.TNC/11).

participating countries had agreed that the GATS would be established as a mechanism separate from but in tandem with the GATT. Many heated disputes persisted. The US proposed the first comprehensive framework for an agreement in October, which for most parties favoured too rapid liberalisation. On the matter of coverage the US, supported by the EC, held that all sectors should be covered by the GATS and be subject to trade liberalisation except for those specified on a 'negative list'. Other states favoured a more gradual approach with a 'positive list', whereby only those sectors specifically added to a country's national schedule would be liberalised (Drake and Nicolaidis, 1992). Proposals on the application of the MFN clause were based on considerations as diverse as economic development needs, mutual obligations and reciprocity, and universality. The US pushed for an immediate and universal application of the GATT norms concerning MFN, national treatment, and open market access.

Another conflictive issue was the treatment of LDCs under an agreement on services. Most of the developing world was at this point convinced that their 'special and differentiated treatment' under Part 4 of the GATT had not been effective (Jaramillo, 1998). This clause had possibly benefited the very poorest states, but ignored many others. It was inflexible in that LDCs, as signatories to the GATT, had to use Part 4 as an escape clause and could only do so in some instances. Instead of having a specific section devoted to their concerns, LDCs now sought to have them woven into the treaty's main framework in a more flexible way which would recognise different stages of development (Nunes, 1998). They reiterated that their service sectors needed time to become more competitive and that they must decide for themselves the desirable rate and steps of liberalisation without fear of retaliation from the industrialised world. They held that they must be allowed, just as developed states had once been, to protect infant industries from foreign competition which would otherwise inhibit their growth and worsen trade deficits. Their objective was to liberalise only certain markets selectively which were of interest to them, and to create a preferential trading system among themselves. The LDCs also asked that their liberalisation measures be linked to technology and financial transfers from richer states, as a result of findings that information technology favours the comparative advantage of services over manufacturing.

Other states with the US in the lead argued that trade liberalisation was the best means to promote economic expansion in the poorer world. Previous experiences of 'free-riders' – of countries benefiting from the liberalisation measures of others without opening up their own markets – under the GATT had caused wariness of differentiated treatment (Hawes, 1998). There was nonetheless widespread recognition that level of development should be considered in the process of removing trade barriers, that LDCs could not be expected to reciprocate on an equal basis, and that their concerns had to be addressed if they were to remain at the negotiating table. The controversies focused instead on the details of how far the principle of special and differentiated treatment ought to be applied. The US chief negotiator stated that his country sought 'some form of "down payment" of liberalisation [from LDCs] so that the agreement [on services] could have some commercial value to our services providers. And, there is no question that we were under considerable pressure by these industries to produce' (Self, 2000b). The EC asked for less from the LDCs, and reportedly favoured measures equivalent in *impact* given differences in levels of development among parties (Falkenberg, 1998). This would allow services industries to get established in the LDCs without too much exposure to international competition. Unlike the US, the EC and LDCs were prepared to accept an unconditional MFN obligation and to defer commitments to market access and national treatment to future talks (Self, 1998).

A compromise reached in early 1990 permitted states to withhold obligations based on the level of development of individual service sectors and the failure of any parties to open up their markets adequately. In July, the Chair of the Group of Negotiations on Services issued a draft revealing persistent disagreement on many questions (Reyna, 1993). One issue concerned whether various provisions should be classified as 'general obligations' for universal application, or as 'specific commitments' under national schedules to be negotiated in future Rounds.

The applicability of an MFN provision in a general agreement on services remained hotly disputed and nearly caused the talks to collapse. In November 1990, the US delegation argued that there should be no automatic application of MFN to all services once the GATS took effect: it should be extended only as a result of negotiated agreements on specific sectors. This would remove the possibility for countries to be free-riders. The US held that the incentives to reciprocate its own and some other states' commitments on market access and national treatment would otherwise be insufficient. The Chair, Mr

Jaramillo, and numerous delegations angrily rejected the position as damaging to the talks and to the substance of an agreement. This US proposal was reportedly not serious about insisting on or endorsing commitments based on specific reciprocity: the main point was to reject other countries' preparedness to conclude the Round by assuming an obligation to MFN in services without measures regarding market access and national treatment. It reflected a time of high tensions which culminated in the so-called 'Night of the Long Knives' immediately prior to a meeting of the Trade Negotiations Committee in Brussels (Self, 2000b).

The MFN issue became the major agenda item at the Brussels Ministerial Meeting in December 1990, which was meant to produce the final agreement. It was chiefly the deadlock reached in the agricultural negotiations over the EC's trade-distorting subsidies which caused the services talks and the entire Uruguay Round to break down in that month. There is reason to doubt, however, that the Brussels talks would have resulted in a successful outcome in any event. The Co-Chairman of the Group of Negotiations on Services believes that if the parties had concluded an agreement at this time, the results would have been disastrous: the thirty-five drafted Articles still lacked clear definitions and detailed provisions as a reflection of remaining disagreements and calls for exemptions (Hawes, 1998). India's chief negotiator agrees, adding that the parties did not even understand the issues fully at this time (Zutshi, 1998).

When the services talks resumed in the spring of 1991 they came to focus on the framework for an agreement, improved national commitments, and sectorial annexes. Offers of trade liberalisation measures were submitted by thirty-five countries in an expanded range of service sectors. The major talks on MFN took place in the autumn of that year. The main dispute concerned whether MFN should apply globally to all sectors, and the conditions under which any exemptions for specific services would be permitted (Jaramillo, 1998). Once more the talks reached a stalemate: the US delegation rejected the EC request for an exemption for telecommunications and broadcasting, and the resistance of LDCs to liberalising maritime industries. Eventually the US indicated a willingness to extend MFN privileges to long-distance telecommunications, if all parties with major markets in this sector committed themselves to implement full market access and national treatment (Reyna, 1993). The Dunkel Draft of December 1991 largely endorsed the text with which the delegates had been working, and provided the basis of the remaining talks. The Draft allowed parties to receive exemptions from the MFN obligations under certain circumstances and for a limited period of time, normally up to ten years.[20]

The signing of the final GATS agreement in April 1994 established a legally enforceable framework to govern international trade in services. Like the GATT, the main text set out norms and rules applicable to all parties, while annexes detailed country commitments and regulations for individual sectors. There were three fundamental aspects to the agreement. First, total coverage: it applied to all services traded and supplied across state borders on a commercial and/or competitive basis (thus excluding government-provided services). However, governments could select the service sectors in which they made commitments to liberalisation. Secondly, national treatment: the GATS forbade most forms of discrimination against foreign suppliers of services in the areas in which commitments were made. Some restrictions were allowed. In contrast to the GATT, national treatment had to be applied only in sectors in which a country had specifically promised to give foreigners access to its market. In other words, parties could limit the scope of the market access and national treatment which they gave. Thirdly, the MFN norm: countries must treat the services and their suppliers of all member countries equally. However, governments could get one-time, temporary exemptions even from this clause, normally for a maximum of ten years. These were listed in the Appendix, and thus permitted more favourable treatment of some GATT/WTO members than others.[21] Other stipulations required that domestic regulations, the principal way to influence the services trade, be transparent, reasonable, objective and impartial. Indeed, numerous aspects of the agreement called for transparency which the parties viewed as essential to fairness. They sought to ensure compliance with commitments, by requesting countries to make their laws on trade in services widely known and by exposing distorting measures.

The GATS called for new rounds of talks to lower trade barriers

---

[20] 'Draft Final Act Embodying the Results of the Uruguay Round of Multilateral Trade Negotiations'. 20 December 1991 (GATT Doc. No. MTN.TNC/W/FA).

[21] 'General Agreement on Trade in Services' in 'The Final Act Embodying the Results of the Uruguay Round of Multilateral Trade Negotiations'. GATT, Geneva, 1995 (GATT 94/4).

further. At the end of the Uruguay Round governments also decided to continue negotiating over four sectors in which they had so far failed to reach agreement: telecommunications, maritime transport, financial services and the movement of natural persons.

Assessing the Uruguay Round: fairness and justice in the agricultural talks

Like other international negotiations, the Uruguay Round of the GATT was not driven foremost by concerns about justice or fairness *per se*. The overall objectives were economic and the driving force the desire to continue liberalising world trade. At the national level efforts to increase economic growth, notably by maximising export opportunities, influenced the positions and behaviour of individual delegations. Few appear to have thought directly about concepts of justice and fairness. Several high-level negotiators stated in interviews that these were 'new' terms which they did not feel comfortable using in discussing the Round. It may be that when an elaborate regime of norms and rules already exists, negotiators do not need to refer to such considerations as often or as openly as when they bargain outside any normative framework (Sjöstedt, 1998). Even if delegates seldom contemplated or directly invoked these concepts during the talks, their behaviour reflected such concerns (Tran, 1998). The US, the EC and the LDCs did make explicit references to fairness and justice when debating the CAP, reciprocity, free-riders, exemptions and preferential treatment, and more so than in previous GATT rounds. According to the Co-Chairman of the Group of Negotiations on Services, the parties discussed the importance of balancing benefits and sought to make roughly reciprocal commitments (Hawes, 1998).

At the core of the agricultural talks were profound disagreements over market access and the conduct of trade, and appropriate pathways to a liberalised agricultural trading system. These disputes caused many deadlocks in the talks. A central conflict concerned the EC's agricultural policy, which prevented a successful conclusion of the entire Uruguay Round for almost two years. The US and the Cairns Group regarded the EC's export subsidies as the most trade-distorting type of support measure and as an aggressive dumping instrument, which harmed their own economies as well as those of LDCs and other exporting states. They held that the CAP stole foreign markets, while preventing outside access to the EC's own markets.

The policy also kept domestic prices high, and was in this sense unfair to consumers (Hellström, 1998).

Stressing that the GATT prohibits such subsidies for all other sectors, the US sought to rectify what it viewed as an unfair situation for US and other agricultural exporters. It wanted to create new trade rules promoting competition on equal terms (Hillman, 1994). The US protested especially against the CAP's export grants to buyers of wheat, which had made the EC a very competitive supplier of flour worldwide and eroded the US market share. Already prior to the Uruguay Round, the US had started to use a retaliatory, tit-for-tat strategy of subsidising its own wheat flour sales. The US insisted on reciprocity and matched EC export subsidies with subsidies of their own, in an effort to trigger change in EC trade practices and regain their full share of the world market. The policy failed to stop the Community from dumping surplus wheat flour outside its borders at subsidised prices. It exemplified nonetheless the new emphasis on ensuring reciprocity and fair competition by use of instruments which contradicted other cardinal GATT norms such as non-discrimination (Rhodes, 1993).

The EC Commission held that its favoured approach of market management would benefit all states, including LDCs, by preventing 'unjustified costs of cut-throat competition' (Ingersent *et al.*, 1994, p. 59). The main argument put forward against the abolition of the CAP was its importance as a pillar of European unity. The EC confirmed its commitment to the goals of the policy, to defend a good living standard for farmers and to ensure reasonable and stable food prices for consumers and equality in prices among EC states. Towards the end of the Uruguay Round, however, the EC Agricultural Commissioner recognised that the CAP was inequitable and unbalanced and proposed reforms. He attributed the problem of the EC's agricultural overproduction to the CAP's guarantee of product prices. While the US and the Cairns Group repudiated the EC request for the option of 'rebalancing' trade barriers as a tactic to avoid major reductions, the Community knew that it had to cut its high spending on subsidies (Murphy, 1998). Unwilling to abandon its support of farmers and without an alternative policy in place, the EC insisted that more gradual cuts in export subsidies were required to permit adjustment than those proposed by the US and other countries.

A difficult dispute concerned the financial compensation for cuts in support prices which European farmers were to receive under the reformed CAP. The GATT Director-General, Mr Dunkel, the US and other parties insisted that these compensatory payments were not sufficiently 'decoupled' from production to qualify for exemption and must therefore be phased out. The EC responded that the USA's own deficiency payments to farmers functioned as trade-distorting export subsidies and should not be exempted. Ultimately the two parties worked out a bilateral agreement, without input from other GATT members: the reformed EC income support (related to hectare of land or head of animal) and the US deficiency payments would both be exempted from being phased out under a separate so-called 'blue box' arrangement. It was a special negotiated deal which addressed the interests and fairness conceptions of the particular parties, and bypassed simple across-the-board application of GATT norms emphasising free trade. The Chair of the Negotiating Group on Agriculture underscored that pragmatism motivated the exemption of the CAP payments: it would have been politically impossible for the EC to move directly to income support which was entirely decoupled from means of production (de Zeeuw, 1998).

Several parties were sceptical about the EC argument that any base year for reforms after 1986 would be unfair, in failing to give credit for European liberalisation measures undertaken since the launch of the Round. According to high-level participants the matter was not really about fairness, but the EC simply sought to limit the steep liberalisation measures which a later year would require (Hellström, 1998). Nonetheless, Mr Dunkel recognised that granting some credit for the EC reforms since 1984 was required to break the stalemate in the talks. The final agreement thus permitted 1986 to be used as a base year for reductions.[22]

Concepts of fairness and justice also influenced the agricultural talks when it comes to the treatment of the LDCs. They had not generally been able to afford subsidising agricultural production and had instead taxed their farmers, in contrast to industrialised states. Heavily dependent on agricultural exports, they had suffered much from their restricted access to rich-country markets. For them, fairness required increased market access and the choice not to reciprocate measures in the process of trade liberalisation. As noted, provisions

---

[22] The final agreement on agriculture defined the years from 1986 to 1988 as the base period for domestic subsidy reductions, and the years from 1986 to 1990 as the base period for export subsidy cuts (Schott and Buurman, 1994).

within the GATT already granted LDCs special privileges. There was broad agreement that they should not have to undertake the same reforms within the same time frame as developed countries, but controversy over the preferable nature and extent of special treatment. Some industrialised states sought to extend it only to the very poorest states, or in other ways phase out or limit differential treatment (Watkins, 1991). When Jamaica and other food-importing LDCs requested compensation for the removal of export subsidies and for supposedly higher food prices, the US held that they too would ultimately benefit from a liberalised trading system and that any price increases would be short-lived. A member of the US delegation held that granting compensation for trade distortions would have been extremely difficult, since negotiators would have had to establish which liberalisation measures had affected what parties adversely and to what extent (Yeutter, 1998).

The final agreements relating to agriculture nonetheless addressed many concerns of the LDCs, partly by compromising on norms of free trade for a period of time. The notions of preferential treatment of these countries, the least developed in particular, and mutual gains (that is, ensuring that LDCs too would benefit from liberalisation) influenced numerous provisions including those on cuts in export subsidies, tariffs and domestic subsidies. Certain government assistance measures to encourage agricultural development in LDCs were endorsed. The new provisions on standards for sanitary and phytosanitary measures embodied a range of fairness considerations, most of which were incorporated also in other parts of the Uruguay Round agreements. They included differential treatment of LDCs to take account of their financial, trade and development needs (e.g., more time for compliance and time-limited exemptions from agreed obligations), harmonisation in accordance with generally accepted scientific standards, non-discrimination, and transparency.[23] Food security was not established as a GATT principle, but its significance for some countries was acknowledged. It was recognised that liberalisation could undermine the availability of adequate food supplies at reasonable prices to LDCs and that international food, technical and financial aid to help meet the needs of the least developed and food-importing

---

[23] 'Agreement on Sanitary and Phytosanitary Measures', Articles 31–4, in 'The Final Act Embodying the Results of the Uruguay Round of Multilateral Trade Negotiations' (note 21 above).

developing states was essential.[24] Japan took the lead in establishing the relevance of 'non-trade concerns' in the liberalisation of agricultural trade, and secured exemptions from tariffication requirements under certain conditions (applicable to rice). In exchange for being allowed to exempt a product from tariffication, however, a country had to accept a higher percentage of minimum imports (which Japan did).

Finally, the formulation of a 'balanced package' based on the consideration of all affected interests, compromise and mutual benefit was reportedly a major factor propelling key governments to accept the final Uruguay Round agreements (Jaramillo, 1998; Hawes, 1998). Several high-level negotiators stated that they regarded parts of the texts as unfair, but that their perception of the overall outcome as one based on largely balanced concessions from a more objective viewpoint prompted them to sign (Yeutter, 1998; Akao, 1998). To mention one example, Japan reportedly thought that its own food security concerns were comparable to those of many countries considered LDCs, such as Korea, and that the latter's more favourable treatment on the matter of food security was unjustified. Moreover, Japan thought that market access should be reciprocal in the sense that food-importing countries such as itself should have a guarantee concerning food supplies from exporters, in exchange for promising access to their own markets for exporting states. The final agreements satisfied Japan only in part, but were sufficient to be seen as a fair deal overall (Akao, 1998).

Fairness and justice in the talks over services

GATT norms became particularly debated in the services talks, in which there was no prior concept of trade. Formulated for goods, they did not readily apply to services given their unique properties. The first major fairness issue emerged long before the official negotiations began. It was the question of whether services should be included at all on the agenda for the new round of GATT talks. The greatest resistance came from LDCs, notably India and Brazil. They argued that they needed more time to develop their own services sectors

[24] 'Decision on Measures Concerning the Possible Negative Effects of the Reform Programme on Least-Developed and Net Food-Importing Developing Countries' in 'The Final Act Embodying the Results of the Uruguay Round of Multilateral Trade Negotiations' (note 21 above).

before being able to negotiate these on a basis of equality with the industrialised world, which controlled about 80 per cent of the trade in that area. Given their own relatively weak and unregulated services sectors, LDCs suspected that the application of GATT rules at the time would freeze existing inequities between the North and the South. The rules might cause LDCs always to remain exporters in less lucrative areas, given their comparative disadvantage in services. The developing world also feared that the removal of protectionist regulations, exposure to international competition and a large influx of foreign companies would erode their sovereignty and increase dependence (Weiss, 1995). Finally, they thought that industrialised states had failed to fulfil obligations in sectors important to them. Market access for LDCs remained particularly limited in the areas of agriculture and textiles. They requested progress on these fronts before more complex issues were added to the negotiating agenda (Winham, 1989).

The concept of balancing diverse interests guided the eventual resolution of this dispute, and permitted the negotiations to move forward. The parties worked to construct a broad agenda which addressed a sufficiently wide range of concerns to win the acceptance of all (Hawes, 1998). Such an agenda was included in the 1986 Punta del Este Declaration, with many concessions given to LDCs. Furthermore, countries agreed at the 1988 Montreal review meeting that progress in the talks on services would be conditional upon progress being made also on issues important to LDCs such as agriculture and textiles (Nunes, 1998).

The US certainly played a dominating role in ensuring that services were placed on the agenda of the Uruguay Round. In earlier GATT rounds, the LDCs had felt excluded and marginalised when it came to matters such as agenda-setting (Sjöstedt, 1998). After opposing the US plan for a long time, LDCs eventually accepted the inclusion of services because of their active participation in the consultations leading to that decision (Zutshi, 1998).

Another agenda-setting matter which was eventually resolved by balancing different interests was the question of coverage: whether the negotiations and the final agreement on services should encompass all sectors or only some and, if so, which ones. This issue was taken to be essential to fairness, because liberalisation in many sectors affected the interests and prospective gains of parties differently. There was a desire to avoid a repetition of how earlier GATT rounds had neglected areas of significance to certain states, such as textiles and agriculture in the case of LDCs. Hence the majority of states considered coverage of all sectors necessary to achieve an equitable balance between competing interests. However, the controversy over a 'negative' versus a 'positive' list persisted. Those who opposed the use of a negative list, including many LDCs, argued that it would force parties to make concessions in every sector. Those who objected to a positive list, including the US and the EC, argued that it would grant parties veto power over the application of the GATS (Reyna, 1993). The final provisions, as described earlier, integrated both approaches.

One question of coverage which evoked fairness arguments and demanded much time was whether an agreement on services should encompass labour. LDCs held that the labour sector, being essential to the supply of services, should be subject to liberalisation and that all types of labour (unskilled, semi-skilled and skilled) should be included. If the agreement was to include capital flows on which industrialised states are so dependent, it should also include labour flows which are so essential to LDCs. The actual talks on the issue did reportedly treat labour and capital on the same footing, although only skilled labour was up for discussion (Self, 2000b). The final agreement established the significance of liberalising the labour sector, and included all types of 'natural persons' engaged in the supply of services. It called for continued negotiations after the Uruguay Round on new commitments in this sector. The agreement was thin on specific commitments to market access: parties were to negotiate directly with each other the terms under which labour would be permitted to supply a service.[25]

The settlement of this matter illustrates a pattern in the Uruguay Round: the treatment of cardinal GATT norms such as MFN, national treatment and non-discrimination not as general automatic obligations but as negotiable commitments, to be made on a conditional (reciprocal) and sectorial basis. The most influential conception which drove this change was that of reciprocity, held notably by the US. It defined fairness as the establishment of an overall balance of concessions and reciprocal benefits from an agreement. No country should

---

[25] 'Annex on Movement of Natural Persons Supplying Services under the Agreement' and 'Decision on Negotiations on Movement of Natural Persons' in 'General Agreement on Trade in Services' (note 21 above).

be able to gain from the liberalisation measures of others without taking adequate steps to increase access to its own markets (Self, 1998). In the early life of GATT, the US had not been so preoccupied by such concerns. As a hegemon it had emphasised a rough balance in the international commercial system as a whole rather than burden-sharing among countries, and shouldered much of the cost of free trade arrangements (Ahnlid, 1996). More flexible and beneficial terms were given to LDCs in the form of special exemptions and privileges, assistance and extended time for adjustment. Starting with the Uruguay Round, the US argued that a general and unconditional application of the MFN norm had undermined reciprocation and fair competition, and encouraged selfishness by allowing countries to benefit irrespective of their own trade liberalisation record. Pointing to the openness of the US services market, the US demanded a better overall balance of liberalisation measures among states. Senior US representatives stated that '[f]or years, we have given many countries a "free-ride" in the trading system . . . [The Uruguay] Round offers us an opportunity to correct that imbalance' and that '[w]e want shared responsibility, no free-riders'.[26]

The conflict over the application of the MFN clause caused deadlock in the services talks on several occasions. With the US proposal of November 1990, discussed above, the US rejected a single negotiating text which treated MFN as an unconditional general obligation, and made national treatment and market access negotiable on a sectorial basis. The US appeared convinced that the text was unfair and that the MFN provision too had to be negotiated by sector (Jaramillo, 1998). Otherwise every US concession would automatically extend to all signatories while foreign markets could remain relatively closed to the US. This position conflicted with those of the EC, many LDCs including India and Brazil, and other countries: they basically held that parties could not compete properly when they had grossly unequal skills and assets, and that this called for much less emphasis on reciprocity. Indeed, fairness required fewer demands for reciprocal commitments from LDCs, which could not necessarily afford opening up their markets for some time. Moreover, the widespread view was that an unconditional application of the MFN norm underpinned the entire world trade system. A new concept steeped in reciprocity, condition-

---

[26] The Chair of the US Senate Finance Committee and the US Trade Representative, respectively, quoted in Ahnlid (1996, p. 74).

ality and case-by-case considerations might threaten that system and the process of multilateral trade negotiations (Nunes, 1998).

The US position on the issue did not change until steps were taken to address its concerns. By 1993, there were between sixty and seventy schedules with specific market access commitments from countries regarding services. MFN obligations were suspended for maritime, telecommunications and financial services until negotiations over these were completed. In other words, there was an indication that MFN would apply in areas in which countries made considerable commitments and not necessarily in others. The US notion of fairness clearly influenced the terms which granted governments the freedom to limit market access and national treatment in particular sectors, and to override the MFN obligation (at least for ten years) by extending more favourable treatment to some countries than others. It also underlay the turn towards treating such GATT norms as malleable items which could be construed and applied to address individual concerns and circumstances as determined by parties in negotiations. Yet the final agreement was a compromise. The chief US negotiator on services stated after the Round that his country still believed that the MFN provision benefited other countries more than itself, as the US is too large, in most situations, to be a free-rider and that, in theory, more liberalisation could be achieved without this rule (Self, 1998, 2000b).

Finally, preferential treatment according to level of development was an influential principle (Falkenberg, 1998). While the US and other countries had generally accepted it already at the 1988 Montreal review meeting, its application in the services talks produced a significant breakthrough (Zutshi, 1998). The principle was expressed in the gradual liberalisation for LDCs, using step-by-step measures matching their ability to open up markets and their benefits to be had from it. The GATS stated that its objective was to liberalise the services trade progressively, in a way which would benefit all member countries and balance their rights and obligations. The point about a 'fair deal' in terms of balanced concessions pertained particularly to developed versus developing states. Most of the essential requests and concerns of LDCs were integrated into the agreement. It explicitly gave LDCs the flexibility to liberalise more slowly, at a pace which would suit their stage of development and favour the competitiveness and profitability of their domestic and export industries. It did so through preferential treatment and exemptions from some GATS rules. Article 4 committed developed states to liberalise markets in sectors of particular importance to LDCs, to help boost their domestic services and access to information networks and services technology, and to take account of 'the serious difficulty' of least-developed countries to accept cuts in trade barriers. The use of a list of schedules to indicate individual commitments to liberalisation allowed LDCs to lower trade barriers in the sectors and to the extent they preferred. Article 5 permitted the establishment of preferential trading systems provided that certain conditions regarding sectorial coverage and the elimination of discrimination were met, but LDCs had to adhere to these only to the extent that their level of development permitted. LDCs were also allowed to adopt or maintain subsidies and other trade barriers in services as a means to tackle serious financial problems, and to support important development programmes (Articles 11 and 15).

Explaining the influence of justice and fairness considerations

Numerous factors drive multilateral negotiations as complex as those over trade. We will here focus on those which best explain the prominent roles played by justice and fairness considerations.

The institutional and normative setting

The GATT provides an unusual, perhaps unique institutional and normative setting which influenced the Uruguay Round extensively. As signatories of the GATT treaties, participating countries were parties to a quasi-legal system and a contract spelling out rules of conduct with ample references to equity. Justice and fairness, such as matters of implementation and compliance, are always inherent in contractual relations: the parties are bound and expected to play by the rules. However, the GATT treaties also specify a set of obligations and objectives concerning trade liberalisation which inevitably inform negotiations undertaken to fulfil them. These range from the reciprocation of mutually beneficial concessions to preferential treatment of LDCs. An automatic extension of a party's commitment for the benefit of all through the MFN provision creates special opportunities for, and concerns about, free-riding. Although competing interpretations of fairness became influential in the Uruguay Round, the pre-conditions and foundations for the talks remained those enshrined in the GATT and the international trade regime. The strong connection between concrete numbers and the relevant norms contributed to the real impact which the latter had at the negotiating table, including in the discussions of minute details. The GATT structure and bodies served to uphold the norms and to ensure continuity. For example, members of the Secretariat played an important role in interpreting the GATT treaties (Sjöstedt, 1998). A factor affecting whether a particular argument was taken seriously was the extent to which it was based on a persuasive interpretation of some major GATT norm.

The GATT (now the WTO) machinery itself relies on procedures considered essential to fairness. Among these are the principle of consensus in decision-making and rules for dispute settlement, which were further strengthened with the creation of the WTO. They reduce power inequalities between parties, and influence which concerns and interests are taken seriously in the negotiation process.[27] The large number of parties involved, the impossibility of accommodating all views and the lead roles adopted by more powerful states meant that weak states were marginalised at times in the Uruguay Round, particularly in the important informal talks outside the negotiating room (Hawes, 1998). Nevertheless, the formal requirement of consensus meant that otherwise economically small countries exercised some veto power. The chief US negotiator on services pointed out that the GATT/WTO forum 'meets requirements of fairness quite well' and that the consensus rule 'gives all countries, big and small . . . a fair degree of equality when it comes to things like decision-making . . . All parties feel that they . . . require reciprocity from other parties' (Self, 1998). He attributed the effectiveness of the WTO to the fairness of its institutional mechanisms. Another high-level negotiator agreed that since it is a consensus based organisation, 'the negotiation process required bringing everyone on board . . . time had to be taken to convince all the parties' (Falkenberg, 1998). For example, although a poor country, India was an important player whose opposition would probably have made an agreement impossible.

Economic interests

Economic interests go a long way to explain the endorsement and influence of many conceptions of fairness in the Uruguay Round.

---

[27] When Costa Rica, for example, filed a complaint with the WTO concerning US barriers to some of its exports, it won the case and forced the US to change its import rules (*The Economist*, 16 May 1998, p. 21).

They shaped countries' positions on the content of the final agreements, including on exemptions to be permitted. A delegate to the talks on trade in services stated in an interview: 'Fairness is dictated by one's own economic interests. One decides on whether something is fair or not based on one's own goals in the negotiations' (Zutshi, 1998). Initially opposed to liberalisation in services, the EC and many LDCs came to support the development of regulations for trade in services in accordance with GATT norms, once they realised that it was in their own interest to do so. The *epistemic community* was important in producing this change of attitude and in getting services on to the agenda: it provided knowledge and policy support which reduced uncertainties, and demonstrated the possibility and benefits of applying norms of trade to services. Until then, most countries were not able to define clearly their own interests and objectives in the talks (Tran, 1998). This support was crucial to LDCs, which more than others suffered from lack of information and expertise on the very complex issues.

Those arguments about fairness which did make a difference were not simply tactically adopted. They became effective partly because they were, and were seen as, genuinely and firmly held rather than merely self serving. US insistence on reciprocity in the Uruguay Round was certainly closely linked to interests in securing better access to overseas markets in agriculture, services and so forth. But the country also sought to stop others from being able to benefit from its own relatively low trade barriers without having to reciprocate. The decline of the US as a hegemon in favour of new economic powers such as Japan and the EC had eroded its willingness to continue to bear a disproportionate share of the costs of global free trade (Ahnlid, 1996). There was little unequivocal endorsement of the US position. The EC resisted reforming the CAP partly because Germany and other member countries did not believe that they could compete well in a liberalised market. Most parties appear to have been convinced, however, that the US concept of fairness was authentically held and that it had to be addressed if the negotiations were to move forward (Hawes, 1998; Nunes, 1998). Japan's arguments about food security, by contrast, were seen as a tactical effort to justify protection of the country's rice monopoly, although its chief negotiator has denied this (Akao, 1998). Notwithstanding Japan's economic power, these claims were not nearly as effective as those put forward by food importing LDCs.

Internal politics

Internal politics also had an impact on the fairness concepts put forward by parties. The strength of certain domestic lobby groups was a factor behind many national positions held on the issue of coverage and requests for exemptions (Hawes, 1998). The insistence of governments on the reciprocation of trade liberalising measures, and their expressed resentment over free-riding, have to be seen in the light of the power of import-competing domestic producers over consumer groups. In the area of agriculture, most countries adopted negotiating positions based on domestic policies addressing the interests and well-being of particular constituencies. During the Uruguay Round agricultural lobbies in EC countries opposing liberalisation were influential, partly because of their unity across national divides and public support (Moyes, 1987). More generally, the complexity of decision-making procedures and conflicting national interests within the EC acted to slow down or prevent reforms of the CAP. With representatives of all EC countries present in the talks and the Council of Ministers adopting decisions based on consensus, liberalisation could only progress at the pace of the most resistant member state, namely France. Until the agreement on reforming the CAP was finally reached, the Uruguay Round could make no real progress on the matter of reducing agricultural trade barriers.

US policy decisions were based on consultation with agricultural advisory groups at home. Larger competitive farms, represented by the Farm Bureau, supported trade reform in the belief that the EC was stealing international markets for US produce. A US negotiator recalls a 'very rebellious farm sector' with 'a lot of resentment directed to the EC' (Yeutter, 1998). It was a factor in the US insistence on reciprocity. Pressures from US service industries (insurance, finance, information technology and other) to better their access to foreign markets continuously influenced the country's negotiating behaviour. They contributed to the US insistence on the liberalisation of this area, its emphasis on reciprocity and opposition to an obligation to MFN without commitments to national treatment and market access, and its limited support for preferential treatment of LDCs. An unqualified, across-the-board application of MFN would erode US leverage to ensure more open overseas markets. The Congress monitored the US delegation's responsiveness to the concerns of these domestic industries carefully. When the Coalition of Services Industries rejected the draft GATS proposed in 1990 as unbalanced, the US informed other countries that unless it could be exempted from the MFN provision several sectors would have to be excluded from the agreement. In sum, domestic interests and politics were a major factor in the US preference for a rapid approach to liberalisation, and have always been so (Self, 1998, 2000b).

Relative power

Relative power, broadly defined, helps to explain why some arguments were influential while others were ignored. The economic powers in the international system played lead roles in the Uruguay Round. Despite its faint support among other countries, the unorthodox and controversial US position on MFN and related matters had to be addressed because of the economic weight behind it. According to the chief negotiator on services the US got in the end what it had essentially sought, including the MFN exemption provisions (Self, 2000b). Disputes over conflicting interests and conceptions of fairness between major parties such as the US and the EC dominated the talks. Smaller or poorer states sometimes felt that their concerns were being neglected. The LDCs were, however, far more active than they had been in previous GATT rounds and the final agreements went a long way to accommodate their concerns and requests. It was well recognised that the Uruguay Round could not come to a successful conclusion without the LDCs' participation and approval, and that this cooperation would not be forthcoming without provisions for better foreign market access for their goods (Hellström, 1998). It was also widely accepted that failure to come to an agreement would do great harm to the GATT regime and to the future of international trade liberalisation, and that only concessions by all parties could avoid this. This *need to reach an agreement* instilled an important element of fairness in the situation. Together with their preferential treatment in the GATT treaties, it granted the LDCs some control over the process and the outcome.

Conclusion

Conceptions of fairness and justice played unusually influential and wide-ranging roles in the world's most significant round of trade talks to date. First, those reflected in GATT norms such as reciprocity, national treatment and the MFN clause served as important guidelines in the talks. They played a facilitating role in providing objectives and in driving the process of negotiation forward towards new agreements on the removal of trade barriers. In a broad sense, they coordinated expectations and concessions, and underlay the ultimate agreements. Particularly influential was the notion of fairness as reciprocity, balance and mutual gains: the reciprocation of trade-liberalising measures, consideration of the interests and concerns of all parties, and the design of agreements establishing a balance of benefits to all countries (Self, 1998). The delegates did expect each other to negotiate broadly according to these notions, and they generally did so. In the earlier days of the GATT, when talks only concerned goods and tariffs, concessions were exchanged within rather than between sectors. The unprecedented scope of the Uruguay Round made it easier to construct an outcome which everyone could accept as a 'fair deal': parties took advantage of the broad agenda to make trade-offs across different issue areas so as to arrive at a final package considered balanced and mutually beneficial overall (Yeutter, 1998).

Secondly, norms of free and fair trade placed some limits on the freedom of action of countries as contracting parties to the GATT, including the pursuit of narrow self-interests. The international pressure arising from their strength helps to explain why the EC eventually had to agree to undertake fundamental reform of its agricultural policy, which it could no longer defend, and why the LDCs had to accept the inclusion of services on the Uruguay Round agenda. Delegates certainly sought to emphasise particular norms or interpretations of them which would serve their own interests, and their partial success in doing so is reflected in many flexible provisions and exemptions in the final agreements. But bound by the norms and process of trade liberalisation, the EC, Japan and other parties had to reduce barriers more than they wanted.

Thirdly, these norms together with other notions of fairness also became a source of conflict and were themselves bargained over in three interrelated respects: their implementation in established areas, including problems with violations or free-riders; their extension to new areas and issues; and the specific meaning and relative importance of particular norms. They already had a general content which guided the discussions. What was negotiated were the application and interpretation of norms, in order to give them a concrete and agreed meaning in particular contexts.

While trade liberalisation is meant to benefit all by promoting global economic growth, there were steps in the process which had been discriminatory and unbalanced in the eyes of some parties. Influential concepts of fairness were introduced into the Uruguay Round, partly to the detriment of traditional understandings of GATT norms although these remained important. Conflict and competition between these norms and concepts of fairness became a key characteristic of these negotiations. Disagreements over the application of market access and the MFN clause caused deadlocks and brought the Uruguay Round to the brink of collapse on several occasions. The reciprocation of market access commitments was a general expectation, and insistence on this from a critical mass of countries goes a long way to explain the failure to reach an agreement on maritime, financial and telecommunications services.

Finally, ethical concepts played a role in the presentation of positions and requests. In previous talks the parties had sought to promote their interests by appealing to the doctrine and shared benefits of free trade, and world economic growth. The Uruguay Round witnessed for the first time the usage of specific arguments about fairness as well to justify claims (Sjöstedt, 1998). Many of these were based on both self-interest and genuine beliefs about equity. A few appear to have been purely tactical. For example, the EC is likely to have called a base year after 1986 for measuring subsidy cuts unfair in order to minimise the commitments that it would have to make (Hellström, 1998).

Will future talks within the WTO also be torn by bitter conflicts over unfair trade practices? Will they be able to preserve the achievements made and continue the work of removing trade barriers which remain? New talks on services got underway in early 2000 and further talks on agriculture were scheduled. However, the failure to launch a new round of talks at the WTO summit in Seattle in December 1999 dealt a major blow to the work of the organisation. Much attention was given to how NGOs and other groups of activists, which reject the world trade system as unethical on a number of grounds, managed to derail the proceedings on this occasion. In fact, the persistent conflicts between the WTO members themselves, which marked the Uruguay Round, were at least as decisive and constitute some of the greatest dangers to the preservation and consolidation of the free trade regime.

One is the continued disagreements over special treatment of and privileges for LDCs, and their demands for better access to rich-country markets. Another has been repeated disputes, including the threat and use of trade sanctions, between two key members, the US and the EU, over tax advantages for firms, European rules on banana and beef imports and a host of other issues. The leaders of both parties, and other governments, have had limited success in convincing important segments of their constituencies about the benefits and fairness of free trade and have often yielded to the pressures of domestic sectorial interests. This helps to explain why the Uruguay Round came to treat cardinal GATT norms as negotiable rather than automatic obligations, a development which some analysts defined in its aftermath as a threat to the trade regime. The formation of regional trade pacts, which liberalise commerce between neighbours but discriminate against everyone else, continues and any failure to make further progress on a global scale will boost their appeal and popularity. There are many other factors to take into account, including differences over engaging the WTO in supporting labour and environmental standards and the sheer complexity of talks meant to regulate the world economy and promote liberalisation. The experience of the Uruguay Round suggests nonetheless that conflicts involving fairness issues, backed by economic weight and interests, are capable of challenging one of the strongest regimes in contemporary international relations.

5   Tackling ethnic conflicts: justice, fairness, and power in the Israel–PLO interim talks

> There is no meaning for justice, if both of us will not survive to enjoy
> the fruits of justice.[1]

Power asymmetry and justice

Violent conflicts of an ethnic nature have emerged as a primary threat
to peace and security in the post-Cold War era. Internal strife, civil
wars and inter-state disputes driven by ethnic and sectarian differences are waged in the Middle East, Europe, South Asia and Africa.
Each struggle has its distinctive origins, history and dynamics, which
warrant caution in making generalisations across cases. Yet this type
of conflict typically involves the demands of an ethnic minority, under
the rule of an ethnic majority, for self-determination or greater
representation in the central government, and for a fairer share of
resources such as territory and economic assets. The achievement of
peace is often elusive owing to deep-seated fears and suspicions, the
ruling party's few incentives to negotiate, intra-party divisions, and
difficulties with containing political violence. The uneven distribution
of power, and threats or actual use of force and coercion, are
influential. At the same time, genuine claims to justice and fairness
are usually at the heart of these conflicts and become at least underlying currents in any negotiations which get underway.

Analysts of international negotiation have always been keen to
examine the role of power, focusing on a party's ability to move the
other side in a particular direction and achieve outcomes favourable
to itself. The voluminous literature on ethnic and internal conflict

---

[1] Meir Ben Meir, Israel's Water Commissioner and chief negotiator in the interim talks
with the PLO on water (personal interview, 1997).

stresses power inequality as a chief reason for the difficulty to negotiate successful outcomes, and the constructive role which third-party intervention can play in creating a balance of strength between disputants more favourable to a peaceful solution (Rothchild, 1997). Fundamental disagreements remain nonetheless over the impact of power symmetry and asymmetry. As noted in chapter 1, conventional wisdom holds that the process and outcome will largely reflect the strength of the respective parties, particularly when it is unequal. The stronger side supposedly behaves exploitatively and reaps greater benefits reflecting its advantage, while the weaker party has no choice but to make the most concessions. Some studies argue, however, that relative power is not a reliable indicator of how an international negotiation will evolve and that the weaker side may well gain as much or more than the stronger one (Ravenhill, 1993; Rubin and Zartman, 1995).

Divergent definitions and measurements of 'power' itself partly explain this discord. Some concepts emphasise the importance of structural endowments, such as military and economic resources. By disregarding that effective bargaining power is often issue or area specific, they are unable to explain how structurally weak parties could 'win' in international negotiations. Other approaches focus on influence gained in the negotiation process through the skilful use of information, persuasion, problem-solving and other tactics. It has been suggested that the greater the structural imbalance between parties, the more likely it is that other elements will determine the outcome. These may include a firm commitment to certain values and goals, organisational unity, and persuasive references to moral principles (Zartman, 1983, pp. 120–1). While this does not hold true for the case covered here, it points to yet other elements of bargaining strength which may come from both structural and non-structural sources. These include access to good alternatives (a high 'BATNA', as discussed in chapter 1) and low time costs. The less a party has to lose from delays in reaching an agreement, and the better its alternatives to a negotiated outcome are, the more it can afford to request concessions from the other side without reciprocating them fully. Superiority in this sense can enable a party to influence the behaviour of the weaker side and the final outcome heavily.

Rough equality, or at least the absence of sharp inequalities, are known to facilitate the negotiation of agreements which are viewed as just and worth honouring, as discussed in chapters 1 and 2. The will to respond to the concerns of others and accept a balanced solution is more likely to exist in largely equal parties, which cannot pursue their interests unilaterally without collaboration. Equality of bargaining power is difficult to define and calculate, particularly independently of outcomes. It has even been termed 'a myth' (Barry, 1965). Ultimately, it is of course the parties' own perceptions of the situation which matter the most. No parties are ever perfectly equal. But a basic element of equality always exists in that each party can veto an outcome which it views as unfair or otherwise unacceptable by walking away from the negotiating table. There is also an additional and significant degree of equality when each party lacks the capacity to achieve its goals by unilateral means at an acceptable cost. Both factors were present and influential in the case analysed in this chapter.

What actually happens to justice and fairness when the weak must negotiate with the strong? Can such considerations genuinely constrain the behaviour of the powerful? What, if anything, could motivate a stronger party to take justice into account? Is it possible to secure an agreement and compliance with it, while entirely ignoring the weaker party's notion of an appropriate settlement? How do strong, and weak, parties define and operationalise these values when they confront each other? The theories of justice summarised in chapter 1, and those on the role of power in negotiation mentioned above, all yield different general answers to these questions. The dearth of empirical investigations into what happens to justice and fairness when ethnic conflicts are negotiated is, however, striking. While it is not possible to seek comprehensive answers to the questions here, we shall examine them in the context of a case which, like few others, combined stark power inequalities with widely recognised ethical issues: the interim talks between Israel and the Palestine Liberation Organization (PLO) under the 1993 Oslo Declaration of Principles (DoP), commonly called the Oslo Accords. They resulted in two major agreements in 1994 and 1995, respectively. However, difficult negotiations over the interpretation and implementation of these agreements continued for many years thereafter.

Following an overview of the interim talks and the justice issues which they raised, we will focus on two areas of particular importance: water resources and economic relations.

The Israel–PLO interim talks: an overview

Force and the predominance of power determined much of the course of the Arab–Israeli conflict during its first forty-five years. The international community and the parties themselves had at the same time stressed the need to negotiate a permanent solution based on justice and mutual consent. Resolving this conflict was considered imperative to prevent further destabilisation and new wars in the region, including the proliferation of weapons of mass destruction. This is why the Israeli–Arab–Palestinian peace process persisted over the years, despite being brought to the brink of collapse on innumerable occasions. The signing of the DoP and the handshake between Israeli Prime Minister Yitzhak Rabin and PLO leader Yassir Arafat on the White House lawn in September 1993 triggered unprecedented hope that a new era of coexistence was in sight. Instead arduous negotiations followed amidst Muslim and Jewish extremist violence designed to derail them, in the belief that compromise could not serve the cause of justice.

The DoP, based on the secret Israel–PLO talks in Norway, established a staged approach and a timetable for reaching a permanent solution. First, the *interim* negotiations would result in Israeli military withdrawal from Jericho and the Gaza Strip, the transfer of power to a nominated Palestinian National Authority, and the beginning of a five-year transitional period of Palestinian self-government under this Authority. Secondly, the Palestinians would elect a Council and achieve early 'empowerment' (self-government) in five spheres in the rest of the West Bank. Thirdly, the *permanent status* negotiations would commence by the start of the third year of the interim period and cover the thorny issues of Jerusalem, Jewish settlements, refugees, water, security arrangements and borders, among others. The final settlement would take effect at the end of the interim phase. The negotiations leading to the Cairo (Gaza–Jericho) Agreement in May 1994 achieved the first objective. The signing of the Taba Agreement, also termed the Interim Agreement or Oslo II, in September 1995 set the stage for a partial implementation of the second goal: Palestinians gained full control over six main West Bank towns and administrative responsibility for almost the entire Palestinian West Bank population. A Palestinian Council was elected in January 1996.[2]

---

[2] 'Declaration of Principles on Interim Self-Government Arrangements' (Israeli Ministry of Foreign Affairs, Jerusalem, 1993); 'Israeli–Palestinian Interim Agreement on the

A most contested issue throughout the interim talks was the nature of Israel's military redeployment required under the DoP. The withdrawal from Gaza, the Jericho area and several other population centres in the West Bank was undertaken, but Article XIII, paragraph 3, of the DoP called for '[f]urther redeployments to specified locations . . . commensurate with the assumption of responsibility for public order and internal security by the Palestinian police force'.[3] Israel argued on numerous occasions that the Palestinian police force had failed to assume adequate responsibility for security. The DoP also held that the interim period should preserve the integrity of the West Bank and Gaza as a single territorial unit. In fact, the areas from which Israeli forces redeployed and over which the Palestinians gained control in the Taba Agreement were scattered and constituted only 4 per cent of the land of the West Bank. With respect to Hebron, Israel enforced the view that the principle of full withdrawal from Palestinian population centres should be waived owing to the small Jewish settler community living in the heart of the town.

On the other hand, Palestinian demands regarding the size and powers of a Palestinian Council were largely met. The fact that Israel's terms largely prevailed on the redeployment issue and caused much Palestinian resentment might have explained its greater flexibility on this and some other issues (Sayigh, 1996; Khalidi, 1996). Previously, including in the Washington peace talks on the Middle East in 1991–3, Israel had insisted on the election of a small twelve-member Palestinian 'administrative council' with limited municipal functions. Elections eventually took place for a large eighty-eight-member council with both legislative and executive powers. Moreover, Palestinian Jerusalemites were able to turn their right under the DoP to 'participate' in the elections for the Council into a right not only to vote but also to stand as candidates if they had a second address outside the city. The Palestinian Council came to include seven Jerusalemites. Finally, despite Israel's earlier objections, the Taba Agreement accorded Palestinian villages in the Jerusalem area the

West Bank and the Gaza Strip – September 28, 1995' (Information Division, Israeli Ministry of Foreign Affairs, Jerusalem, November 1995); *Middle East International*, 6 October 1995, pp. 2–5; Boutwell and Mendelsohn (1995). Detailed accounts of the Israel–PLO interim talks and the background to them can be found in Joffe (1996), and *The Middle East and North Africa 1997* (Europa Publications Ltd, London, 1997).

3 'Declaration of Principles on Interim Self-Government Arrangements' (Israeli Ministry of Foreign Affairs, 1993), p. 26.

same status as other West Bank villages by placing them under Palestinian civil rule. The significance of this move became the subject of varying interpretations. Some Israelis regarded it as a dangerous tampering with the *status quo* and even as a prelude to a Palestinian capital in Jerusalem, while others saw it merely as a continuation of Israel's old strategy to appease its subjects with limited rights falling short of undermining its own rule over the city. The Palestinians themselves, fully aware of Israel's intention to retain exclusive sovereignty, took the opportunity to assert their political presence and national claims to the city through institution-building and diplomatic initiatives.

Negotiations continued after the conclusion of the interim agreements, to work out the details of the commitments made and ensure their full implementation. Deep-seated disagreements came to plague these talks. Like the final status negotiations, which commenced officially in May 1996 when Israel's Labor Party was still in power, they were repeatedly suspended and resumed. The Labor government and the PLO shared nonetheless a degree of trust and a basic vision. Their ability to work together was expressed in the informal agreement which Israeli negotiator Yossi Beilin and Palestinian negotiator Mahmoud Abbas (Abu Mazen) reached on the permanent status issues. It had just reached Prime Minister Rabin's desk at the time of his assassination in November 1995 (Novik, 1997). Foreign Minister Shimon Peres, a key architect and driving force behind the Oslo Accords, succeeded him. But the suicide bombings in Israel in February and March 1996 fatally undermined his chances to survive in the national elections which followed.

The subsequent installation of a Likud government under Benjamin Netanyahu, a critic of the Oslo Accords, worsened the political climate for reconciliation even further. In his view, the Accords had been 'very poorly negotiated, the aspect of security [for Israel] was not really treated . . . and, as a result, for the past two-and-a-half years there was an outbreak of terrorism from Palestinian-controlled areas'.[4] He emphasised that as long as the terrorist threat persisted, border closures and other security measures had to take priority over everything else. In September 1996 Netanyahu decided to open a second entrance to a tunnel in the Old City of Jerusalem, running

[4] Statement by Prime Minister Benjamin Netanyahu in an interview on the BBC1 TV programme 'Panorama' on 21 October 1996.

alongside the Temple Mount or *Haram al-Sharif* area which is sacred to both Moslems and Jews. To Palestinians, this move confirmed that the Prime Minister intended to ignore or renegotiate the agreements concluded by the previous government in accordance with his own beliefs about the country's interests. It sparked off the worst Israeli–Palestinian confrontations since the 1967 Israeli–Arab War. Moreover, Islamic fundamentalists continued to launch terrorist attacks inside Israel. Netanyahu's decision in March 1997 to begin building the Har Homa Jewish settlement in Arab East Jerusalem caused yet another crisis, and the peace process with the Palestinians was suspended.

The Israel–PLO Wye River Agreement of October 1998 was designed to break the deadlock by tackling the remaining matters of the interim period, and then allowing the parties to move on and settle the final status issues. It established a new agenda for completing the implementation of the DoP and the interim agreements.[5] Netanyahu endorsed for the first time the principle of trading territory for peace, and Israel was scheduled to withdraw further from the West Bank in three stages over three months. After the second phase of redeployment the Palestinians would control about 40 per cent of the West Bank, and a committee would in due course handle the question of the extent of the third withdrawal on which there was no agreement. Among other provisions, Arafat pledged to take serious steps to fight terrorism under close US supervision and Israel promised to release 750 Palestinian prisoners. The final status talks were scheduled to produce a framework agreement by February 2000, and a fully fledged permanent Israel–PLO treaty by September 2000. The first phase of Israeli redeployment under the Wye River Agreement, focusing on the Jenin area in the West Bank, was completed in November 1998.

The second and third Israeli withdrawals never took place as foreseen and had yet to be undertaken by early 2000. Netanyahu, struggling to hold his government together, stated that the Palestinians had not honoured their part of the Agreement. Elections in Israel soon returned the Labor Party to power, and Ehud Barak became Prime Minister in May 1999. A supporter of the Oslo peace process, he promised to get the peace process back on track rapidly. In

---

[5] 'The Wye River Memorandum', signed by Israel and the PLO on 23 October 1998 in Washington, DC. Document available at the website of the Embassy of Israel, London, at http://www.israel-embassy.org.uk/web/pages/peace.htm.

the Sharm el-Sheikh Agreement of September 1999, Israel and the PLO confirmed their commitment to 'full and mutual implementation of the Interim Agreement and all other agreements concluded between them since September 1993', with an emphasis on their obligations under the Wye River Agreement.[6] In the following month, they agreed to specific procedures for ensuring safe passage between Israel, the West Bank and the Gaza Strip.[7] Repeated and disruptive disagreements followed nonetheless over the extent of further Israeli redeployments, continued Jewish settlement in the disputed territories, terrorist incidents and the closure of Israel's borders to the Palestinian territories, and virtually all the final status issues.

Is there any justice in the Oslo peace process?

The Israel–PLO interim talks raised a range of justice and fairness issues at different levels and stages. These concerned the *structure* of the negotiations (the conditions under which they took place including power relations, the starting point for the deliberations, and the ordering of issues on the agenda); the bargaining *process* (for example, the use of competitive and coercive tactics); the *outcome* (the principles to underlie an agreement); and the *post-agreement phase* (matters of giving substance to and implementing commitments made).

From another perspective, the interim talks raised both narrow (contextual) and broad (external) issues of justice and fairness. The narrow ones concerned the reasonable interpretation and implementation of the DoP serving as the framework for the talks, and of commitments made under the subsequent interim agreements. These issues became very contested and influential in the negotiation process. One reason for this was the vagueness or silence of the DoP on several core questions, some of which arose in the interim talks while formally deferred to the final status talks. According to the DoP,

---

[6] 'The Sharm el-Sheikh Memorandum on Implementation Timeline of Outstanding Commitments of Agreements Signed and the Resumption of Permanent Status Negotiations', signed by Israel and the PLO on 4 September 1999 in Sharm el-Sheikh, Egypt. Document available at the website of the Embassy of Israel, London, at http://www.israel-embassy.org.uk/web/pages/peace.htm.

[7] 'Protocol Concerning Safe Passage between the West Bank and the Gaza Strip', signed by Israel and the PLO on 5 October 1999 in Jerusalem. Document available at the website of the Embassy of Israel, London, at http://www.israel-embassy.org.uk/web/pages/peace.htm.

agreements reached in the interim period should not prejudice the outcome of the permanent status talks, but it was well known that they were likely to do so. Acts and threats of terrorism affecting Israeli security, and the arrival into power of a new Israeli leadership critical of the Labor government's undertakings in the Oslo process, were other factors which also made issues of implementation prominent. Palestinians genuinely perceived Israel as having failed to honour the spirit and letter of its Oslo commitments, and *vice versa*. Israel supposedly violated the DoP by, for example, continuing to build settlements during the interim period, including in East Jerusalem. The Palestinian Authority clearly failed to eradicate terrorist operations against Jewish targets.

The broad issues raised in the interim talks involved principles of international law and distributive justice, some of which are endorsed in UN Security Council and General Assembly resolutions concerning the Arab–Israeli conflict. They led the Palestinians to question the legitimacy of the Oslo process itself, but had little impact on the actual conduct of the talks. Virtually all Palestinians agreed that a truly just solution required a reversal of the creation of the state of Israel in 1948 and the establishment of a bi-national state in Palestine. This notion was based on their historical presence in Mandatory Palestine, and Israel's perceived usurpation of their national rights through military conquest and territorial expansion. All major PLO factions had agreed to compromise on this conception when they endorsed the 1988 Algiers Declaration of Palestinian Independence and a two-state solution. In the hope of regaining some rights most Palestinians thus accepted the existence of the Jewish state and the formula of 'trading territory for peace' in UN Resolution 242, which was adopted after Israel's capture of new Arab lands in the 1967 Six Day War. However, Palestinians believed that the situations prior to 1948 and prior to 1967, even if they could no longer be restored, should be used as references in the negotiations to ensure some degree of compensatory justice: they would help others to appreciate how the Palestinian positions already reflected large losses and concessions to Israel over time (Said, 1995).

Instead, the 1993 DoP framework came to endorse Israel's occupation of the West Bank and Gaza as the legitimate starting point for negotiations and compromise. Palestinians perceived this point of departure as unjust historically and legally and as an unfair exploitation of their weakness. It failed to take account of past events and activities which contributed to Israel's superior power at their expense. Among these were Israeli practices in the territories occupied since 1967, illegal under international law and prevailing international opinion, notably the confiscation of land and natural resources for the purpose of Jewish settlement (Quigley, 1995). To the Palestinians, other important principles which the DoP failed to recognise were the right of return for Palestinian refugees, endorsed in UN General Assembly Resolution 194, and their right to an independent state with Arab East Jerusalem as its capital (Tamari, 1997; Zureik, 1996).

Having accepted reluctantly the post-1967 situation as the basis for compromise, Palestinian negotiators still harboured many grievances about the Oslo process. To them the DoP largely reflected Israeli security interests and deferred all issues of essence to the Palestinians to the final status talks, without assurances of how (or whether) these would be resolved. Some of their fears were vindicated when Israel chose to consolidate its position even further during the interim talks. For example, Prime Ministers Rabin, Peres and Netanyahu all continued or stepped up the policy of establishing a strategic presence in territories claimed by the Palestinians through land confiscations and Jewish settlement. They thus sought to undermine Palestinian aspirations, especially to a capital in Jerusalem. Palestinians held that these practices violated international law and the spirit of the Oslo principles, prejudiced future bargaining over the final status of the disputed lands, and contributed an element of threat and coercion to the interim talks. They constantly increased the cost of no agreement to the Palestinians and pressurised them to give in to Israeli demands. Unless they accepted certain terms soon, Palestinians risked being worse off than before negotiations started while Israel would have further fortified its position. Fair bargaining would have required a freeze on Israeli settlement activity (Khalidi, 1996).

There was thus a consensus among Palestinians that the Oslo peace process could not result in a just solution. Their differences concerned whether it was preferable to work for a settlement which would be minimally acceptable and 'fair under the circumstances' (that is, in reference to the mandate of the DoP and given the real situation), or insist on justice and risk losing even more. Disagreement over this question created deep splits within the Palestinian community and bolstered the Islamic fundamentalist camp, especially when the interim period failed to fulfil expectations about improved economic conditions.

Israel did not consider the interim talks unprincipled or amoral. A high-level influential negotiator in the Israeli team, the lawyer Joel Singer, maintained that they were unique and that there are no clear international legal norms by which they could be judged. Moreover, interpretations of international law are politically biased (Singer, 1996). The Oslo framework reflected a situation which was largely brought about by Israel acting in self-defence against Arab armed aggression, and it should be maintained until Israeli security requirements could be guaranteed by other means (Hirsch *et al.*, 1995; O'Brien, 1991). The DoP and subsequent accords were considered legitimate by virtue of having been agreed freely by Palestinians and Israelis acting in their own interest. Israeli negotiators stressed that fair agreements had to be mutually beneficial, and that the Palestinians had already gained extensively from the Oslo peace process. It did not simply reflect the distribution of power between the two sides. Indeed, this case supposedly demonstrated that the weak can turn their feebleness into strength by arguing, as PLO leader Arafat did on several occasions, that any further concessions would break them.

National security interests naturally drove the Israeli government's decision to negotiate with the PLO. These were defined, among other matters, as an Israeli pull-out from the Gaza Strip, an end to all violence against Israel, including the Palestinian uprising and terrorism, and new opportunities for peace treaties with Jordan and other Arab states which an agreement with the PLO would open up (Slater, 1993). From an Israeli perspective, the genuine issues of justice and fairness arising in the interim talks concerned applying and adhering properly to the letter and intent of the DoP (Singer, 1996). They did not in Israel's view involve matters which could threaten its own security and survival, such as a right of return for Palestinian refugees from the 1948 Israeli–Arab war and their descendants to what is now Israeli territory, nor questions on which precise commitments had yet to be made. The Israeli government pointed out repeatedly that with Oslo it had not committed itself to freeze Jewish settlement in the disputed territories, share political rule over Jerusalem, or to a number of other Palestinian demands.

The Israel–PLO interim negotiation is a case in which both parties, and the outside world, clearly recognised the power asymmetry between the two sides. Indeed, a critical factor in the Israeli government's decision to negotiate with the PLO was the Palestinians' political and financial weakness in the wake of the 1990–1 Gulf War. It was seen as an unprecedented opportunity to obtain a peace agreement from a position of strength and to tackle long-term regional security threats, notably from Iran and Iraq. Behind PLO leader Arafat's preparedness to enter talks with Israel was a recognition of the vulnerability of his own authority and the need to demonstrate progress in recovering Palestinian land and resources (Makovsky, 1996).

The substance and sharpness of the inequality varied somewhat between issue areas. Generally speaking, Israel's *de facto* control over the resources being negotiated and its stronger economy, the deferral of the major disputed questions to the final status talks and, related to this, Israel's ability to strengthen its position on the ground throughout, were unbeatable assets. The Israeli teams had better knowledge of the issues, more experience in international negotiation, and far better bargaining skills. Palestinian negotiators lacked important expertise and information, coordinated and consulted poorly among themselves partly as a result of internal divisions and mistrust, and had no well-developed bargaining strategies (Sayigh, 1996). PLO leader Arafat and the Palestinian Authority suffered from fragile support within their own community, a financial crisis as a result of the loss of funding from Gulf states, and from dependency on Israeli markets for Palestinian goods and employment. They had far more to lose with each delay and disruption in the talks, not at least in terms of their perceived legitimacy and standing at home. This limited their ability to resist Israeli demands for concessions on many occasions. Finally, the Palestinians had no powerful patron to offset the strong support of the US Clinton Administration for Israel's approach to the peace process. They represented an entity of ambiguous status, not a country, and had to engage in talks with a well-established state over their own future.

Were the Israel–PLO interim talks then dictated by this power asymmetry between the two sides, and did they confirm references to principles of justice and fairness as empty commitments for public consumption? Did these negotiations largely witness the weak capitulating to the demands and interests of the strong, as some analysts have argued (Said, 1995; Usher, 1995; Ashrawi, 1995)? If the terms of the DoP and the interim agreements reflected imbalance in bargaining power, does this mean that they are illegitimate? Answering these questions is precarious. It depends on what measuring rods, and conceptions of justice and power, are used. There is much confusion and dispute over what legal and ethical principles, if any, and interpretations of these apply to the Israeli–Palestinian conflict. The reference against which the gains and concessions of each party should be assessed – for example, the pre-1967 situation versus the post-1967 context – is also contested. Israelis and Palestinians came to evaluate their respective concessions differently. Their full significance were still not clear several years after the conclusion of the interim agreements, as talks on their implementation and on a permanent settlement continued. Finally, as already noted, the negotiation of many crucial issues was postponed to a later stage. A detailed examination of the interim talks in two key areas, water resources and economic relations, does nonetheless shed considerable light on the subject matter. We will now turn to these.

Conflict and cooperation over water

Water is a dwindling resource of great strategic significance in the Middle East. The increasing demand for fresh water from growing populations has led to a situation in which usage now exceeds replenishment (Kemp and Harkavy, 1997). It has triggered competition and armed conflict among several states in the region for decades, and continues to do so. The main sources under Israeli control fall into two categories: surface water (notably the trans-boundary Jordan, Litani, Yarmouk, Hasbani and Banias Rivers, and Lake Tiberias) and ground water from which most supplies are drawn (including the Eastern Aquifer inside the West Bank, two aquifers cutting across the border between pre-1967 Israel and the West Bank, and aquifers along the coastal plain in Israel and the Gaza Strip). In the 1994 peace treaty with Jordan, Israel agreed to share the waters of the Yarmuk and Jordan Rivers with Amman and to transfer additional water annually from its northern region. However, water remained an important issue in the conflicts between Israel on the one hand, and the Palestinians, Syria and Lebanon on the other by early 2000. A stable and comprehensive Arab–Israeli settlement, and sustainable water usage through methods such as desalination, recycling and the development of alternative supplies, could not be achieved without a resolution of these water disputes.

Israel gained control over most of the Jordan River basin in the 1967 Six Day War, and then put in place military occupation orders which limited Palestinian access to water. Restrictions on pumping from

Palestinian wells and on the drilling of new Palestinian wells, combined with over-pumping from newly created and older Israeli wells, led to a steady decline in the volume of usable water available to the Palestinians in favour of Jewish settlers in the West Bank and the Israeli population as a whole. The Palestinian population grew by about 84 per cent between 1967 and 1987, but its water supply for domestic use increased only by 20 per cent and its supply for agriculture and industry was frozen (Baskin, 1993). A sharp inequality in access to water and consumption soon emerged between Israel, and Palestinians in the West Bank and Gaza. In the first part of the 1990s, the latter received about 110 million cubic metres or less than 20 per cent of the West Bank water supply while the former drew about 490 million cubic metres. Israel had a three to five times greater per capita consumption which depended heavily on supplies from aquifers beneath the West Bank and Gaza (Gleick, 1993). The shortage forced the Palestinians to buy additional water from Israel, at a higher price than that paid by Israelis whose water consumption was subsidised. The water shortage and costs hampered the development and productivity of Palestinian agriculture and the Palestinian economy. For Palestinians, the problem contributed to unfair competition and distorted trade relations between the two sides.[8]

The multilateral talks over regional issues in the Middle East were initiated at a conference in Madrid in October 1991. In the area of water they focused on desalination, recycling of waste water, data collection and other projects of shared interest. The Israeli–Palestinian bilateral track was set up to resolve the conflict over ownership and usage of water in the West Bank and Gaza. Contrary to the discussions in this forum, the secret Israel–PLO talks in Oslo eventually succeeded in producing an agreement on a provision concerning water rights. This was later included in Annex III of the DoP, which called for an Israeli–Palestinian committee to work out cooperative arrangements for water management, and to make proposals concerning 'water rights of each party' and 'the equitable utilisation of joint water resources' during and after the interim period.[9]

An Israeli participant in the Oslo back channel, who wished to remain anonymous, recalled that this formulation came about after a

---

[8] *Middle East International*, 8 September 1995, p. 6; Boutwell and Mendelsohn (1995); Sayigh (1996).

[9] 'Declaration of Principles on Interim Self-Government Arrangements' (Israeli Ministry of Foreign Affairs, 1993), Annex III, paragraph 1.

lot of 'pushing and pulling'. The Palestinians sought to achieve a recognition of their water rights, an issue which the Israelis insisted on deferring to the final status talks. The agreed formulation lacked any explicit commitment to Palestinian water rights, but represented nonetheless a significant concession for Israel: the country agreed to use the controversial term 'rights' and recognised water rights as an important issue to be discussed. According to Noah Kinarti, head of the Israeli water delegation until August 1995, the official Israeli negotiators were dismayed eventually to learn about this as well as several other 'concessions' made to Palestinian demands. Informed about and engaged in the Oslo talks only at a very late stage, they proved unable to revoke the provision regarding water rights (Kinarti, 1997). Clearly, most members of Israel's official negotiating team opposed the DoP's reference to water rights despite its vagueness and resisted discussing the matter in the interim period.

Opposing views of the problem and the negotiable issues

The signing of the DoP set the stage for the Israel–PLO interim negotiations, in which water became a central matter. It involved the questions of the control or ownership of water resources in the West Bank and Gaza, the allocation and management of these resources, and the development of new supplies. The talks came to focus more specifically on Palestinian water needs, allocations and rights; the licensing of water abstraction in the West Bank; price-setting for additional water supplies to Gaza; and cooperation in waste water management (Al-Sharif, 1997). We shall examine how these issues were negotiated and eventually tackled in the 1994 Cairo Agreement and the 1995 Taba Agreement.

The two parties entered the talks with sharply conflicting notions of the problems at hand. The Palestinians partly emphasised principles, while the Israelis stressed practicalities. The former insisted that an explicit Israeli recognition of their water rights in the West Bank and Gaza had to precede discussion of all other issues. In their view, the core dilemma to be resolved through negotiation was the inequitable control and distribution of existing water resources resulting from Israel's confiscation of Palestinian sources and high water consumption. Any stable solution would have to include a reduction in Israel's water usage to the benefit of that of the Palestinians.

The Israeli team defined the essential problem as one of severe water scarcity affecting national security. Therefore, the interim talks should focus on pressing practical and technical matters of protecting and managing the scarce supplies more effectively and developing new sources. They particularly stressed the urgency of fulfilling Palestinian 'humanitarian rights' to water, defined as basic needs for drinking water and excluding water necessary for agriculture (Ben Meir, 1997). They argued that water rights in a legal or political sense, including the question of control over the disputed supplies, was a matter to be settled in the final status talks together with the issues of borders, Palestinian sovereignty and refugees. In sum, Israel was not willing to negotiate water rights in the interim phase.

For several months after the signing of the DoP, these conflicting agendas caused deadlock in the interim talks over water. The Palestinians held that the DoP had recognised their water rights implicitly, that international legal principles such as the Helsinki Rules on the Uses of the Water of International Rivers should define these rights more precisely, and that they certainly included rights to the Jordan River (Q'Awash, 1997). Already at the 1991 Madrid Conference, however, Yitzhak Rabin of the Labor Party had stressed that progress in the peace negotiations depended on Israel retaining total control of Palestinian water sources. When Labor came into power the following year, Prime Minister Rabin retained this hardline approach. In the early stages of the interim talks, the Israeli team continued to reject the Palestinian demand for a discussion of water rights and to argue that the primary task was to fulfil basic water needs. A statement by Gidon Tsur, Israel's Water Commissioner at that time, captures the approach well: 'the issue of water rights is secondary. Not one cubic meter of water has been created by a declaration of rights. And I'd like to see us begin to talk about real water . . . creating new quantities of water' (Collins, 1995).

Negotiating water: from stalemate to breakthrough

The two sides were nonetheless able to sign the Cairo Agreement on 4 May 1994.[10] The Palestinian Authority thereby gained the power to

---

[10] 'The Cairo Agreement on the Gaza Strip and Jericho, 4 May 1994'. *The Middle East and North Africa 1997* (Europa Publications Ltd, London, 1997).

manage and develop water resources, including to dig new wells, in the newly autonomous Jericho and Gaza Strip. The Palestinians established a Water Authority and appointed a Water Commissioner for these areas. Israel retained control over wells in the Jewish settlements and military installations, but agreed to freeze the settlers' water consumption at the existing level and to exchange data relevant to protecting water quality and quantity.

The dispute over water rights continued to plague the talks over an interim agreement which would expand Palestinian autonomy in the West Bank. The head of Israel's delegation to the multilateral talks, Avraham Katz-Oz, broke sensationally the country's traditional stance in the same year by agreeing to discuss water rights. The sudden change of policy was reminiscent of what had happened in the secret Oslo talks. Like many of his 'dovish' colleagues, including Yossi Beilin and the academics Yair Hirschfeld and Ron Pundik who took a lead role in the Oslo back channel, Katz-Oz had come to realise that enforcing Israel's position on the Palestinians would not lead to peace. Unless they were more forthcoming on Palestinian concerns about water rights, there might never be any agreement. More hardline Israeli negotiators did not share this view. In an interview, Israel's Water Commissioner at the time described Katz-Oz' move as 'an accident' (G. Tsur, 1997). The head of the Israeli bilateral team, Noah Kinarti, attempted to ignore the turn of events and to remain focused on water supplies and the development of new resources in his discussions. But now debated in the multilateral talks, water rights became impossible in due course to avoid in the bilateral track.

As late as 4 August 1995, Foreign Minister Shimon Peres was reportedly denying that Israel could possibly recognise Palestinian water rights or reduce its own water consumption so as to increase Palestinian supplies.[11] Israel demanded continued unilateral control over water sources also in the Palestinian autonomous areas. The Palestinian team kept insisting on their rights to the three main aquifers and the surface water in the West Bank. They argued that water and land were inseparable, that they had to gain control over the water in and underneath the territory from which Israel withdrew, and that Israeli offers of cooperation to develop new supplies through desalination and other means were too expensive for them and unacceptable.

---

[11] 'Water Rights Latest Obstacle in Talks'. *Palestine Report* (Jerusalem), 4 August 1995, pp. 4–5.

When Israel and the PLO had resolved other contentious issues and appeared to be on the verge of signing an agreement, the question of water rights remained as the major obstacle. A turning point occurred when Peres in the same month drafted a recognition of Palestinian water rights to certain West Bank aquifers. This was done in preparation for his meeting with PLO leader Arafat, and was approved by Rabin and the Israeli water team. Arafat refused Peres' proposal on several grounds. It failed to recognise the Palestinians' rights to the Jordan River, and to provide them with water from Lake Tiberias as outlined in the Johnston Plan (discussed below). Moreover, the Palestinian delegation required an additional 100 million cubic metres from the Jordan River, so as to reach their goal of equalising Palestinian and Israeli per capita consumption of drinking water at the Israeli level of 100 cubic metres per year (Rodan, 1995a, 1995b). According to Israel's Minister of Agriculture at the time, Yaakov Tsur, the Israeli negotiators rejected these demands as impossible. They also held that the requests were unfounded, because per capita water consumption was related to standard of living: given their relatively low living standard the Palestinians supposedly needed less water than Israel (Y. Tsur, 1997). Peres and Arafat failed to reach an agreement in their meeting.

Gideon Tsur replaced Kinarti and became head of the Israeli bilateral water team on 20 August 1995. The latter's toughness no longer seemed to serve the Rabin government's desire to reach a speedy agreement with the Palestinians on the next stage of Palestinian self-rule. Tsur met immediately with Abu 'Ala (Ahmed Qurei), the head Palestinian negotiator. On 24 August, they signed an agreement in which Israel formally recognised Palestinian water rights in the West Bank.[12] Senior Israeli officials justified the decision by saying that the head of Israel's multilateral team had already set the precedent. The Palestinians conceded on their demand for rights to the Jordan River, because it would have required Jordan's involvement. According to Agriculture Minister Tsur, they also stopped insisting that the term 'equal rights' to water be included when realising that Israel would not yield any further on the issue at that stage. Rabin had instructed the bilateral team not to go beyond the compromises made in the multilateral talks (Y. Tsur, 1997). But

---

[12] 'Water after Oslo II: Legal Aspects of Water in the Occupied Territories'. *Palestine Yearbook of International Law*, Vol. 8, 1994–5, p. 104.

Foreign Minister Peres made further concessions in early September on a related issue. Following media exposure of the grossly unequal water distribution between 120,000 Palestinians and 400 Jewish settlers living in Hebron, he agreed to allocate an additional 2,000 cubic metres daily to the former and to increase the overall annual water allocation to Palestinians by 28 million cubic metres. Israel also expressed an intention to ensure long-term growth in Palestinian water supplies, specifying that it had to come from new sources developed with international assistance rather than from a reallocation of existing supplies reserved for Israeli consumers.[13]

The much delayed Israel–PLO Interim Agreement was eventually signed in Taba on 28 September 1995. It represented a significant compromise for both sides. Israel recognised the Palestinians' water rights in the West Bank in principle, in exchange for the latter agreeing to defer the negotiation of the substance of these rights until the final status talks.[14] A Joint Water Committee was established with equal representation and veto power for each side. It would oversee the implementation of the Agreement and coordinate water and sewage issues, and make decisions by consensus. The issues included the licensing of new wells, increased extraction from existing water sources, the establishment of annual extraction quotas, and cooperation in managing water supplies in the West Bank. The Palestinians were then required to obtain Israeli approval within the Committee to drill new wells also in the autonomous areas. The parties devised a scheme to meet Palestinian immediate water needs, whereby Israel would provide one-third of the required supplies and the Palestinians would obtain the remainder by developing the Eastern Aquifer and 'other agreed sources in the West Bank'. They also produced an estimate of the Palestinians' future water needs. The Agreement did not clarify whether Israel's own water consumption would be reduced to meet any of these needs. Shmuel Kantor, adviser to Israeli Water Commissioner Meir Ben Meir, stated in an interview that Israel was willing to cut its water use in the agricultural sector to meet Palestinian domestic needs. He and Ben Meir referred to a plan whereby Israel would eliminate the use of fresh water in agriculture to increase supplies for domestic use (Kantor, 1997; Ben Meir, 1997).

[13] *Middle East Monitor*, Vol. 5, No. 10, October 1995, p. 2.
[14] 'Israeli–Palestinian Interim Agreement on the West Bank and the Gaza Strip – September 28, 1995', Annex III (Protocol Concerning Civil Affairs). Information Division, Israeli Ministry of Foreign Affairs, Jerusalem, November 1995.

Fadel Q'Awash, deputy head of the Palestinian Water Authority, argued that the additional water created by this project was targeted for the Israeli economy and not the Palestinians (Q'Awash, 1997). The two parties did, however, agree to pay the same price for water, based on a pricing mechanism reflecting actual production and transportation costs, and to share relevant data.

Negotiations continued within the Joint Water Committee from September 1995 onwards over the implementation of the Taba Agreement, normally on a bi-monthly basis. Vagueness on several core issues had facilitated its conclusion, but also left room for conflicting claims to be asserted later. For example, Palestinians interpreted the Taba reference to 'other agreed sources in the West Bank' which they could develop as other aquifers in the West Bank. Israel argued that it referred to new sources which might materialise such as desalinisation plants or water imports from Turkey. While the Netanyahu government was pleased with the functioning of the Committee and the steps taken, Palestinians accused it of delaying and attempting to obstruct the implementation of many provisions. Both the Palestinian Water Commissioner and the deputy head of the Palestinian Water Authority argued that the Joint Water Committee's procedures for licensing the drilling of new wells were excessively and intentionally slow, and that it approved only a fraction of the Palestinian requests for a permit (Al-Sharif, 1997; Q'Awash, 1997). Israel held that it was acting to protect the quality of the water resources. Palestinians also complained that Israel had not shown that the price charged for water was the supplier's actual cost, as required by the Taba Agreement. Each side accused the other of withholding relevant data which should be shared, and each side vehemently denied the charge. The Israeli Water Commissioner said that some of the Taba provisions might not be implemented exactly as foreseen, because the principle of meeting humanitarian needs for water had to take priority. Palestinians, however, blamed the Likud government for not working to fulfil even this basic goal.

Power inequality restrained by 'relative fairness'

The Israel–PLO interim talks reflected the ambiguity and disagreement concerning what principles apply to water rights and the 'equitable utilisation' of water resources. Some pointed to the 1954 Johnston Plan on regional cooperation and allocation quotas for the

Jordan River as a relevant customary regime in international water law, although it was never ratified (Elmusa, 1996b). The 1966 Helsinki Rules on the Uses of the Water of International Rivers set forth many widely accepted factors to weigh in the settlement of disputes. They include the extent to which the water sources are located within the sovereign borders of states, past and present utilisation of the water, the water needs of each state, and its costs of meeting those needs by alternative means. Each principle and each interpretation of it can lead to a dramatically different resource distribution, and the question of which should be applied is therefore often disputed. Prior use and sovereign control are influential factors in practice, and Israel used them to support its own claims to the water sources in the West Bank. However, the fact that Israel captured these by force from another country, Jordan, and that her negotiating partner, the Palestinians, was not a state complicate such considerations. An Israeli negotiator argued that international law played almost no role in the interim talks over water because it had nothing to do with the situation on the ground. Lawyers were called in after an agreement had been reached to present it in a more legal form (Kinarti, 1997).

The absence of a salient, let alone agreed, standard meant that legal or ethical principles could not coordinate the Israel–PLO water talks. The two parties based their respective positions and claims on different principles and concepts, which were at once genuinely held and used tactically to serve their own interests. We have seen that these opposing stances, especially on the issue of water rights, caused serious delays and deadlocks in the talks leading to the Taba Agreement. Eventually they became subject to negotiation and compromise in order to make an agreement possible. In efforts to implement the Taba provisions, controversial fairness issues arose once more as Israel and the Palestinians accused each other of interpreting and implementing the terms in arbitrary ways.

Israelis hardly used the language of equity in the negotiations. Emphasising severe water scarcity as a matter of national security, they presented their approach as one concerned with maximising the protection and efficient management of the finite resource: 'Not justice, not fairness; water scarcity is what governed our approach' (Kantor, 1997). Specifically, the argument was that effective management of the West Bank's water resources required a continuation of Israeli unilateral control. Israel's Water Commissioner explained in an interview: 'There is no meaning for justice, if both of us will not survive to enjoy the fruits of justice' (Ben Meir, 1997). Israel feared that management by Palestinians could lead to overpumping and depletion in efforts to provide water to their growing population, including refugees who might return in future years. In order to avoid losing supplies on which the country depended so critically, Israeli negotiators stressed the development of new water resources.

Israel's approach was nonetheless justified on grounds which it considered to be moral and which were reflected in the final Taba Agreement. One aspect was the focus on the basic water needs of all residents of the area, and Israel's and the Palestinians' shared obligation to meet those needs. Senior Israeli negotiator Joel Singer held in a personal interview that the permanent solution should take account of principles for the equitable distribution of water resources, such as proportionality and need. He stressed that such a solution could be worked out and such principles could be considered only in the final status talks once population sizes, the ultimate fate of the territories and borders were better known (Singer, 1996). Another aspect was the idea that it would be unreasonable to ask Israel in negotiations to jeopardise its national security interests or to worsen the situation for its own population; for example, by agreeing to lower the Israeli standard of living as a means to increase water supplies to the Palestinians. Israeli negotiators emphasised that the agreed arrangements must bring gains to both sides over the existing situation. They pointed out that earlier Israeli proposals for regional cooperation had been rejected. As a result of this, the country ended up using its own capital (reportedly over US$30 billion since 1948), advanced technology and management skills successfully to develop the water resources which it now used. This was a considerable investment which had to be taken into account (Y. Tsur, 1997).

The water talks naturally raised a number of justice and fairness issues for the Palestinians. Their basic viewpoint was that the negotiations concerned water sources on and under Palestinian territories which were rightfully theirs, and that Israel had come to control and exploit these by force to the detriment of the indigenous population. Even moderate Palestinian negotiators regarded the water talks and their outcome as a legitimisation of Israeli claims to their national resources. In particular, the Taba provision for joint Israeli–Palestinian management and sharing of the water sources under Palestinian jurisdiction was viewed as unjust historically and legally (Pacheco, 1995). However, by agreeing to negotiate on the basis of the DoP, the

Palestinians accepted in fact the post-1967 situation as the starting point for concessions. Their actual negotiating behaviour was driven extensively by pragmatism and, related to this, the concept of equality between the two sides as the meaning of 'fairness' under the circumstances.

The concept of equality was reflected in many of the Palestinians' requests. These included the recognition of their water rights and their entitlement to greater control and a larger share of the region's resources; and the equalisation of per capita water consumption and prices, and of access to water sources, between Palestinians and Israelis. The Palestinian team based these demands on international water law, notably principles of equitable utilisation of shared water resources set out in the 1966 Helsinki Rules. Many references to international law and justice were largely rhetorical. But on issues such as water rights, the Palestinian negotiators were very firm with the Israelis. At the same time, they were driven by pragmatic considerations of what could realistically be achieved given their weakness (Haddad, 1997; Sayigh, 1996). They were acutely aware that insisting too much on their principles or on a, in their eyes, more balanced implementation of the DoP, might simply result in further losses and even greater injustice for them.

Whose concerns and ethical conceptions eventually drove the interim talks on water, and what role did power play in securing their influence? The Israeli notion, incorporated into the DoP, that both parties must gain from the process based on the prevailing situation, and that historical grievances about injustice and legal doctrine had to be set aside, clearly served as the foundation (Pundik, 1997). The negotiation agenda and the ultimate agreements reflected Israel's security interests extensively with the focus on water needs and allocations, and effective management, rather than the details of rights and ownership (H'Maidi, 1997). The principle of meeting basic and immediate water needs became central in the Taba formula, as advocated by Israeli negotiators. The Taba Agreement, notably the establishment of the Joint Water Committee, also legitimised Israel's claims to have a considerable say over and a share of resources under Palestinian jurisdiction. The Palestinians were explicitly permitted to develop only the Eastern Aquifer whose supplies were not yet fully exploited. No concessions were made on major Israeli water sources such as the Western Aquifer. Israeli negotiators were able to bypass many Palestinian requests including a substantial discussion of water rights, and a commitment to reduce their country's water usage and to equalise the per capita consumption of the two parties. They even claimed later that their recognition of the Palestinians' water rights in the Taba Agreement should be understood merely as a recognition of their right to have basic needs for drinking water met (Kantor, 1997).

The prevailing power inequality was very influential in securing these gains for Israel. The country was able to use its *de facto* control over the water resources, its superior knowledge about the issues, and professional skills to influence what the Palestinians eventually accepted and to override some Palestinian conceptions of justice and fairness. The Palestinians' desperate need for more water pressurised their representatives to secure a deal which would increase supplies quickly. This was certainly a factor in their acceptance of the Taba Agreement, whose terms they did not view as just. Although Israel's negotiation strategy could have been better coordinated (e.g., the positions of its multilateral and bilateral teams on the issue of water rights), Palestinian representatives suffered far more from poor preparation and inadequate practical expertise. According to Kinarti, the first head of the Israeli bilateral team, they were unable to translate the principles of international law and water rights which they put forward into concrete proposals, did not know the actual water needs of Palestinian towns, and did not know how to operate water pipes. Israel reportedly had to inquire with the towns directly about their water needs, and this information was then used in drafting the terms of the agreement (Kinarti, 1997).

But power inequality alone did not direct the water talks. Both parties were determined to reach an agreement, and had much to lose from failing to do so. This meant that Israel had to take some account of the Palestinians' notions of a reasonable solution. The great importance which they attached to water rights and to fairer water allocations played a key role in changing the Israeli position on the issues. In this case and in the interim talks generally, the inexperienced Palestinian team never developed elaborate bargaining strategies or tactics. When their arguments became influential, they appear simply to have communicated persuasively and successfully the depth of their concerns. At the conclusion of the agreement in August 1995 with Abu 'Ala, which recognised Palestinian water rights, Water Commissioner Tsur admitted that Israel had gone a long way towards the Palestinian demands: 'A year, a year and a half ago, nobody dreamed of giving them what we are prepared to give today. When we started the talks, we thought that to discuss water rights was out of the question' (quoted in Rodan, 1995b).

The Palestinians improved their overall conditions and came out far better than if no agreement had been concluded or if the *status quo* had prevailed. The Cairo Agreement placed the power to manage water resources in Jericho and Gaza in their hands, and froze the Jewish settlers' water consumption there. At Taba they gained a recognition in principle of their water rights in the West Bank and of the need to settle these in the final status talks, as well as equal representation within the Joint Water Committee for the interim period. Their annual allocation of water increased substantially, to the point of meeting at least basic survival needs. Many Israelis came to believe that these concessions would in due course threaten their own water requirements. The Taba Agreement stipulated that the two peoples should pay the same price for water, and in this respect the Palestinian negotiators were also successful.

The talks did not meet Palestinian criteria of justice based on history and international law. But they took an important step towards a more equitable sharing of control and use of water resources. Israeli power was restrained by the need to give the Palestinians a fair share of benefits based on the existing situation, in order to secure an agreement. As mentioned earlier, Israeli representatives stressed that negotiation must be a mutually beneficial exercise and that the Palestinians got a fair deal under the circumstances. The concept of 'relative fairness' referred to working for and accepting what was practically possible, rather than insisting on 'absolute' (external) principles which might be politically unrealistic and lead to even greater injustice. It has been endorsed by Faisal Husseini, a prominent Palestinian spokesperson (Joffe, 1996).

Unequals negotiate economic autonomy and cooperation

Nearly thirty years of occupation, the Palestinian uprising from 1987 to 1993, and the aftermath of the Gulf War had devastating effects on the Palestinian population in the West Bank and Gaza. After the 1967 War, the West Bank and Gaza economies became heavily dependent on Israel. Arab states' economic boycott of the Jewish state and various Israeli restrictions limited opportunities for exporting Palestinian goods. Isolated from many foreign markets and lacking control over natural resources and borders, the Palestinians had little scope for developing their own economy. High levels of unemployment created a flow of cheap Palestinian labour from the territories into Israel. From 1967 and onwards, Israel also controlled banking services and introduced its own currency in the West Bank and Gaza. The government set trade tariffs and value added tax (VAT) rates for these territories, and kept the income from the tax collection. Palestinians protested against unfair terms of trade: security, health and quality controls in Israel reportedly limited Palestinian imports into the country while Israeli goods, often subsidised, were exported freely to the territories, resulting in a large Israeli trade surplus. Israeli restrictions on the use of water and land impeded agricultural and industrial development in the West Bank and Gaza where, in the late 1990s, nearly three million Palestinians lived.[15]

The idea that gains from economic cooperation, integration and growth would be the motor of the peace process and ensure its success was at the heart of the philosophy of Shimon Peres, the Israeli statesman who had been so influential in the Oslo breakthrough (see Peres, 1993). It was widely recognised among Palestinians and Israelis as well that the prospects of their dialogue would partly depend on strengthening the West Bank and Gaza economies (Hirschfeld, 1997). They shared an interest in reaching an agreement which would improve Palestinian living conditions through measures such as free trade with Israel and the creation of new jobs. This would encourage support for the Oslo peace process and for Arafat's Palestinian National Authority among the Palestinian public, and bolster Israel's security. An Israeli–Palestinian agreement on trade, tariffs, labour mobility and other core issues was also seen as a first step towards building new economic and trade relations between Israel and the larger Arab world.

Informal discussions on economic issues had already covered certain groundwork and built a rapport between some Israeli and Palestinian negotiators by the time official negotiations began in November 1993. Israel's Deputy Foreign Minister Yossi Beilin and Abu 'Ala, then the PLO's treasurer who headed the PLO team in the secret Oslo talks, shared ideas on economic cooperation and integration as the basis for a peace agreement. These were later reflected in

---

[15] *Al Quds* (East Jerusalem), 27 February 1998.

the DoP, with its extensive references to new economic arrangements. The DoP transferred all responsibility for education, health, social welfare, direct taxation, culture and tourism to the Palestinian Authority. Some Israeli control would remain in more strategic areas through the establishment of an Israeli–Palestinian Economic Cooperation Committee. It would handle issues of water, energy, financial development, transportation, trade, industry and labour, among other matters. The DoP connected Palestinian economic progress to a Middle East development programme, which would end the Arab boycott of Israel and integrate Israel into regional trade and various cooperative ventures.[16]

Among numerous economic issues covered in the Israel–PLO interim talks, some disputed items arose already in October 1993 within the Middle East multilateral track. One concerned customs. Israel wanted a full customs union with the Palestinian autonomous areas, whereby their customs duties and purchase taxes would remain at the (high) Israeli level. This would prevent the country from losing business to the Palestinian territories. The Palestinians held that lower duties and taxes would better serve the need to improve their living standards and weak economy. The fear was that a customs union would force them into protectionism owing to factors such as Israel's trade restrictions with various Arab countries, and that Israel's high taxation levels would reduce the competitiveness of Palestinian exports. Palestinian negotiators at first insisted that their VAT rate be lower than that of Israel, but then considered that a higher rate could contribute much needed funds to the Palestinian Authority. They kept insisting on a VAT rate different from the Israeli one, however, to signify Palestinian autonomy (Hulleileh, 1997a).

Israel responded that it might set up border controls to prevent cheap goods from being smuggled into the country unless the Palestinians agreed to harmonise taxes and customs. So as to give their farmers time to adjust to free trade, Israel proposed a sliding scale of restrictions on certain Palestinian agricultural exports over three years. Palestinian negotiators argued that any such exceptions must be applied to both sides, and threatened to institute reciprocal protectionist measures. Yet another dispute arose over Arab states' economic boycott of Israel. While Israel thought that time had come

---

[16] 'Declaration of Principles on Interim Self-Government Arrangements' (Israeli Ministry of Foreign Affairs, Jerusalem, 1993), Articles 6, 11 and 16 and Annexes 3–4

for the Palestinians to call for its end, the latter wanted to wait until a detailed agreement had been reached (Ozanne, 1993).

When the official Israel–PLO bilateral talks opened in Paris in November 1993, the parties established subcommittees on trade and labour, banking and finance, and fiscal matters. The Israeli delegation, headed by Finance Minister Avraham Shohat, made clear that they wanted to retain close links with the autonomous areas. While supporting this goal the Palestinian team, led by Abu 'Ala, emphasised that their economic relationship had to be based on equality and parity.[17] He disclosed that the PLO was almost bankrupt and that international donors had not fulfilled their pledges of financial aid. The flow of assistance to the Palestinian territories did improve in due course, however. At a session later in the month, Palestinian negotiator Nabil Sha'ath rejected once more Israeli calls for a customs union with the Palestinians and Jordan.[18]

Israeli negotiators opted to make some concessions in December 1993. They agreed to let the Palestinians export agricultural produce into Israel freely (subject to certain exceptions), and to import goods from Arab countries hostile to Israel and to import cars duty-free into the autonomous areas. The Palestinians themselves were still concerned that Israel would merely replace political rule of the territories by economic control and remain too influential in their economy. They therefore continued to reject the idea of a customs union, and preferred an independent customs authority.[19] To them, such an authority would also have considerable symbolic value as an element of sovereignty. Another major dispute afflicting the Paris negotiations was the Palestinians' request to establish their own central bank. It would issue a Palestinian currency, direct monetary policy, and control commercial banks. With this initiative the Palestinians sought once again to achieve an element of sovereignty, to reduce their dependency on the Israeli shekel, and to undermine Israel's ability to pressurise them in the ongoing talks through monetary instruments. A principal Israeli negotiator says that his country, together with experts from the US and the International Monetary Fund, rejected the notion of an independent Palestinian bank during the interim period on the grounds that the Palestinian economy was not sufficiently

[17] 'Economic Ties'. *MidEast Mirror*, 17 November 1993, p. 9.
[18] 'Economic Union'. *MidEast Mirror*, 24 November 1993, p. 14.
[19] 'Open Economic Market Agreed with the PLO'. *MidEast Mirror*, 16 December 1993, pp. 22–4.

mature for it. Israel felt that there were no sound economic reasons behind the request, but also resented the symbols of sovereignty which such a bank and an independent currency would constitute (Brodet, 1997). The Palestinians' economic agreement with Jordan of 7 January 1994 provided for twenty-six Jordanian bank branches to be reopened in their territories and confirmed the use of the Jordanian dinar there. They then put the plan for a central bank on hold, in order to focus on establishing a development bank which could channel foreign aid into the autonomous areas (Kuttab, 1994).

The PLO suspended the Paris talks on 21 January 1994. The apparent motive was to prevent an economic agreement from being reached before the interim negotiations had made substantial progress on other issues, notably Israeli troop withdrawal. Barely had the economic talks resumed before the question of a customs union produced deadlock in mid-February. The Palestinian request for the freedom to set their own tariffs on imports into the autonomous areas caused Israel to fear that cheap products from third countries would flood its market. Shohat, the head of Israel's delegation, warned that if they could not agree on the issue by the end of that session, he would propose to close the country's market to the Gaza Strip while the *status quo* would remain in the West Bank. Palestinian negotiators insisted that the West Bank and Gaza must be treated equally.

The talks continued nonetheless and resulted in an agreement by mid-April on agricultural products, industry and energy. The conditions of Palestinian workers in Israel, trade, currency and the VAT rate in the autonomous areas remained difficult sticking points. Palestinians wanted Israel to guarantee entrance for a certain number of workers for the next five years until their economy had recuperated. At first potentially flexible, Israel hardened its position on the issue after two terrorist bombs exploded in the country in early 1994. Furthermore, the Palestinian delegation held that their workers in Israel had not received benefits corresponding to their pension, income tax and social insurance contributions. Israeli negotiators eventually agreed to new tax and pension arrangements for the future, but refused to discuss compensation to Palestinians for past social security contributions. They argued that much of the collected taxes had gone back into 'administering' the West Bank and Gaza since 1967, and that it would be complicated to calculate the credits and debts arising from this administration (Fischer, 1994). In a different area, the dispute over trade escalated when Palestinian negotiators doubled the number of items for which they requested exemption from customs duties at the Israeli level. The two sides adjourned the talks on 22 April, after failing to agree also on customs procedures.[20]

On 29 April 1994, Shohat and Abu 'Ala finally signed the Paris Protocol on Economic Relations.[21] It stipulated that Israel and the Palestinians would have similar import policies and regulations, and form a limited customs union bound by a number of concessions to the latter. The Palestinian Authority would determine its own customs rates for many products deemed essential for economic development, which were indicated on three lists. These included goods from Arab and Islamic countries, which could be imported up to the point of meeting Palestinian market needs, and basic foodstuffs. For all other products, except the import of some motor vehicles, the Israeli customs rate was to serve as the minimum Palestinian rate. The accord provided for the establishment of a Palestinian Monetary Authority (not an independent central bank) to regulate and supervise banks and foreign exchange transactions, among other matters, in the autonomous areas. The parties agreed to continue to discuss the possibility of a Palestinian currency.

The protocol allowed Palestinian agricultural produce to be exported freely into Israel, except for six goods protected by import quotas for four years, and into any other country. The Palestinians would pursue their own direct taxation policy. The dispute over VAT (indirect taxation) was settled by allowing the Palestinian rate to be slightly lower, by about 1–2 per cent. There was no provision for compensating Palestinians for past social security contributions. However, in the future income tax and other contributions of Palestinian employees in Israel would be transferred to the Palestinian Authority and a Palestinian social security system. Of the infrastructure used by Palestinian workers in Israel, about 25 per cent was estimated to be Israeli and therefore the Palestinian Authority would receive 75 per cent of the income taxes collected from them. Israeli negotiators did not agree to guarantee entrance to a minimum number of Palestinian workers, nor to pay compensation for the

[20] 'Economic Talks in Paris Reach Impasse on Customs Policy'. *MidEast Mirror*, 22 April 1994, p. 10; 'Paris Talks'. *MidEast Mirror*, 13 April 1994, p. 6; Cooley (1994).

[21] 'Protocol on Economic Relations between the Government of the State of Israel and the PLO, Representing the Palestinian People'. Israel Information Service Gopher, Information Division, Israel Foreign Ministry, Jerusalem.

periodic closure of borders. They argued that Israel was not to blame for the need to undertake this security measure owing to terrorist attacks and threats, nor for its negative effects on the Palestinian economy (Shohat, 1997). Article VII, which affirmed each side's authority to decide about 'the extent and conditions of the labour movement into its area', lent some support to Israel's proclaimed right to seal off its borders. A Joint Economic Committee, consisting of an equal number of Israeli and Palestinian members, was set up to oversee the implementation of the protocol.

The protocol, as the framework for future economic relations between Israel and the Palestinian self-governing areas, was incorporated into the Cairo Agreement of May 1994 as Annex 4 and into the Taba Agreement of September 1995 as Annex 5. Shohat pointed out that Israel had made painful compromises affecting its economic interests for the sake of peace, but praised Abu 'Ala as 'an honest and fair negotiator'.[22] Abu 'Ala stressed that success in implementing the protocol would depend on factors such as Israeli cooperation on the ground and Palestinian economic development.

A 'relatively fair' agreement fails in implementation

Israeli negotiators adopted a pragmatic approach to the economic talks, as to the interim negotiations generally. The focus was on formulating a solution acceptable and beneficial to both sides, using the existing situation as the starting point. They held that considerations of past injustices were backward-looking, and too controversial to permit an agreement (Novik, 1997). The parties could at best acknowledge that injustice had been done on both sides, but then had to move on and work out practical arrangements. This attitude was reflected in Israel's refusal to discuss compensation to Palestinians for past social security contributions, and in its willingness to agree to a new tax and pension system for the future. At the same time, Israeli negotiators emphasised that they sought an agreement which would protect basic interests on both sides. Some Palestinian negotiators concurred that their counterparts tried to be as fair as possible (Hulleileh, 1997a). For Israel's part those interests concerned economic

---

[22] 'With Self-Rule Kick-Off Set for May 4 and Economy Accord with PLO Sealed in Paris, Peace Focus Now Shifts to Syria'. *MidEast Mirror*, 29 April 1994, p. 4.

and national security, balanced by the need to improve Palestinian economic conditions in order to reach a stable peace. The Israeli delegation, influenced by a strong agricultural lobby at home, clearly negotiated issues such as the customs union and VAT so as to avoid a significant loss for its own constituents. Concerns about national security and public opinion were at the forefront when Israel insisted on the right to close its borders in the event of a terrorist attack or threat, and refused to guarantee entrance to a minimum quota of Palestinian workers.

Several sources of power backed Israel's negotiating approach. Its economy was far stronger, and more diversified and independent, than that of the Palestinians.[23] Israel provided a vital market for Palestinian workers and goods, and the inhabitants of the West Bank and Gaza suffered substantially when it was closed off. By contrast, Israel was relatively invulnerable to disruptions in its intake of Palestinian labour and produce, especially since starting to employ foreign nationals. The country's favourable position with respect to the control of land and access to expertise and information also had an impact in the talks.

The chief concern of the Palestinians was to achieve a more equal and fair economic relationship with Israel. They defined this as greater separation and independence from the Israeli economy and autonomous decision-making on trade, monetary policy, import policy and other issues. They also thought that such a relationship required greater parity between the two sides on matters such as standard of living and the possession of sovereign economic institutions. These goals drove the Palestinian negotiating positions throughout, including their demand for a separate currency and a central bank. Eager to demonstrate progress before constituents and to advance their agenda for the final status talks, they sought at times symbolic elements of sovereignty rather than real economic gains. For example, the importance of a Palestinian VAT rate which was only slightly lower than the Israeli one was that it symbolised two separate economies. Other Palestinian goals in the talks were to integrate the West Bank and Gaza economies, strengthen economic ties with Jordan and Egypt, and lower Palestinian consumption costs.

---

[23] According to one estimate, Israel's GDP was on average eighteen times the Palestinian GDP in the early 1990s (Elmusa and El-Jafaari, 1995). Over 80 per cent of the West Bank's exports went to Israel.

The Palestinians ultimately accepted less than what they considered fair on some issues. They were well aware of the need to accept the best deal they could get in many areas. Apart from the weak power base already discussed, the Palestinians suffered from lack of preparation and organisation. The Palestinian Authority had not yet been established and all members of the Palestinian delegation had not been selected by the time the economic talks with Israel began in November 1993. The Palestinian delegates had to spend the first couple of months asking questions, learning, and consulting with their leaders in Tunis. They did not formulate their negotiating positions until about February 1994. Views on whether this inadequate preparation influenced the Palestinians' ability to secure a balanced agreement differ, however, partly because Egyptian and Jordanian government representatives and the private sector assisted them (Elmusa, 1996a).

It is difficult to assess precisely the extent to which the protocol took into account and balanced the concerns of each side. Its preamble stated that principles of reciprocity, equity, fairness and mutual respect for each other's interests would govern the relations between Israel and the Palestinians in various economic spheres. These principles were reflected extensively in the wording and in the terms of the protocol, at least at face value. In practice some clauses, while nominally based on reciprocity, equality or some other concept of fairness, would mainly benefit Israel. Drawing on their superior power position, Israeli negotiators were certainly able to secure favourable terms and to override certain Palestinian concerns about economic independence. For example, they achieved a customs union with some limitations. The Palestinian delegation ultimately felt that they had no choice but to accept such a union. Without it, borders would have to be delineated between the two parties and Israel would have insisted on retaining Jerusalem on its side. This would be widely seen as prejudicing the final status negotiations concerning sovereignty over the city, which the Palestinians could not accept.

Israel achieved for its farmers a period of adjustment to free trade in certain agricultural products, which it viewed as a fairness issue. Nominally the list of exceptions to free trade applied equally to Palestinian farmers, but in fact it protected largely Israeli produce. The protocol also granted each side the authority to decide about labour movement within its own boundaries. In reality, the provision was a victory for Israel's right to close its borders over the Palestinians' request for secure employment in that country. Israel obtained the regulations on health and quality standards which it had advocated, and the protocol only mentioned that Israel could change import policy for health, safety and environmental reasons (Article 3(10)). Finally, Israel refused to discuss and compromise on several issues including the payment of compensation for border closures and for past Palestinian social security contributions. The Palestinians did not secure a minimum quota for their workers in Israel, nor a central bank. The Governor of the Palestinian Monetary Authority pointed out that the lack of an independent currency 'deprives us of a major monetary tool'.[24] Critics argued that the protocol would maintain economic distortions and inequalities with respect to agricultural trade, subsidised Israeli production, and Palestinian imports from countries other than Israel. The Palestinians' Minister of Economy and Trade judged that the provisions still limited their trade with Arab countries substantially (Masri, 1997).

Nonetheless, Israeli and Palestinian negotiators did generally consider the terms of the Paris Protocol fair and mutually beneficial under the circumstances. Despite the difficulties, a sense of good will, good cooperation and mutual respect reportedly prevailed throughout the talks (Shohat, 1997). The strong was not perceived as simply imposing its will on the weak. Both parties were determined to reach an agreement restructuring their economic relations in a manner which would promote Palestinian economic growth and public support for the peace process. Considering the *de facto* situation on the ground, the terms of the protocol favoured the Palestinians considerably and perhaps more so than could have been expected from the DoP framework. Several provisions reflected substantial compromises on both sides rather than the sharp inequalities between them. On the main issue of agriculture, Palestinians gained free and full access to the Israeli market subject to some fixed-term quotas to be eliminated in 1998. The creation of a Palestinian Monetary Authority involved the transfer of certain economic powers from Israeli hands. The customs union reduced Israel's fears of an influx of cheap products, but also addressed Palestinian concerns about fairness by permitting them to trade goods essential to economic development freely without restric-

---

[24] Comment by Fouad Bseiso in 1996, reported in *The Palestinian Monetary Authority and the Banking System: Summary* (Centre for Palestine Research and Studies (CPRS), Economics Department, December 1996).

tions, including with Arab countries. The resolution of the dispute over VAT balanced concerns on both sides: the agreement on two slightly different rates involved a low risk of smuggling for Israel, and the symbolically important concession of a separate rate for the Palestinians. Accused of unfair practices in the past, Israel agreed to begin transferring income taxes and social security contributions collected from Palestinians working in Israel to the Palestinian Authority. The protocol also treated the West Bank and Gaza economies similarly as one unit, as requested.

The serious charges of injustice and unfairness which emerged in due course related to problems with implementing the Paris Protocol. They surfaced because of developments on the ground rather than dissatisfaction with the terms of the agreement *per se*. The problems centred on Israel's closure of its borders to the Palestinian territories after terrorist attacks by Islamic fundamentalists. These attacks, which peaked in early 1996 and in the summer of 1997, killed dozens of civilians and injured hundreds of others mainly in Jerusalem and Tel-Aviv. The role and wisdom of the border closures in combating terrorism were much debated, even among Israeli policy-makers. Chief Israeli negotiator Brodet admitted that a major goal was to reassure and satisfy the Israeli public (Brodet, 1997). Officially Israel stressed that the measure was an act of self-defence necessary to protect its population, given that Arafat was unwilling or unable to prevent such political violence. Palestinians held that the closures violated the Paris Protocol and mounted to mass punishment for the acts of a few extremists. To them, the negotiation of the protocol had balanced concerns on both sides but in this later phase Israeli power and security interests dominated over all other considerations. PLO leader Arafat's vulnerability and weakness had also become more obvious, especially before his Islamic opposition. Negotiators on both sides did concur, however, that the border closures damaged the Palestinian economy which the protocol was meant to bolster through an open flow of goods, workers and capital with Israel.

In the spring of 1995 Abu 'Ala and the Palestinian Director-General for Trade, Samir Hulleileh, called for a renegotiation of the Paris Protocol. They argued that Israel's imposed border closures had prevented its proper implementation. The Palestinians now wanted to import more products from third countries than those specified in the agreement, which the Israeli officials involved initially accepted (Maltz, 1995). Both Prime Minister Rabin and PLO leader Arafat reportedly refused to renegotiate the protocol, because it could set a precedent for reopening other agreements. Israel therefore responded mainly by undertaking measures designed to allow trade to continue despite border closures, and by issuing more work permits for Palestinians. In early 1996, Hulleileh stated that almost all Palestinian factory production and other economic activity had stopped and that Palestinian trade had declined because of Israel's border closures.[25] Together with Finance Minister Muhammad Nashashibi and other Palestinian officials, he announced soon thereafter that the measures and their devastating impact had in effect annulled the Paris Protocol.

In addition to terrorist attacks and border closures, the arrival into power of a new government in Israel in June 1996 undermined the implementation of the agreement. The replacement of most members of the Israeli negotiating team by Likud representatives removed the good working relationships which had developed with the Palestinians over the years. Distrust and suspicion grew on both sides. Palestinians came to view Israel's stated security concerns increasingly as an excuse to avoid implementing the Paris Protocol (Novik, 1997). Following yet another terrorist attack in a Jerusalem market in July 1997, Prime Minister Netanyahu froze the transfer of tax and customs payments to the Palestinian Authority. He held that the money was used to pay Palestinian police officers suspected of involvement in attacks on Israel and that the payments, crucial to the Authority's survival, would not be resumed until Arafat worked wholeheartedly to destroy the terrorist infrastructure in the Palestinian self-rule areas. In August 1996 the Israeli government announced that 30 per cent of the tax rebates would be transferred in response to the Palestinian Authority's 'partial cooperation' in investigating the Jerusalem market bombings. Insisting on full payment the Palestinians claimed that withholding the funds was illegal, unrelated to security, and designed to strangle their leadership and political aspirations.[26] Israel eventually resumed the transfer of all tax payments following reproaches from the international donor community. The two parties confirmed in the 1998 Wye River Agreement their

[25] M. Jamal, 'Separation Due to Irreconcilable Differences'. *Palestine Report* (East Jerusalem), 15 March 1996, p. 12; 'Dependence on Israel Unhealthy'. *Palestine Report* (East Jerusalem), 14 June 1996, pp. 6–7; 'Paris Protocol: Null and Void'. *Palestine Report* (East Jerusalem), 26 April 1996, pp. 12–13.

[26] 'PA to be Given 30 Per Cent of Withheld Funds'. *Jerusalem Post*, 19 August 1997, p. 1; 'The Closure: Security Boost or Ticking Bomb?'. *Jerusalem Post*, 22 August 1997.

recognition of the importance of speeding up economic development in the West Bank and Gaza, and of ensuring safe passage between these areas and Israel. The Wye River Agreement called for a resumption of the earlier joint work on economic issues and for a number of new initiatives.[27]

Conclusion

Issues of justice and fairness arose persistently in the Israel–PLO interim talks. These issues, among others, caused deadlocks and crises calling into question the continuation of the entire peace process. The predominance of Israel's power, reflected in the DoP, meant that the country's concerns, especially with regards to national security, influenced the process extensively. Israeli negotiators did not think that they could 'afford' being driven primarily by questions of justice. As defined by the Palestinians and much of the international community, they would undermine vital Israeli interests and any gains to be had from the process. Successful bargaining and peace required a pragmatic approach which set aside contentious historical and legal charges of injustice. While making ample references to international law and morality, the Palestinians were acutely aware of the need to make large concessions to secure an agreement. They could not risk incurring greater losses by insisting on their understanding of a principled solution. Both Israeli and Palestinian negotiators admitted in interviews that considerations of justice were not the primary factor which ultimately determined the course and outcome of the talks.

At the same time, power inequality alone cannot explain the Israel–PLO interim talks. A fundamental objective was to restructure the Israel–Palestinian relationship towards greater equality in the political, economic, trade and other spheres. They partly aimed to transfer authority, territory and other resources from 'the strong' to 'the weak', and enabled the Palestinians to fulfil some basic preconditions of what constitutes a state. In working for that goal, Palestinian negotiators were not without their own sources of influence. One was the threat that a failure to produce agreements minimally acceptable to the Palestinian public could fatally erode support for Arafat and the

---

[27] 'The Wye River Memorandum', signed by Israel and the PLO on 23 October 1998 in Washington, DC. Document available at the website of the Embassy of Israel, London, at http://www.israel-embassy.org.uk/web/pages/peace.htm.

moderate Palestinian leadership, which Israel needed to obtain its own critical goals in the negotiations. This would bolster the appeal of Islamic fundamentalist organisations whose power was already growing in the Israeli-held territories, partly because of the financial bankruptcy and decline of PLO institutions. The fact that both Israel and the PLO needed the peace process and would suffer substantially from its collapse meant that neither side could merely dictate the terms at the expense of the other. The Palestinians managed to compensate for some of their weakness merely by putting forward certain notions of fairness convincingly, without resort to sophisticated negotiating strategies. These notions, and their perceived authenticity and depth, moved the Israeli government into making considerable concessions on several occasions. Israel's recognition of Palestinian water rights is one example.

The DoP's and Israel's emphasis on avoiding zero-sum issues and creating agreements benefiting both sides could be seen as incorporating a notion of 'relative fairness' (Pundik, 1997; Baram, 1997). From this perspective, Israel could not be expected to introduce or accept claims to justice which would leave the country worse off than when the talks first started. It justified using the post-1967 situation as the starting point for negotiations and the exchange of concessions. Many Palestinian negotiators agreed that they secured reasonable terms under the circumstances, and this perception ensured their acceptance of them. As always there were people on both sides who were unsatisfied, and there was certainly a widespread conviction among the Palestinians that the DoP and the interim agreements defied international legal principles. But most of their subsequent complaints concerned the implementation of the terms and not their substance.

In the years following the conclusion of the interim agreements, a primary threat to the Israeli–Palestinian peace process lay exactly in the failure or delays to implement many of their provisions. Disputes over Israeli troop withdrawal, terrorist incidents, the continued expansion of Israeli settlements and border closures deepened resentment and feelings of betrayal on both sides. Perhaps most damaging of all was the failure of the 1994 Paris Protocol to improve economic conditions in the West Bank and Gaza, and the actual deterioration in Palestinian living conditions. The development of the Palestinian economy was and remains fundamental to a stable and comprehensive settlement of the conflict, and ultimately to Israeli security. But the repeated border closures made a mockery of the vision of free trade with Israel as an engine of Palestinian economic growth. The customs union arrangements with Israel rendered the Palestinians especially vulnerable to such restrictions on the movement of people and goods, and they imposed heavy burdens in terms of soaring unemployment rates and falling export revenues. The level of private investment in the Palestinian territories dropped considerably after the signing of the DoP in 1993. Overall, the general economic stagnation coupled with a high population growth caused an actual and substantial decline in per capita income. The Palestinian GDP per capita reportedly fell by an estimated 12 per cent in 1995 and by 6 per cent in 1996, and the GNP per capita dropped by 10 per cent in 1995 and by 7 per cent in 1996.[28] This bleak picture stood in sharp contrast to the optimistic model of economic exchange and mutual benefit set forth in the Paris Protocol.

The talks over the implementation of the interim agreements and the final status issues were still ongoing in early 2000. In February of that year, at a time when Israel accorded great priority to a military withdrawal from Lebanon and a peace treaty with Syria, Barak and Arafat failed to agree on the scope of Israel's second delayed withdrawal in the West Bank. Moreover, they did not come up with the framework for a permanent settlement foreseen under the Wye River Agreement. They had yet to complete the most difficult substantial negotiations of all, on resolving the final status issues. The Israeli and Palestinian positions remained very far apart on the right of return for Palestinian refugees, the borders of a Palestinian state, the political status of Jerusalem and other questions. Indeed, solutions which could address deeply held notions of justice and win the necessary domestic political support on both sides seemed elusive. Both the Israeli Prime Minister and the PLO leader remained constrained and threatened by severe internal divisions and opposition at home. These pressures were likely to increase as the talks came close to a final deal. As another round of final status talks opened in Washington, DC, in early April 2000, Faisal Husseini, the PLO official for Jerusalem, warned that the Palestinians were prepared to return to violence unless they got a fair deal.[29] On the question of Jerusalem, he held that they could not settle for less than Palestinian control over the eastern part, including the Old City. Israel had earlier stressed the

---

[28] *West Bank and Gaza Update,* March 1998.
[29] 'Husseini Warns of Violence over Jerusalem'. *Jerusalem Post,* 7 April 2000.

principles of a united Jerusalem as Israel's capital and no return to the 1967 borders.[30]

The grievances and despair in the Palestinian territories over how little the peace process had delivered, and might deliver even in the final phase, appeared to continue to play into the hands of Arafat's strong opponents, particularly the Islamic fundamentalist camp. Several other factors, including any involvement by key Arab states and the US, were set to have a bearing on the ultimate outcome. Both Israeli and Palestinian leaders had, however, confirmed their commitment to certain fundamental principles and goals, partly for the sake of their own political survival. The experience of the interim period had demonstrated vividly that any long-term, durable settlement would have to balance concerns on both sides rather than merely reflect the balance of forces, and include the strongest provisions possible for timely and evenhanded implementation.

[30] 'Opening of Negotiations on the Framework Agreement on Permanent Status, 8 November 1999'. Document available at the website of the Embassy of Israel, London, at http://www.israel-embassy.org.uk/web/pages/peace.htm.

6   Can justice and fairness ever matter in arms control? Negotiating the extension of the Nuclear Non-Proliferation Treaty

> When the parties were presented with a package which included a set of principles and objectives and a strengthened review process, they felt that it was a fair package which satisfied all their needs.[1]

Negotiating growing threats of mass destruction

The past few years have raised many hopes, and many fears, regarding human safety in face of the proliferation of non-conventional weapons. The conclusion of the Comprehensive Test Ban Treaty (CTBT) in 1996 was lauded as a monumental achievement in the history of arms control, which would end nuclear explosive tests and go far to prevent the spread and further improvement of nuclear weapons capabilities globally. Within two years, in May 1998, India and Pakistan each exploded several nuclear devices underground. The tests reinforced long-held views that these bitter enemies are among those most likely to be drawn into a nuclear conflict, and to develop into new fully fledged nuclear states. In October 1999, another setback emerged with the failure of the United States (US) Senate to ratify the CTBT. Similarly, the decision of the 1995 NPT Review and Extension Conference to extend the Nuclear Non-Proliferation Treaty (NPT) indefinitely and to strengthen future reviews of its operation was initially welcomed as a significant step towards complete nuclear disarmament. But the three PrepComm meetings, held subsequently under the new review process, demonstrated that the old conflict between the Western nuclear weapons states (NWS)

---

[1] Ambassador Jayantha Dhanapala, President of the 1995 NPT Review and Extension Conference and UN Under-Secretary-General for Disarmament Affairs (personal interview, 1998).

and the non-nuclear weapons states (NNWS) over the conditions for nuclear disarmament had persisted. Evidence indicates that North Korea has attempted to resume a clandestine nuclear weapons programme, in violation of its obligations under the NPT and its 1994 non-proliferation agreement with the US. Another weapon of mass destruction was entirely outlawed in the 1993 Chemical Weapons Convention, adopted after more than two decades of negotiations. It established a strong implementation and verification regime, and has fortified the global norm against chemical weapons. Will the regime be able to deter and reveal violations despite increasingly sophisticated weapons technologies? Will non-signatory states such as Iraq, North Korea and Syria stifle the achievement of its objectives? This remains to be seen.

The record of conventional arms control stands in sharp contrast to these considerable international efforts to eliminate weapons of mass destruction (chemical, biological and nuclear). Conventional arms have proliferated far more, and have been used to wage the most deadly conflicts since 1945. Yet the attempts to control their widespread availability and use have been half-hearted and ineffective. The negotiation of the 1997 Ottawa Treaty banning anti-personnel landmines is an exception in this area. A number of factors have led the international community to conclude that the proliferation of weapons of mass destruction is instead the prime threat to global security. In the Middle East and South Asia, the regions most prone to a nuclear confrontation, few of the conditions which made nuclear deterrence relatively reliable during the Cold War exist. Geographic distances are short, many countries are internally unstable, command and control systems are poor, conflicts over territory and other scarce resources are rampant, political uses of violence are standard, and the possibility of nuclear and similarly destructive weapons falling into the hands of terrorists and brutal leaders is real (Evron, 1994; Kemp and Harkavy, 1997). The Gulf War of 1990–1 shed new light on the significance of preventing proliferation and working to eliminate weapons of mass destruction.

During the Cold War, 'arms control' referred to efforts to regulate the competitive buildup of arms, nuclear in particular, through agreement on freezes and other limits on specified types of weapons. The process helped more generally to manage the US–Soviet rivalry by keeping channels of communication open and reducing the risks of accidental war or escalation. Greater aspirations today have broadened the term to include disarmament, the abolishment of entire categories of weapons, and the creation of new international norms. The end of the US–Soviet competition has enhanced the prospects for attaining such goals. At the same time, in a world deprived of the relative predictability and security of bipolarity, the desire of several countries in conflict-ridden regions to acquire their own deterrent weapons capabilities has increased.

Arms control talks are conducted in time of peace over a longer period, unlike other military negotiations which are often *ad hoc* and one-time encounters between warring parties. At the multilateral level they take place in established fora, including the Conference on Disarmament and the Conference on Security and Cooperation in Europe. A number of features, while not unique, distinguish arms control talks from many other international negotiations. These have, as we shall see, implications for justice and fairness considerations. Negotiations over arms control involve vital issues of national security and survival for states. They typically engage parties whose relations are damaged by long-standing conflict and mistrust. While conducted in time of peace, they take place in the shadow of the threat of use of force and arms competition. It is not unusual for parties to develop and deploy new weapons as a means either to improve their bargaining power, or to circumvent or compensate for mutually agreed arms control measures. As in other international negotiations, perceptions of national interests shape the process and the outcome extensively. In this area, however, the political relations among negotiating countries and the larger international security situation determine largely how they are defined (Goldblat, 1996)

Can arms control ever be about justice and fairness? An overview

It is common to regard the sheer importance of national security issues as irreconcilable with serious ethical considerations. Negotiators clearly enter into arms control talks in order to serve the security interests of their own countries, and not for the sake of behaving morally in a broader sense (Ledogar, 1998). Such negotiations have nevertheless important justice and fairness dimensions, two of which are of a general nature.

First, countries engage in arms control talks because alternative ways of providing for their security, including through a continuous buildup of arms, are less effective or more costly and risky. There is ample room in this process for the pursuit of self-interest. But it is restrained by the need to take into account the security requirements of others. Arms control agreements can only be durable when they balance the essential concerns of all parties, avoid enhancing the national security of some at the cost of others, and are mutually beneficial. Like other international agreements, they must secure the voluntary approval and compliance of states. This means that they cannot be seen as unreasonable or unfair in the sense of ignoring or damaging the vital security needs of anyone whose signature is important.

Secondly, arms control is about mutual obligations and mutual rights. As signatories of arms control treaties, countries are parties to a legally binding 'contract' spelling out norms and rules of conduct regarding permitted and forbidden military activities. The duty of compliance with obligations under agreements, which parties have negotiated and entered into freely, is a fundamental principle of international law. It raises particularly stark issues of justice and fairness in this area, however, because of the stakes involved and the potentially fatal consequences of violations. In arms control agreements a state agrees to give up or limit specified military activities, in exchange for other parties doing the same, as a means to provide for its security. Such agreements are fully effective only if all comply; violations may directly threaten the security of complying states. Parties often associate justice and fairness not only with compliance in itself, but also with the establishment of verification procedures which deter and detect breaches and reflect the seriousness of their obligations.

The literature on military negotiations focuses on well-known driving forces such as considerations of national and international security. Some studies suggest that certain conceptions of fairness relating to procedure and outcome were influential in US–Soviet arms control talks during the Cold War. The meaning attached to fairness by both sides supposedly entailed reciprocity, parity and equality. These values were reflected in agreements on equal ceilings or freezes and equal percentage reductions in existing arms arsenals. They were also expressed in the bargaining process, as the superpowers moved from their opening positions to a compromise agreement by reciprocating each other's concessions (Jensen, 1983; Druckman, 1990; Jensen, 1963; Zartman *et al.*, 1996). One study reviews six cases of international negotiations, including those resulting in the Strategic Arms Limitation Talks (SALT) I Agreement, and the SALT II and Partial Test Ban Treaties. It suggests that among various patterns of reciprocity the US and the Soviet Union often practised 'comparative responsiveness', whereby each side acted based on a comparison of its own and the other's tendencies to concede (Druckman and Harris, 1990).

Fairness in this sense thus played a facilitating role by coordinating the parties' expectations and concessions and helping them to reach agreement. One must ask what made this possible, in light of the conflicting and disruptive arguments about fairness witnessed in more recent arms control talks. The emphasis on quantitative measures meant that principles such as equality could be translated relatively easily into uniform ceilings and reductions. The considerable parity existing between the US and the Soviet Union as nuclear powers, and the shared goal of using arms control to reinforce mutual deterrence (for example, by ensuring roughly equal second-strike capabilities), were certainly important. These factors correspond well to what the theoretical literature proposes: parties who are roughly equal in power, and who recognise a mutually prominent solution or foresee an agreement based on equality, tend to use procedures based on reciprocity (Schelling, 1960; Bartos, 1974). It is when parties perceive themselves as largely equal – for example, in dependency on or gains to be had from a negotiated agreement – that they realise the need to search for a balanced solution and acquire the motivation to reciprocate concessions to arrive at such a solution (Zartman, 1991). Their equality implies that other procedures or other types of agreements may cause costly delays and even fail.

The cited studies on US–Soviet arms control talks point to the importance of fairness only in the sense that the pattern of concession-making and the terms of concluded agreements match some concepts of fairness found in the academic literature. It is not clear from these studies whether US and Soviet negotiators practised reciprocity, equality, parity and so on because these principles corresponded to their own sense of fairness. The principles may well have been used for political and tactical reasons. Chapter 3 showed that even in a far less sensitive area such as transboundary air pollution, Cold War hostilities and mistrust pervaded negotiations in the 1970s and 1980s and left little room for ethical concerns: the parties employed equal percentage reductions and uniform ceilings because of their simplicity, not because they were seen as fair. These approaches seemed most likely to produce results under the circumstances, and to help sell the agreements to domestic constituencies. Solutions based on equality often serve as 'focal points' in negotiation more generally, for many reasons other than a concern about fairness or morality (Schelling, 1960). However, a high-level US negotiator stated in an interview that the US and the Soviet Union could never have accepted a treaty which was unfair in the sense of being 'unbalanced' or failing to benefit both sides. He recalled how the head of a Soviet arms control delegation had likened the process to an exercise in mountain climbing: the two sides would reach the mountain top more easily if they assisted each other as partners (Earle, 1998). The SALT II Treaty never entered into force, partly because US opponents held that its failure to restrict Backfire bombers and heavy intercontinental ballistic missiles on the Soviet side made it militarily inequitable.

Important US–Russian bilateral talks continue today, notably over reductions in strategic arms. Evidence of the growing proliferation of weapons of mass destruction has at the same time intensified efforts within multilateral fora such as the Conference on Disarmament and the Conference on Security and Cooperation in Europe. The global context, format and goals of these talks differ dramatically from those conducted between the Soviet Union and the US. They are large-scale, complex negotiations between numerous parties divided by divergent security requirements, military capabilities and technological and other resources. Do concerns about justice and fairness enter into this environment? If so, how? Do only procedural and outcome fairness understood as reciprocity and uniform measures matter, as observed in earlier US–Soviet arms control talks? There have been no systematic or empirical studies to date which can answer such questions.

A variety of justice and fairness issues do arise in multilateral arms control efforts. For example, the Chemical and the Biological Weapons Conventions, like the CTBT, recall the principles of equality and reciprocity: all parties are subjected to identical bans and requirements and to the same verification procedures, although these can affect them unequally as in the case of the CTBT. The three agreements are often singled out as non-discriminatory in this sense and as distinct from the NPT, which permits the NWS to keep their weapons until 'general and complete disarmament' takes place. The talks on a Chemical Weapons Convention were concluded successfully once Western chemical weapons states, especially the US and France, abandoned their attempts to retain certain privileges (Bernauer, 1993). The Convention requires all parties to destroy their chemical weapons and production facilities, at the same percentage rates. The greater security value which Western states attach to nuclear weapons certainly helps to explain why agreement on uniform obligations was possible in the case of chemical and biological weapons, often labelled 'the deterrent of the poor'. The final document of the 1996 Fourth Review Conference for the Biological Weapons Convention stressed that all cases of non-compliance must be confronted decisively, without selectivity or discrimination (Zaluar and Monteleone-Neto, 1997).

But justice and fairness assume meanings which go far beyond the narrow notions which reportedly guided US–Soviet talks. They have also done little to coordinate expectations or otherwise facilitate negotiations to date. The talks within the Conference on Disarmament which led to the Biological and Chemical Weapons Conventions, and which have since continued to ensure effective implementation, raised two contentious issues with fairness dimensions: any negative impact of the Conventions on the development of LDCs, and implementation and verification. In the talks on chemical weapons, countries of the Non-Aligned Movement (NAM) opposed verification involving national requests for 'challenge inspections' on the grounds that it would disproportionately target them and could be abused for espionage. Their activities would be more closely monitored by industrialised countries, given their technical superiority, than *vice versa* (Stern, 1994). The final provisions had to balance the demand of industrialised states for some intrusive challenge inspections to ensure compliance, with the need to protect legitimate national security, commercial and other interests of targeted countries.[2] The Convention requires governments to enact export controls on commercial chemicals, despite protests by LDCs that these do more to hinder their economic development than prevent weapons proliferation. It also obliges chemical weapons states to bear the bulk of the high implementation costs, in order to alleviate this burden on developing and less-resourced states. By early 2000 negotiations were still ongoing on a protocol to the Biological Weapons Convention, to

---

[2] 'Convention on the prohibition of the development, production, stockpiling and use of chemical weapons and on their destruction (Chemical Weapons Convention)', published in Goldblat (1996).

contain measures for implementing and verifying compliance with its provisions which the original treaty text lacks.[3]

The negotiations leading to the indefinite extension of the NPT illustrate with particular richness how justice and fairness can enter into today's major arms control efforts. The full meaning of this experience remains the subject of varying interpretations and prophecies, and can only become clearer with time. Yet the decision to make the NPT permanent, and to improve implementation and compliance with the Treaty, is surely a critical step in the process to halt the development and spread of nuclear weapons. What meaning do international negotiators themselves give to concepts of justice and fairness in formulating agreements of this significance and complexity? Which conceptions have they acted upon, if any, and why? How do national and international security concerns, the multilateral structure of the negotiations, power relations, and coalition building affect such values? Can justice and fairness considerations help to explain recent successes and setbacks with the NPT? We will now turn to these questions.

The 1995 NPT Conference: disputing the fulfilment of mutual obligations

The 1968 Treaty on the Non-Proliferation of Nuclear Weapons entered into force in 1970 with the aims to prevent the further spread of nuclear weapons, promote peaceful nuclear cooperation and an end to the arms race, and to pave the way for nuclear disarmament. To achieve these ends it established a bargain between the NNWS and the NWS, defined as those countries which manufactured and exploded a nuclear weapon or other device before 1 January 1967 (the US, the Soviet Union/Russia, the UK, France and China). The obligations and privileges associated with this bargain have ever since provided the framework and the agenda for follow-up Review Conferences. They have also been the focus of accusations and

---

[3] 'Convention on the prohibition of the development, production and stockpiling of bacteriological (biological) and toxin weapons and on their destruction (Biological Weapons Convention)', published in Goldblat (1996). The Convention explicitly bans the development, production and stockpiling of bacteriological and toxin weapons, but not their use. Some parties to the Convention have reserved the right to employ biological weapons for retaliatory purposes, or against countries which are not parties to the 1925 Geneva Protocol prohibiting the use of such weapons.

disputes concerning compliance, and other matters with justice and fairness implications.

For their part, the NWS pledged to negotiate 'in good faith' effective measures 'relating to cessation of the nuclear arms race at an early date and to nuclear disarmament, and on a treaty on general and complete disarmament' (Article VI). They agreed not to transfer nuclear weapons to other states, and to refrain from encouraging in any way an NNWS to acquire nuclear explosive devices (Article I). Moreover, the NWS undertook to contribute to the development of peaceful uses of nuclear energy in the NNWS (Article IV) and to share the benefits from any peaceful applications of nuclear explosions with them (Article V). In exchange for these commitments the NNWS agreed not to develop or acquire nuclear weapons (Article II) and to accept a set of safeguards, in accordance with the safeguards system of the International Atomic Energy Agency (IAEA) and a list of other specifications and conditions, to verify their compliance with this obligation (Article III). They had 'the right to participate in, the fullest possible exchange of equipment, materials and scientific and techno- logical information' for peaceful uses of nuclear energy (Article IV).[4] As of January 2000 the NPT had 187 signatory states, including North Korea and Iraq. India, Pakistan and Israel, all possessing nuclear weapons capabilities, remain outside, as does Cuba.

The NPT called for conferences to assess its implementation every five years, in part because the Treaty set out the disarmament obliga- tions very vaguely and briefly without any procedure for verification (Dhanapala, 1998). Of the first five NPT conferences, the parties were able to agree on a joint Final Declaration only in two, in 1975 and 1985. They made progress on several issues and objectives, but disagreed sharply and persistently over the compliance of the NWS with their disarmament obligations and the right of the NNWS to acquire and develop nuclear technology for peaceful purposes. The fourth Review Conference held in 1990 gave an indication of the disputes to come: some states made clear that they would seek to make an extension of the NPT conditional upon specific disarmament measures. Others objected that this would weaken the Treaty to the point of endan- gering its very existence.

---

[4] 'Treaty on the Non-Proliferation of Nuclear Weapons', published in Goldblat (1996). Under Article X, a party has the right to withdraw from the Treaty if it judges that 'extraordinary events, related to the subject matter of this Treaty' threaten its 'supreme interests'.

The NPT Review and Extension Conference was held from 17 April to 12 May 1995 in New York, with Ambassador Jayantha Dhanapala of Sri Lanka serving as its President. The participants included 175 of the then 178 signatory states. Representatives of ten non-party states, including Pakistan and Israel (not India), and about 200 non-governmental and international organisations attended as observers. The Conference had two distinct objectives: to review the operation of the NPT, particularly in the last five years, and to decide as stipulated in Article X whether the Treaty should now, twenty-five years after its entry into force, be extended indefinitely or for one or more fixed periods. The talks in these two areas proceeded simultaneously, covered much of the same ground, and involved the same parties (Westdal, 1995). When the initial plenary sessions opened there was still no agreed rule on the voting method to be used, should a vote became necessary to decide about the extension. The parties had repeatedly failed to reach agreement on this issue in earlier preparatory meetings, which they had held over eighteen months to decide about procedural rules. The Conference President was now charged with resolving the matter by 27 April (Sanders, 1995).

The negotiations proceeded on several tracks. The review of the implementation of the NPT took place in three established Main Committees. These handled disarmament and security assurances to NNWS, safeguards and nuclear-free zones, and peaceful uses of nuclear technology, respectively. By contrast a small *ad hoc* group of twenty-five hand-picked countries conducted the major talks on extending the Treaty. Referred to as 'the President's Consultations', they came to draft a set of principles and goals for nuclear disarmament and non-proliferation, and to work out how the extension would be linked to a strengthened review process. The group included representatives of the NWS, the NAM and of other geopolitical interests. Ambassador Dhanapala resolved to conduct these consultations because he, like many parties to the Conference, was concerned that the decision on the NPT extension be taken by consensus: 'It is impossible to negotiate in a huge assembly hall with over a hundred parties. What is needed is to get representatives of . . . the most important parties to test ideas . . . it allowed a solution to be worked out in a smaller group and to be accepted by a larger group' (Dhanapala, 1998).

A number of contentious issues emerged at an early stage which, while formally falling within the domain of either one of the Main

Committees or the President's Consultations, transgressed organisational divides and came to dominate the entire Conference. These related more or less to the core bargain between the NWS and the NNWS contained in the NPT of 1968. They concerned the question of how far the parties had fulfilled their respective pledges associated with the Treaty, and what conclusions should be drawn from this record when it came to extending it. These disputed issues all evoked considerations of justice or fairness, as we shall see. On the issue of *disarmament* the NWS admitted that they had not always lived up to their obligations in the past. However, they had now effectively ended the nuclear arms race. They were undertaking significant measures in line with what they regarded as their core commitment under Article VI, to negotiate nuclear disarmament 'in good faith'. The NWS fiercely opposed the introduction of any specific timetable, and argued that they could eliminate their nuclear arsenals only as the international security situation permitted, 'in the context of general and complete disarmament' (Weston, 1998; Simpson, 1998). In the meantime, it was critical to prevent other countries from acquiring these weapons. The US stressed that as long as other countries possessed nuclear forces, it must reconcile arms reductions with the maintenance of deterrence and had to test its own weapons needed for deterrence for safety purposes (Earle, 1998).

The usual allies of the NWS and other industrialised countries were divided between those supporting this position and those demanding firmer and faster progress on disarmament. Norway, New Zealand and Australia were among the latter. Sweden, Ireland and Austria believed that the EU had adopted 'a complacent view tailored to the needs of France and Britain' on the matter (Johnson, 1995a). The NAM countries, while meeting in Bandung (Indonesia) in late April 1995, voiced 'deep concern' that the NWS had not honoured their NPT obligations fully. They requested that the NPT Conference adopt specific measures to achieve genuine nuclear disarmament (Sanders, 1995). They sought a time bound framework to reach this goal, as well as more immediate steps such as the conclusion of a CTBT and the negotiation of a 'non-discriminatory' ban on nuclear weapons fissile material.

The differences surrounding disarmament led to disagreements over the best *form of extension* for the NPT. Many Western and Eastern European countries favoured an indefinite and unconditional extension of the Treaty (Dhanapala, 1995). In the run-up to the Conference all the NWS, except China, lobbied vigorously to achieve this end. They approached the governments of NAM countries known to object to a permanent or unconditional renewal, and attempted to persuade them to change their minds. Apart from Sweden and Switzerland, several states supporting an indefinite extension agreed that linking it to time-bound disarmament commitments was impractical. However, they stressed that the NWS must not abuse such an extension to escape their disarmament obligations and that they must progress with implementing these more rapidly. From the outset the Canadian delegates took a lead role in advocating and rallying support for this position on 'permanence with accountability'. They solicited signatures on an *aide-memoire* which later became a resolution for indefinite extension (Leigh-Phippard, 1997). Canada argued that a permanent Treaty would provide a more secure international environment in which disarmament could take place in 'a rational and structured way' (Sinclair, 1998). A fixed-term renewal would evoke uncertainty which the NWS could use as an excuse not to proceed with disarmament, and reduce international pressure on them to do so.

The opposing notion that an indefinite extension would rather reinforce the weaknesses and inequalities of the Treaty was widespread among NAM countries (with the notable exception of South Africa, further discussed below). They were deeply concerned that permanence would deprive them of leverage on disarmament matters, and remove all pressure on the NWS to honour their pledges. Some believed that a time-limited renewal would help to avoid this, while others felt that a comprehensive review of the NPT was in order prior to any decision. When meeting in Bandung, the NAM countries failed to adopt a common position on the conditions to be attached to an NPT extension so as to ensure serious nuclear disarmament.

Another dispute concerned the nature of *security assurances* provided by the NWS. In exchange for renouncing the nuclear option the NNWS had, ever since the negotiation of the NPT, requested protection to minimise threats to their security which could otherwise arise from their forfeiture of nuclear weapons. They requested security guarantees of two kinds: 'positive' assurances entailing a commitment to act in support of an NNWS threatened by a nuclear attack, and 'negative' assurances defined as a pledge by the NWS not to employ nuclear weapons against them. It had been argued in 1968 that it was impossible to formulate provisions within the Treaty catering to the diverse security needs of all states concerned for an indefinite future.

Instead the US, the UK and the Soviet Union provided positive and negative assurances in a joint resolution to the UN Security Council and in separate policy statements. The US asserted that it would seek Security Council action to defuse a nuclear threat against any NNWS which was a party to the NPT (or an equivalent treaty), and that it would not use nuclear weapons against such a party unless it was allied with another NWS at the time of an attack on the US or its allies.[5] Just prior to the NPT Review and Extension Conference, the NWS reconfirmed these positive assurances in a UN Security Council Resolution (UNSC 984 (1995)) and the negative ones in a statement to the Conference on Disarmament. Many NNWS, however, considered these promises inadequate for their security needs.

The question of *accession* to the NPT by new states became another stumbling block in the negotiations. A group of Arab states invoked the principle of universality to argue that all countries should accede to the Treaty and be bound by the same terms. They singled out Israel's nuclear weapons programme, and pointed to the imbalance and threat to Middle East security which a permanent renewal of the NPT would perpetuate unless Israel joined. The principle of universality is not stated explicitly in the 1968 NPT text. The signatory states assumed nonetheless at the time of its adoption that they would work to include more parties, especially those with nuclear potential, and that the Treaty would eventually become universal in order to attain its objectives (El-Araby, 1998). The Egyptian Foreign Minister stated that since the NPT 'is incapable of safeguarding [its] national security ... Egypt ... cannot support the indefinite extension of the Treaty because the regional situation ... remains volatile and ... unsatisfactory.'[6] He went further to propose that the Conference be suspended until the NPT was universally accepted. Jordan, Syria, Kuwait and Lebanon also refused to agree to a permanent extension unless Israel became a party to the NPT.

Export controls and *peaceful uses of nuclear technology* became another subject of intense debate. Developing countries argued with resentment that nuclear export controls had come to disadvantage them, and violated their 'inalienable right' under the NPT to develop

---

[5] 'Treaty on the Non-Proliferation of Nuclear Weapons'. US Arms Control and Disarmament Agency, Washington, DC (obtained from http://www.acda.gov/treaties/npt1.htm (undated)).

[6] Statement by Egyptian Foreign Minister Amre Moussa, quoted in 'Israel's Nuclear Weapons Continue as Stumbling Block'. *ACRONYM NPT Update*, No. 5, 21 April 1995.

nuclear energy for peaceful pursuits without discrimination (Article IV). The NPT spells out that such safeguards must not hamper their economic or technological advancement, nor international co-operation on peaceful nuclear activities.

Disagreements over *rules of procedure* to employ in the event of a vote on the NPT extension persisted to the very end. The Treaty itself already stipulated that this decision should be taken by 'a majority' (Article X). Moreover, when the Conference opened on 17 April 1995, a majority of parties already favoured a permanent extension. The NAM countries insisted on a consensus decision, by contrast, while the US and other NWS sought a large substantial majority (Earle, 1998). The most controversial matter was whether the vote should take place by open or by secret ballot. Western and Eastern European delegations generally favoured an open vote on the grounds that it was the normal procedure, and that it would ensure transparency and accountability. Many NAM countries argued that only a secret ballot would protect them from distorting pressures and allow them to vote freely without fear of repercussions. The NWS had already urged and pushed them to agree to an indefinite extension. Some NAM representatives said that the tactics used against them, particularly by the US, the UK and France, had been aggressive and coercive and that they had reason to think that they would be employed again.

Explaining progress: the steps and the new bargain to ensure better compliance

How could the negotiations move forward in this complex situation, with a large number of parties disagreeing over multiple issues? A web of forces were at work, and there is no single-factor explanation. A decisive ingredient was the fact that the vast majority of countries, despite their differences over the NPT, were united in their belief that it was a tremendously important regime and that the Conference had to succeed. No country wanted to be held responsible for undermining a treaty of such a widely recognised international significance. The proposals which became influential sought to strengthen the NPT in two ways: by making it permanent and by tying the parties more firmly to their commitments, especially on disarmament matters.

In the review of the operation of the Treaty, as well as in the talks over its extension, the greatest obstacle to an agreement was the question of the implementation of Article VI. Despite weeks of argumentation in Main Committee I, the parties could not resolve their deep divisions over whether the nuclear arms race had effectively ended and what the NWS had done or failed to do to fulfil their disarmament obligations. The Chair of the Drafting Committee, followed by the Conference President, intervened with their own initiatives to try to break the deadlock but no progress was made. The conflicts surrounding Article VI is the single most important explanation behind the failure to reach agreement on a Final Document on the results of the review. The issue of whether the NNWS had honoured their part of the bargain by complying with Article II was hardly questioned or discussed, other than in the case of countries such as Iraq and North Korea (Earle, 1998). The focus remained on the NWS, and on nuclear-capable states outside the NPT regime.

After much hard bargaining, the countries included in the President's Consultations managed to tackle the dispute over disarmament by tying progress on the issue to the decision on extension. They worked on formulating a package deal acceptable to all parties by using this linkage. Inspired by a South African proposal, it concentrated on setting forth a new 'bargain': an indefinite extension of the Treaty, in exchange for a strengthened review process and a set of criteria to evaluate compliance with disarmament and non-proliferation obligations. Although critical of the slow implementation of Article VI, South Africa believed that failing to make the NPT permanent would worsen the record on nuclear disarmament and proliferation issues even further and threaten '[t]he right of the people to avoid exposure to these weapons' (Goosen, 1998). However, the NNWS should ask for something in return for their willingness to support an indefinite extension. At the start of the Conference South African Foreign Minister Alfred Nzo, as a representative of a major NAM country, had changed the course of the talks by declaring support for an indefinite extension. In due course other NAM states followed his example, thus removing the prospect of a strong NAM opposition to a permanent Treaty. South Africa also convinced some sceptical neutral countries to support permanency by proposing objectives and principles which would fortify obligations in the new life of the NPT. Based on these suggestions, the states involved in the President's Consultations could eventually agree on steps to reinforce future reviews and on criteria to assess state compliance with Treaty obligations. They strengthened the linkages between these two elements, as proposed by the Indonesian Foreign Minister, and the

President then presented the suggestions to the Conference together with the recommendation to make the NPT permanent. On 11 May 1995 the Conference adopted the three proposals, without a vote.

This outcome allowed the parties to avoid a potentially divisive vote both on voting procedure (whether an open or secret ballot should be employed) and on the extension decision itself. Continuous efforts were made beyond the deadline of 27 April 1995 and throughout the conference to reach agreement on voting procedure. The consultations did lead to the adoption of a rule stating that any vote should be by written ballot, but the issue of whether it should be open or secret remained intractable and was never resolved. The Secretariat made arrangements for both options (Dhanapala, 1995). Despite the Treaty stipulation regarding a majority decision President Dhanapala worked from the outset to build consensus, as had been done in previous Review Conferences. His strategies and proposals were all engineered to avoid a vote altogether. He was convinced that a vote would display disunity and undermine the goals of the NPT. A consensus decision, by contrast, would strengthen the Treaty and its ability to convince countries still outside it to join. The result was successful in the sense that the Conference adopted the final decisions without a vote and without formal opposition from any of the participating parties. Some countries said that this reflected their reluctant acceptance of the existence of a majority favouring a permanent extension, and not a positive consensus (Johnson, 1995a).

The issue of universality, particularly Israel's refusal to join the NPT, threatened for long to block a consensus decision on making the Treaty permanent. A mere three days before its scheduled conclusion, the Conference witnessed the submission of an Arab draft resolution. It called upon Israel to accede to the NPT and to subject its nuclear capabilities to IAEA safeguards, urged Middle East states to establish a zone free of weapons of mass destruction, and requested the NWS to extend security assurances to NPT parties in this region (Sanders, 1995). Pinpointing Israel in this fashion proved unacceptable to some states. Their objection meant that a vote might be required not only on the draft resolution, but also on the three proposals which President Dhanapala was about to present to the Conference at large. Intense talks, notably between Egypt and the US, led to a revised draft which urged all remaining states in the area to join the NPT without mentioning any by name. So as to distance themselves from this new diluted version, the Arab states asked the NPT's depositary states (the

US, the UK and Russia) to submit it to the Conference. It was accepted without a vote on 11 May together with Dhanapala's three proposals. Without the inclusion of the resolution on the Middle East, Arab states would have refused to extend the NPT indefinitely without a vote (Dhanapala, 1998; El-Araby, 1998).

Security assurances to NNWS, entrusted to Main Committee I, became another fiercely debated subject. The central question was how to strengthen these assurances and preferably make them legally binding, and what new form they would take. Many NAM countries as well as Switzerland considered the existing NWS assurances insufficient. Egypt stressed that NPT parties in nuclear-weapon-free zones needed much better security guarantees. Those contained in UN Security Council Resolution 984 (1995) were not legally binding, so a policy change among the NWS could easily undermine them. The NAM countries now requested an 'unconditional, comprehensive . . . and legally binding instrument' banning the use of nuclear weapons against NNWS, and committing the NWS more firmly to combat threats of their use. They also sought the universal adoption of a 'no-first-use' policy as the best safeguard against nuclear weapons. While formally adopted by China, the other NWS rejected such a policy as detrimental to nuclear deterrence (Johnson, 1995a, 1995b).

On 4 May 1995 Main Committee I had a draft text containing three options: a protocol to be attached to the NPT, a convention on no first-use, and a treaty on negative security assurances. It had made much progress by the last day of the Conference, although the NWS never agreed to enter into legally binding obligations concerning security guarantees (Dhanapala, 1998). This progress could not be translated into an official agreement, however, given the failure of the Review to produce a Final Document.

There were intense debates in Main Committees II and III, and in some plenary sessions, over whether nuclear export controls had discriminatory effects and whether the NWS had broken their promise to help others develop nuclear resources. Iran took a lead role among the NAM countries in arguing that the operation of nuclear export controls discriminated against them. They reproached the NWS for using export controls to escape promises made under Article IV of the NPT, to assist the NNWS particularly in the developing world to develop nuclear resources. They held that, while the NWS had supplied non-party states such as Israel with nuclear materials and knowledge in violation of Article I, the NNWS parties to the NPT had been deprived of any comparable benefits. Most parties, including Conference President Dhanapala, acknowledged that the NWS and others had offered little assistance of the kind foreseen in Article IV and that parties to the NPT had hardly received any more aid than non-signatory states (Dhanapala, 1998). A number of NAM countries insisted that nuclear exports and indeed the NPT as a whole be implemented in a more transparent way, to prevent arbitrary treatment and ensure compliance with Treaty obligations. Much discussed was Iran's proposal that an international body administer nuclear exports (Sanders, 1995). These concerns were reflected in the final text of the 'Principles and Objectives' document. It emphasised the right of NNWS parties to the NPT to develop nuclear energy for peaceful purposes. It stated explicitly that efforts promoting the exercise of this right should give preferential treatment to NNWS parties, particularly in the developing world, and that nuclear-related export controls should be made more transparent.[7]

It proved impossible, as already explained, to reach agreement on a final document on the results of the NPT review. The parties ended the Conference on 12 May 1995 by adopting its Final Report, containing a package of agreements formulated earlier. They emphasised the need to implement every provision of the NPT effectively. The legal decision to extend the NPT indefinitely stressed the need for full compliance and universal adherence, and the goal of eliminating nuclear weapons completely.[8] It was linked politically to three other decisions, of a political nature and not legally binding: on principles and objectives, a strengthened review process, and the Middle East.

The 'Principles and Objectives' document set forth a set of standards and goals to evaluate progress in implementing the NPT in future review conferences. These were: universal adherence, non-proliferation, nuclear disarmament, the establishment of nuclear-weapon-free zones, security assurances, safeguards (including a binding commitment not to acquire nuclear weapons and acceptance of IAEA safeguards as preconditions for the transfer of nuclear

[7] Articles 14–17 in 'Principles and Objectives for Nuclear Non-Proliferation and Disarmament'. Decision adopted at the 1995 NPT Review and Extension Conference, New York, 17 April–12 May 1995 (NPT/CONF.1995/32/DEC.2).

[8] 'Extension of the Treaty on the Non-Proliferation of Nuclear Weapons'. Decision adopted at the 1995 NPT Review and Extension Conference, New York, 17 April–12 May 1995 (NPT/CONF.1995/32/DEC.3).

materials to NNWS), and peaceful uses of nuclear energy.[9] The document emphasised full implementation of Article VI on the disarmament obligations of the NWS, and specifically the immediate negotiation of a 'non-discriminatory' and 'universally applicable' ban on the production of nuclear weapons fissile material, the conclusion of a CTBT by 1996, and systematic efforts towards the elimination of all nuclear weapons.

The decision to strengthen the NPT review process provided for annual PrepComm meetings to be held. Unlike past meetings these would focus on substantial issues, such as the full implementation of the NPT and the 'Principles and Objectives' declaration, rather than on procedures. Review Conferences, to be held every five years, 'should look forward as well as back'.[10] The Resolution on the Middle East pointed to countries still outside the Treaty operating unsafeguarded nuclear facilities. Reaffirming the importance of universal adherence, it urged every single state in the Middle East to join the NPT and to place their nuclear facilities under IAEA safeguards. All countries in the region should also take steps to establish zones free of weapons of mass destruction, and the NWS should 'exert their utmost efforts' to ensure the realisation of this objective.[11]

In the aftermath to the 1995 Conference, the three non-party states with nuclear capacities continued to refuse to adhere to the NPT on the grounds of national security and fairness. Israel argued that its ambiguous and covert nuclear option was needed to deter threats to its national survival.[12] The country said that it could not rule out attacks by one or more Arab states, several of which possess or seek to develop weapons of mass destruction. Israel held moreover that its security could not be ensured with existing NPT mechanisms for verifying compliance, especially in a region dominated by undemocratic and closed societies. Incidents such as the IAEA's failure to detect Iraq's development of a nuclear weapons programme in the early 1980s had pointed to the inadequacy of these mechanisms.

---

[9] 'Principles and Objectives for Nuclear Non-Proliferation and Disarmament' (footnote 7 above).

[10] 'Strengthening the Review Process for the Treaty'. Decision adopted at the 1995 NPT Review and Extension Conference, New York, 17 April–12 May 1995 (NPT/CONF.1995/32/DEC.1).

[11] 'Resolution on the Middle East'. Adopted at the 1995 NPT Review and Extension Conference, New York, 17 April–12 May 1995 (NPT/CONF.1995/32/RES/1).

[12] See Evron (1994) for a detailed assessment of Israel's nuclear doctrine and alternative policies.

Pakistan's position recalled arguments made by Arab states refusing to agree to a permanent NPT extension unless Israel joined: Pakistan said it would become a party to the NPT only if India did the same. Signing unilaterally would place Pakistan at the mercy of India, given its superior conventional forces and nuclear capability (Mahmood, 1995; Akram, 1998). It would also further undermine the regional balance in South Asia. India for its part continued to argue that the NPT is unequal and discriminatory in allowing the NWS to keep their nuclear weapons while asking others to forego them. If the NWS needed to retain nuclear weapons until 'complete disarmament' has taken place, as they argue, so did India given its tensions with China and Pakistan and their nuclear capabilities. In sum, India would sign the Treaty only if and when it binds the NWS to a firm commitment and a timeframe for eliminating their nuclear arsenals (Ghose, 1998).

The influence of justice and fairness considerations

A range of issues with justice or fairness connotations arose in the 1995 NPT Review and Extension Conference. These related to the structure, process, procedures and outcome of the negotiations, and to implementation and compliance. Most of these were at the same time essential matters of international and national security, and to varying extents framed as such by the negotiators and countries involved. The basic agenda and collective purpose of the talks stemmed from the norms underlying the NPT itself: the unacceptability of the danger of massive indiscriminate harm posed by nuclear weapons, and the significance of preventing the proliferation and use of them and of ensuring nuclear disarmament. Many parties regarded these not solely as matters of physical safety and well-being for themselves, but also as broader ethical issues. The international community as a whole has increasingly come to consider the threat and use of nuclear weapons as immoral and as prohibited under international and humanitarian law, other than possibly in extreme circumstances of self-defence. This was expressed in the July 1996 advisory opinion of the International Court of Justice.[13] The prevention of such threats or

---

[13] The International Court of Justice concluded in its advisory opinion of July 1996 that the threat or use of nuclear weapons is almost always prohibited under international and humanitarian law. The Court could not decide conclusively whether it was legal or illegal for a state to use nuclear weapons in extreme cases of self-defence, to ensure

uses has also become equalised with an obligation to negotiate agreements leading to nuclear disarmament and even the abolishment of this entire category of weapon. Analysts and negotiators alike refer to the value of the NPT in both moral and security terms.

The 1995 Conference is another case in which the parties naturally focused on the details of the issues and proposals on the table. Personal interviews and primary documentation confirm that they seldom used the language of justice and fairness directly during the talks, or reflected on such considerations at a general abstract level. The sources also indicate, however, that justice and fairness were underlying currents and at times very influential. These values affected the talks in many more ways than they reportedly did in US–Soviet arms control negotiations during the Cold War. We will consider the major issues in turn, and then examine the circumstances and the factors which led negotiators to act upon (or ignore) them.

A structural fairness issue was *the terms and principles of the 1968 NPT itself*, which served as the fundamental framework for and basis of the talks. The Treaty divides signatory states into two groups: the NWS (understood as the US, the UK, Russia, China and France) and the NNWS (all other countries). It then establishes obligations and privileges, many of which are different for each group. The central differentiation is that five countries may keep and even upgrade their nuclear weapons until 'complete disarmament' takes place at some unspecified point in the future, while all other states are prohibited under the Treaty from possessing these same weapons irrespective of their security requirements.[14] In exchange the NWS are obliged to engage in arms control talks, avoid contributing to the spread of nuclear weapons materials in any way, and to help others develop peaceful uses of nuclear energy. Parties representing all geopolitical camps recognised in interviews that the NPT is founded on this bargain, involving mutual obligations and rights.[15] However, they expressed widely different understandings of the exact terms.

---

its very survival. At the same time it held that the continued international differences over the question of the legality of nuclear weapons were destabilising and harmful, and that states were obliged to engage in negotiations leading to nuclear disarmament. See further 'Legality of the Threat or Use of Nuclear Weapons', Advisory Opinion, International Court of Justice, General List No. 95, 8 July 1996.

[14] As already noted, every party has the right to withdraw from the NPT in exceptional circumstances when its vital interests are threatened.

[15] A list of the interviews conducted appears in the list of references.

Many NAM countries and some other NNWS held that the NPT is grossly unfair in the sense of being unbalanced and discriminatory. The obligations imposed upon them are more specified and re- stricting, and the total burden of sacrifices is much greater, than those applying to the NWS. India, Pakistan and Egypt, among others, stressed that 'the bargain' permits the NWS to keep their weapons without having to commit themselves to serious disarmament mea- sures, security assurances for NNWS, or even to the stringent safe- guards and verification system which applies to all other parties. A fair regime, they held, would aim to establish equality and subject the NWS to a time-bound programme leading to the complete elimination of their nuclear arsenals (Ghose, 1998; Akram, 1998). Referring to recent nuclear tests in South Asia, one negotiator said: 'It is not surprising what is happening now with India and Pakistan, as it is exactly what the NWS did in the past. The NWS have already done it' (El-Araby, 1998).

Members of the South African and Canadian delegations argued, by contrast, that the different characteristics of the NWS and the NNWS required differentiated obligations: unequal parties could not be treated equally in this case, and unequal treatment did not make the NPT discriminatory. In fact, it establishes a mutually beneficial balance of duties and benefits concerning disarmament and non-proliferation (Goosen, 1998; Sinclair, 1998). The heads of the US and UK delegations indicated that they did not consider the NPT unfair for two reasons. First, accession to it is entirely voluntary. Secondly, it does not license the NWS to have nuclear weapons permanently so their privileged status is only transitionary: Article VI entails a firm commitment to proceed towards the elimination of all nuclear weapons, although the NWS could not do so immediately (Weston, 1998; Earle, 1998). In sum, they portrayed the NPT as a pragmatic bargain needed to serve the moral cause of reducing the dangers of these weapons.

The NPT does express the obligations of the NWS in vaguer and briefer terms which leave room for different interpretations and complicate the task of assessing its fairness in many respects. However, the extension decision and the 'Principles and Objectives' document resulting from the 1995 Conference did specify for the first time that the goal is to eliminate all nuclear weapons. They clarified that the norm underlying the NPT is that ultimately no state has the right to possess nuclear weapons, and that the Treaty aims to remove them from the hands of every party.

Two other questions are of particular interest here: how can the NPT have attracted nearly universal adherence if its terms are discriminatory in the eyes of so many countries? What impact, if any, did this perception have during the 1995 NPT Conference? India invoked the inequality of the NPT, along with the failure of the NWS to honour their disarmament obligations, as the reason for remaining outside: the balanced bargain envisioned when a non-proliferation treaty was first proposed, that countries with nuclear weapons would eliminate them if others refrained from acquiring them, had simply not materialised (Ghose, 1998). However, the vast majority of countries have acceded to the NPT voluntarily whether or not they consider the terms fair. They have done so for reasons of security and pragmatism. The Treaty reflects the reality in 1968, that certain states already possessed and refused to relinquish nuclear weapons and there was a danger that other countries would follow suit. The best option was to accept the NPT as an instrument to prevent nuclear proliferation and promote disarmament. Many NNWS also expected to benefit from increased access to nuclear technology.

The 1995 Review and Extension Conference confirmed the widespread acceptance of the NPT, despite its inequality. There was no serious attempt to renegotiate the basic bargain on which it is founded. But the uneasy compromise between the haves and the have-nots under the Treaty, and the sense among resentful NNWS that its division of obligations is unbalanced, filtered into the Conference in another way: in the conflicts surrounding the question of how far the parties had *implemented and complied with their Treaty obligations*, and particularly with Article VI (Dhanapala, 1998). This was the issue which, more than any other, defined the 1995 Conference. It was at the very centre of the crucial bargaining and raised influential questions of justice and fairness.

We noted earlier that the duty of compliance acquires particular significance in arms control agreements, and that signatory states have always considered the NPT as a package of mutual obligations and mutual rights. Countries accepted the Treaty on the assumption that there would be full compliance with the bargain. It was with the expectation that the NWS would at least fulfil their promises regarding disarmament, the sharing of nuclear technology and so forth that the NNWS accepted the inequality of this deal. The view permeating the Conference was that the NWS had not even done this adequately, despite the favourable terms extended to them. Their poor compliance record added to already existing resentments and the sense of injustice regarding the unequal bargain. The brevity and ambiguity of Article VI inevitably gave rise to different interpretations, ranging from an obligation on the part of the NWS simply to negotiate disarmament in good faith to a duty to eliminate all nuclear weapons (Simpson, 1998). Nonetheless, they were generally seen as having pursued their own interests in non-proliferation while neglecting other issues of importance to the NNWS. The NPT had allowed the privileged few to be complacent, while imposing a number of restrictions on all other parties.

The perception that the implementation of the Treaty had been unbalanced in this sense fed directly into the 1995 Conference. It largely explains the impasse in Main Committee I over Article VI and the failure to agree on a Final Review Document. It also explains the refusal of NAM and other countries simply to agree to an indefinite extension of the NPT, and the need for a new bargain linking renewal to a better process for ensuring compliance based on specific criteria. According to the Conference President, 'the determination of the NNWS to pin down the NWS' on the disarmament issue secured the explicit reference for the first time to the elimination of all nuclear weapons as the ultimate goal (Dhanapala, 1998). The 'Principles and Objectives' statement went a considerable way to fulfil the steps towards nuclear disarmament which the NAM countries requested at the Bandung meeting in April 1995. The terms of the final Conference decisions suggest that one conception of justice was particularly influential: the notion that parties must honour their obligations under agreements which they have entered into freely, avoid profiting from the compliance by others without reciprocating, and thus ensure that all parties benefit from the agreed bargains as originally foreseen.

The entire negotiation over the NPT extension was driven by this notion, although the parties had different ideas of how to address it. The NAM countries were certainly concerned that a permanent treaty would undermine their leverage and their chance to be heard in future disarmament talks, which could be seen as a process fairness issue. In fact, the NAM saw a periodic and conditional extension as the principal means to keep the NWS accountable for fulfilling their obligations. An indefinite extension would not only relieve them of pressures to do so, but might also suggest a right of the NWS to keep nuclear weapons and perpetuate their monopoly in this area indefinitely (Dhanapala, 1998; El-Araby, 1998). The head of Indonesia's delegation summed up the predominant NAM view: 'an indefinite extension would mean the permanent legitimisation of nuclear weapons' permitting 'the five privileged powers . . . to keep their nuclear arsenals while others are barred forever from acquiring them. It will thus lead to a permanent division of the world into nuclear-haves and have-nots, ratify inequality in international relations and relegate the vast majority of non-nuclear nations into second class status.'[16]

A periodic extension, by contrast, would obligate the NWS to undertake specific measures towards the elimination of nuclear weapons. Their performance in this area would then be reviewed and affect decisions on the renewal of the NPT at regular intervals. Indonesia argued that this was a reasonable compromise between an indefinite or unconditional renewal and a single fixed-period extension, which would serve the interests of all parties. The other major position prevailed, that conditional renewal would call into question an entire treaty of paramount significance and that there were better ways to ensure compliance. But the adopted 'Principles and Objectives' document and the reinforced review process expressed the same concern about 'permanence with accountability', with an alternative channel for exercising leverage and securing compliance (Sinclair, 1998).

The insistence of President Dhanapala (and the NAM) on taking the extension *decision by consensus* enhanced the influence of the notion of duty of compliance. It also reinforced the need for a 'package agreement' seen as establishing a *fair balance* between the concerns, interests and obligations of the various parties. New measures reinforcing accountability, on the part of the NWS in particular, were simply necessary to get the overwhelming majority of parties to agree to make the Treaty permanent. The requirement of consensus, which gives every party veto power, has always been the preferred work method at NPT Review Conferences. It is an established rule of procedure in other arms control fora including the Conference on Disarmament. It can be seen as a pragmatic recognition of the fact that all states are equal in their status as sovereign entities, and that no country is likely to accept an arrangement which affects its security

---

[16] Statement by Ambassador Izhar Ibrahim, head of Indonesia's delegation to the 1995 NPT Review and Extension Conference, on 19 April 1995, quoted in *Nuclear Proliferation News*, No. 24, 17 May 1995.

interests adversely (Jurrjens and Sizoo, 1997). In the 1995 Conference, however, the President and most countries thought that a consensus decision was vital above all for the moral authority and moral credibility of the NPT. The future effectiveness of the Treaty was seen as depending directly on that kind of legitimacy. This overriding concern goes a long way to explain how the parties could avoid a vote on the extension decision and bypass the controversy over a secret versus an open ballot. Several high-level negotiators acknowledged in personal interviews that the NAM countries had been pushed to acquiesce to an indefinite extension, but disagreed over whether these pressures were unusual or unfair in any way. The NAM argument that voting should be secret so as to ensure freedom of expression without fear of repercussions failed to prevail. Had the parties put the extension to a vote, it would first have been necessary to vote on whether the procedure should be open or secret.

The debate over the implementation of the NPT to date extended, as we have seen, to nuclear export controls and nuclear cooperation. The Treaty, in light of the negotiations which led to its adoption in 1968, points clearly to a bargain: as a reward for renouncing nuclear weapons and as a precaution against any economic discriminatory effects, the NNWS would gain access to nuclear technology for peaceful uses with aid from the NWS. Indeed, the NPT is often described as a deal between the NWS and other countries interested in nuclear technology. Non-party states would supposedly be denied the benefits of cooperation and trade in this area, while parties to the bargain would be protected against negative economic or technological effects of accepting nuclear safeguards.[17] The widespread acknowledgment that the NWS had not honoured their part of this bargain adequately, and the concerns which NAM countries voiced on the matter at the 1995 Conference, were reflected in the outcome: the 'Principles and Objectives' statement established, for the first time, the principle of preferential treatment of non-nuclear parties to the NPT in activities to facilitate their right to develop nuclear energy. The document also emphasised non-discrimination and transparency.

In another area, the NNWS sought to *strengthen their bargain with the NWS concerning security guarantees*. We noted earlier that the NWS refused to include any such guarantees in the NPT itself and the

---

[17] See, for example, *Safeguards to Prevent Nuclear Proliferation*. Nuclear Issues Briefing Paper 5, March 1998 (Uranium Information Centre, Melbourne).

reasons for this. They did, however, provide alternative pledges and all parties to the 1995 Conference agreed that some kind of bargain on security assurances already existed. The head of the UK delegation to the 1995 NPT Conference confirmed that the NWS had undertaken to give both positive and negative assurances, and that the UK at least considered these 'politically binding' (Weston, 1998). The NAM countries argued that they did not simply have an interest in such assurances: the voluntary renunciation of nuclear weapons had endowed the NNWS with a legitimate *right* to compensation, in the form of guarantees that these same weapons would not be used against them. This right could be realised only through a legally binding document, making withdrawal difficult, and not through looser promises such as those expressed in UN Security Council Resolution 984 of 1995 (Goosen, 1998). A quest for justice in this sense thus motivated the NAM countries, while security and domestic political considerations explain the reluctance of the NWS to agree to anything of the kind. Some NNWS reportedly considered existing assurances unfair also because they had not been negotiated multilaterally with input from the states whose very security was at stake (Sinclair, 1998). No single view prevailed in the end. The outcome of the 1995 Conference recognised but never resolved the dispute over security assurances. The 'Principles and Objectives' document calls upon parties to consider further steps to protect NNWS parties to the NPT against nuclear threats, which 'could take the form of an internationally legally binding instrument' (Article 8).[18]

Arab states argued similarly when requesting *universal adherence* to the NPT. They held universality to be a matter of justice in the sense that complying states, in volatile regions such as the Middle East, could endanger their own security unless all countries were bound by the Treaty. Egypt argued that the NPT, without Israeli adherence, created a regional military imbalance and could not safeguard its national security. Moreover, it has been suggested that Egypt was led to believe that the Treaty would become universal and was thus 'duped' to sign it (El-Araby, 1998; Sinclair, 1998). The Arab countries undoubtedly saw the Conference as a good opportunity to rally international opposition against Israel's unsafeguarded nuclear facilities. Their preparedness to agree to a permanent NPT extension in

---

[18] 'Principles and Objectives for Nuclear Non-Proliferation and Disarmament' (see footnote 7 above).

exchange for the Middle East resolution underscores that their real interests focused on Israel. The head of the Egyptian delegation says that the resolution compromised his country's concerns about 'universality' by failing to refer to Israel by name. Egypt accepted it because there was no other option, other than withdrawing from the NPT altogether (El-Araby, 1998).

Universality became a major issue at the 1995 Conference, because some parties saw it as a matter of justice and virtually all saw it as central to the proper functioning of the Treaty. The principle was seen as persuasive on both these grounds. It influenced the four major decisions of the Conference, especially the 'Principles and Objectives' statement and the Middle East resolution. There are no signs to date, however, that the principal threshold states (Pakistan, India and Israel) have come any closer to signing the Treaty. Egypt's reservations about being a party to the NPT without the adherence of Israel, with whom it has a peace treaty, may be less compelling than those stated by Israel for not signing the Treaty. The latter country faces several hostile Arab countries which are thought to possess weapons of mass destruction. Israeli nuclear forces played a decisive role in deterring Iraq from using chemical weapons during the Gulf War (Kemp and Harkavy, 1997; Evron, 1994). Nonetheless, Arab state parties to the NPT including Syria, Libya, Iraq and Iran regard Israel, given its nuclear capabilities, as a 'free-rider' reaping the benefits of the regime without paying any costs.

What considerations drove the behaviour of the negotiators, including their decisions to act upon certain conceptions of justice and fairness and to ignore others? The principal factors were international and national security concerns, coalition building and fragmentation, the complex multilateral structure of the negotiations, and the exercise of leadership.

First, certain ethical conceptions had an impact because they served the overarching purpose of the Conference: to abate the threat and use of nuclear weapons and to make the NPT regime more effective. Those concerning mutual compliance with obligations, universality and agreement by consensus are obvious examples. The paramount importance of reaching an agreement on extending the NPT guided how different conceptions were eventually balanced, bridged and 'packaged'. It also ruled out using a fixed-term or otherwise overtly conditional renewal of the NPT, as a means to safeguard NAM leverage in future disarmament talks and to ensure better compliance by the NWS. Ideas of justice and fairness among individual state delegations often overlapped with their national security interests. Examples include the emphasis placed by NNWS on full compliance with obligations concerning nuclear disarmament, security assurances and the sharing of nuclear technology. The conditions attached by the NWS to these matters reflect in turn their concerns about national security and domestic politics. For instance, the US Congress would never have approved unconditional 'blanket' security assurances implying protection for states such as Libya, Iraq and North Korea, or intervention against other nuclear or threshold states (Simpson, 1998). India genuinely resents the NPT's inequalities, but avoids membership also because it believes that the nuclear option best protects the country against two nuclear enemies, China and Pakistan.[19] Negotiators participating in the 1995 Conference confirmed in personal interviews that when essential security interests and perceptions of fairness conflicted, they naturally felt required to prioritise the former.

Notions of national interests led to the emergence of new coalitions, and to the fragmentation and weakening of the NAM camp formerly driven by ideology. Virtually all NAM countries agreed that the implementation of the Treaty to date had been unbalanced. But divergent security interests drove them into different coalitions, and impeded an NAM consensus on an alternative to making the NPT permanent. Some NAM countries formed a coalition with traditional allies of the NWS among the Group of Eleven, which had come to believe that nuclear weapons threatened rather than safeguarded their security in the post-Cold War period.[20] They now called for the abolition of all these weapons. Other NAM countries recognised that a conditional or limited extension of the NPT would not serve their security interests, and thus moved into the camp favouring a permanent extension (Leigh-Phippard, 1997). This is an important background to the final outcome: an indefinite extension linked to the principles of compliance, universality and the elimination of nuclear weapons.

The 1995 NPT Conference was extremely complex in several regards. No less than 175 parties with many conflicting interests had

---

[19] In a speech to the Indian Parliament in 1968, Prime Minister Indira Ghandi held that the country's decision not to sign the NPT was based on 'enlightened self-interest and the consideration of national security' (Ghose, 1997, p. 242).

[20] The Group of Eleven refers to Australia, Austria, Canada, the Czech Republic, Denmark, Finland, Ireland, the Netherlands, New Zealand, Norway and Sweden.

to tackle multiple controversial issues for an overriding purpose which was dual and unprecedented. This complexity created a need for the exercise of leadership to manage the process and bring it to a successful conclusion. South Africa and Canada played lead roles in proposing solutions which bridged opposing positions, and identified elements of a final overall agreement. Dhanapala's leadership was most decisive. His insistence that the moral authority and legitimacy of the NPT required a consensus decision on its extension, the creation of the President's Consultations, and his work on designing a balanced package agreement, had a significant impact on the outcome emphasising permanence with accountability. The fact that the President's Consultations included relatively few countries, and at the same time high-level representatives of all major positions, was essential to their success. Some analysts argue, however, that the forum diverted senior negotiators away from the Main Committees and contributed to the failure of the review track. Too many junior negotiators with less authority and flexibility were supposedly left to try to tackle difficult stumbling blocks on their own, including those which plagued Main Committee I.

Conclusion

The 1995 NPT Review and Extension Conference raised justice and fairness issues relating to many components of the negotiations. The extent to which they were acted upon varied considerably. We noted that most parties do not consider the NPT's differentiation of rights and obligations based on different circumstances (some countries possessing nuclear weapons before 1967 and others not) to be fair. Yet they continued to accept this inequality as an inevitable reflection of historical conditions and pragmatic politics. The single most influential issue during the Conference was instead the extent to which parties had implemented and complied with the NPT. This question set much of the agenda for the Conference, influenced positions and proposals in the bargaining process, caused stalemates and deadlocks, and shaped the package agreement which was eventually adopted. The conception that parties must honour obligations which they have accepted freely, and that the NWS had not done so adequately, prevailed. Several contentious matters were settled by balancing rights and duties, and different interests such as non-proliferation and disarmament. High-level participants report that the final package was seen as fair in this sense, and was therefore accepted (Dhanapala, 1998; Earle, 1998; Weston, 1998).

The NPT has succeeded in halting the proliferation of nuclear weapons, and in attracting new members. It is remarkable that despite its unequal terms, the Treaty has acquired more signatory states than any other arms control agreement. Moreover, it is clear that its implementation has been uneven, and that the NNWS have not seen many benefits promised in exchange for their compliance materialise. For them the benefits are fundamental issues of national security and well-being rather than mere incentives or 'sweeteners'. There are at least two reasons to believe that continued inadequate compliance with the NPT may pose a growing threat to the effectiveness of the regime.

The first reason is that the experience of the 1995 Conference, and the decisions resulting from it, raised new expectations about improved compliance. A large number of NNWS decided to support an indefinite extension of the NPT in the belief that the 'Principles and Objectives' declaration and the strengthened review process would lead to a more evenhanded implementation of the Treaty, including Article VI. A member of the Canadian delegation said: 'The point of strengthening the Review process was to force a more demonstrated seriousness on the part of the NWS that they would take their commitments seriously' (Sinclair, 1998). It is true that the NPT itself was not amended and that the extension was not linked to the 'Principles and Objectives' document concerning disarmament in a legal or explicit way. But the bargaining and the compromises whereby it was finally agreed, and the new reference to the abolition of all nuclear weapons as the ultimate goal, placed at least a political conditionality on the extension decision. It is also true that the 'Principles and Objectives' do not specify a timeframe or specific measures for achieving this final goal, other than the conclusion of a CTBT by 1996 and a ban on the production of nuclear weapons fissile material. The exact meaning of the 'strengthened review' remained unclear and disputed in the aftermath of the 1995 conference. The widespread understanding was nonetheless that future reviews should be more substantial and focused on objectives such as full implementation (Sinclair, 1998).

The second reason is that while expectations about improved compliance increased, the differences over the way forward appear to have deepened. The three PrepComms held following the 1995 Con ference, for the purpose of preparing for the review of the NPT in 2000, were a testimony to this. They revealed the persistence of old disputes over nuclear disarmament, universality (particularly as applied to the Middle East and Israel), security assurances and other core issues, as well as profound differences over the status of the 1995 decisions and the purpose of the new review process. In the first PrepComm in April 1997, the Western NWS repeated that general and complete disarmament and regional stability must be a precondition for complete nuclear disarmament under Article VI. Stressing his country's commitment to this goal, the head of the UK delegation later specified that he understood 'general and complete disarmament' to include the elimination of all weapons of mass destruction, including chemical and biological weapons which are of major concern to the NWS. He added that the US and Russia must implement the Strategic Arms Reduction Treaties and reduce their nuclear arsenals, before the UK and other NWS could be expected to cut their smaller forces any further (Weston, 1998). The US and France argued that they had already made significant arms reductions, and would continue to do so as far as their concerns about maintaining stability and ensuring verification permitted. Canada was at the forefront in opposing the NWS' various conditions for nuclear disarmament. The NAM reiterated their call for specific time-based commitments leading to the elimination of all nuclear weapons.

The 1997 PrepComm had to drop a recommendation in its final report regarding issues to be discussed at the next PrepComm. The controversy was over giving nuclear disarmament any extra attention (Roche, 1997). Mexico insisted that nuclear disarmament be singled out, in order to ensure the achievement of 'balanced obligations'. Disagreement also emerged over whether the new review process should focus on the NPT or, as most NAM states argued and the NWS resisted, consider the 'Principles and Objectives' document and the Middle East Resolution equally important and binding. These same problems go a long way to explain the setbacks in the 1998 Prep-Comm, although it formally collapsed over pressure to implement the 1995 Middle East Resolution (Johnson, 1998). The parties were unable to agree on any substantial recommendations or procedural rules for the 2000 Review Conference, and did not adopt any final report. The Third PrepComm, held in May 1999, witnessed continued intense disagreements over nuclear disarmament, the elimination of nuclear weapons, and the Middle East. It succeeded in adopting a final report which contained essential procedures, but no recommendations on substantial issues, for the 2000 Review of the NPT.

Issues of justice and fairness will continue to shape the functioning of the NPT in the future. States signed the Treaty in the belief that it would reduce dangers to their security, and provide gains in exchange for required sacrifices, in a more effective or less costly way than other alternative options. In so doing they accepted a set of contractual obligations and mutual rights, which are different for different parties but constructed so as to provide a bargain which benefits everyone. This arrangement naturally provokes resentment and charges of injustice when some parties are seen as neglecting, or simply violating, their pledges while profiting from the compliance by others.

Because the NPT is a bargain, it is conditional. This was clearly shown at the 1995 Extension and Review Conference, when the pact between the NWS and the NNWS had to be substantiated in order to permit an extension of the Treaty. After the Conference, despite this reconfirmation of mutual undertakings, more NNWS appeared to believe that the NWS were using arguments about general disarmament as a tactic to seek to remain nuclear indefinitely. Having secured a permanent extension of the Treaty, they were suspected of not being genuinely prepared to relinquish their nuclear status and of attempting to limit the understanding of what they had promised in 1995 (Goosen, 1998). The US Senate's rejection of the CTBT in October 1999 obviously called into question the US' commitment to a full implementation of Article VI of the NPT on the disarmament obligations of NWS, particularly as specified in the 'Principles and Objectives' document. It also dealt a moral and political blow to the efforts to persuade other key states, whose ratifications are necessary for the CTBT to enter into force, to endorse it. By early 2000 progress towards the entry into force of this Treaty, so vital for nuclear arms control and non-proliferation, remained blocked by Russia, China and the US, which had failed to ratify it, and by India and Pakistan, which had only made conditional pledges to sign.

If the NWS are committed to every part of the NPT as they say, a statement detailing the exact conditions and the steps they envision for carrying out their obligations could enhance confidence and facilitate progress on nuclear disarmament. Indeed, if a timebound framework is unpractical, it is all the more important to discuss and agree on specific measures, bilateral and multilateral, to be taken in the entire process towards achieving this goal. They should engage all five NWS and clarify the relationship between disarmament in different areas (conventional weapons, nuclear weapons, and other weapons of mass destruction).

A continued slowness on the part of the NWS to implement their commitments would deprive the NPT of moral clout and credibility, and feed non-party states with convenient and persuasive arguments for refusing to join. The NWS say that they have been unable to reduce their nuclear arsenals more for reasons of security and deterrence, and that they must continue with sub-critical tests although these may contribute to the further development of nuclear weapons. The ways in which threshold states such as India and Israel claim a right to possess nuclear weapons and justify their nuclear policies are almost identical. Unlike the five NWS recognised in the NPT, they are not bound by this regime and have not formally pledged eventually to eliminate all their nuclear weapons. When key parties are seen as escaping their responsibilities, the non-proliferation regime cannot persuasively request states outside it to join, and its continued existence cannot even be taken for granted. Mexico, Egypt and South Africa are among the states which have stated that they would consider leaving the Treaty if the NWS do not implement Article VI fully.

The President of the 1995 Conference warned after its conclusion that a mass exodus from the NPT may result if the NWS do not disarm more swiftly. It is difficult to estimate the real likelihood or full repercussions of such ominous scenarios. Given the irreplaceable value of the NPT for international security, however, every possible measure should be taken to strengthen it. In this case, justice understood as mutual compliance with treaty obligations is indeed a cornerstone of effectiveness.

7 Conclusion

> Parties seek a fair deal because it is best for all. An agreement has to
> be fair and balanced for it to be successful.[1]

This study began by posing the question of whether justice and
fairness play a genuine role in international negotiations. We asked if
and when such concepts impact upon the bargaining process in any
way and how they are (to be) defined and operationalised. Furthermore, the book set out to examine empirically what factors motivate
negotiators to take justice and fairness into account, and what circumstances enable them to do so. What then can we conclude at this
stage? The purpose of this chapter is not to review the details of the
preceding case studies, but to address the major questions which
underlay all of them. What do the cases suggest collectively that was
disputed or not known before?

Justice and fairness matter, in many ways

First of all, the engine running international negotiations is not limited
to the pursuit of private interests and the maximisation of individual
gains in a narrow sense. Negotiators do regularly act upon ethical
considerations. Arguments about justice and fairness are taken
seriously and can be very influential. In the words of one senior
diplomat, '[j]ustice and fairness issues are always lurking behind or
on the stage when negotiating international agreements' (Björkbom,
1998a). Another seasoned negotiator explained why he regarded such
principles as inherent in any talks: 'any deal must be possible to

[1] Ambassador Ralph Earle, acting head of the US delegation to the 1995 NPT Extension
and Review Conference (personal interview, 1998).

implement and must therefore give each party its share . . . a deal should be negotiated to move the parties forward, to improve the situation, and this requires a sharing of benefits' (Tran, 1998). He pointed out that justice and fairness act as a positive force in this manner, although it may be absent in unequal power relationships which thus threaten the implementation of agreements.

There are numerous examples in the preceding chapters of how considerations of equity changed the course and the outcome of a particular negotiation. All the cases covered raised major controversial issues of justice and fairness, and had they been ignored it is unlikely that the talks could ever have been concluded successfully. The principle of 'no harm', and scientific evidence of some countries suffering unprovoked damage from foreign sources of air pollution, secured the onset of the acid rain talks within the UN-ECE in the mid-1970s. Concerns about justice and fairness were at the centre of the process which led to the Second Sulphur Protocol. Their persuasiveness led negotiators to compromise on the recommendations of the RAINS model by differentiating emission reduction requirements according to economic ability, and to call for equity in the distribution of the cost burden in future abatement plans. The widespread judgment during the 1995 NPT Review and Extension Conference that the NWS had neglected their disarmament obligations, while benefiting from the compliance of others with the Treaty, resulted in the explicit reference to the elimination of all nuclear weapons and in new measures emphasising balanced implementation. Israeli negotiators accepted compromises during the interim talks with the PLO which they described as painful, costly and unexpected, in order to address some Palestinian needs. Objections to distorted terms of trade in agricultural goods led to agreement in the Uruguay Round of the GATT on steps towards a fairer liberalised trading system with preferential treatment (less onerous and fewer requirements) for LDCs. At the same time the US emphasis on the importance of reciprocal benefits and the prevention of free-riding challenged well-established GATT norms and influenced the Final Act.

Concerns about justice or fairness were influential in these and other instances, yet virtually all the negotiators interviewed reported that they did not perceive or discuss the issues in those terms. They typically said that their minds and the talks had focused on specific practical matters, not on 'abstract concepts', 'philosophical questions' or 'such ideas' (Goosen, 1998; Ramaker, 1998; Singer, 1996; Y. Tsur,

1997). Some said that they had never heard about or 'never come across principles of justice and fairness in the negotiations' (Falkenberg, 1998). Many were uncomfortable employing these words to analyse their negotiating experience, and said that they did not like and would avoid using them (Akao, 1998; Ledogar, 1998). When questioned further, however, the interviewees did reckon that principles commonly associated with fairness or justice had been important; for example, notions of reciprocity, the differentiation of obligations according to economic ability, and the duty to implement freely negotiated agreements (e.g., Jaramillo, 1998). It is clear that although negotiators may not have framed or even thought consciously of the issues as matters of justice and fairness, such concepts were frequently reflected in their behaviour.

The issues in international talks are not limited to the principles to govern the allocation of benefits and burdens in an agreement (that is, to the outcome and distributive justice), as conventionally thought.[2] Collectively, the cases in this study underscore the importance of the range of justice and fairness issues which the analytical framework in chapter 2 identified. They emerge from the earliest preparatory phase when the agenda is set, to the final stage involving implementation and compliance. They are all significant in the notion of justice as the balanced settlement of conflicting claims, set forth in this study. Negotiators themselves clearly do not associate justice and fairness with outcomes only, although these are obviously important. Every kind of issue arose in the Uruguay Round of the GATT, starting with the matter of establishing an agenda which would balance the conflicting interests and concerns of parties. A US negotiator who participated in this process pointed out that the unprecedented broadness of the final agenda had 'a fairness element to it, in that it ensured that countries could do what they believed to be fair . . . that they had enough flexibility to put together a balanced package' (Yeutter, 1998). Questions about the justice of the bargaining process and the procedures and tactics used, and of the implementation of negotiated agreements, dominated the 1995 NPT Review and Extension Conference as well as the Israel–PLO interim talks: 'While there were problems with the Interim Agreement that made it unfair . . . [w]hat was unacceptable was the failure to implement the terms of the Interim Agreement' (Q'Awash, 1997). Only in the European acid

---

[2] See the literature review and discussion in chapters 1 and 2.

rain talks, whose structure, process and procedures are well established and accepted, did the focus remain on the terms of agreements.

The motivation to act upon grounds which others can accept as reasonable

What then motivates negotiators to act upon considerations of justice and fairness when they do? Virtually all practitioners interviewed denied that these had been the primary concerns prompting their entry into and conduct during negotiations. The principal question asked was not 'What would be a just and fair solution?' The overriding purpose was to reach cooperative agreements serving goals which could not be reached as well unilaterally. In the European acid rain talks, the parties worked to achieve the environmentally most effective emission cuts at the lowest cost possible. Within the GATT, member states sought to reap economic benefits and promote economic growth through the continued liberalisation of world trade. The Israel–PLO interim talks aimed to enhance the national security of one party in exchange for granting greater self-determination to the other. In the NPT Review and Extension Conference negotiators endeavoured to promote international security by strengthening the Treaty's objectives concerning disarmament, non-proliferation and universal adherence.

Justice and fairness are nevertheless an important aspect of reaching long-term, stable agreements in these and other areas. The design of workable arrangements can rarely rely on hard-nosed bargaining and the promise of mutual benefits alone. In order to win the respect and voluntary approval of the parties and their constituencies, the provisions must be seen as worth honouring partly by appealing to their sense of fairness. They must include principles for the allocation of rights, duties, benefits and costs among parties who are joined in a cooperative venture, and reflect their voices and concerns. Negotiators are thus motivated to formulate terms, and behave more generally, on grounds which others can freely accept as reasonable and authoritative rather than merely self-serving. This facilitates the achievement of broadly supported agreements. In every preceding case study, political compromise required taking concerns about justice or fairness into account in some way. The parties, when upholding conflicting principles, usually addressed these so as to arrive at an agreement which all could accept as balanced and appropriate under the circumstances. Thus, the notion of 'relative fairness' became influential in the Israel–PLO interim talks, which endorsed solutions acceptable and beneficial to both sides given the existing situation over options entailing net losses for any one party. The principle of burden-sharing resulted in differentiated obligations based on economic ability rather than in one-way resource transfers in the Second Sulphur Protocol, and the principle of complying with freely negotiated commitments led to a strengthened process for reviewing the NPT rather than in a conditional extension of it.

As discussed earlier, some philosophers and the vast majority of the negotiators interviewed associate the meaning of justice with acting upon grounds which others can freely accept as reasonable and balanced. Doing so is obviously pragmatic as well, in the sense that it promotes consensus and successful outcomes, which in turn serves the objectives and interests of negotiating parties. They use principles of justice and fairness as instruments to reach agreements and to regulate their interaction, in light of opposing claims and interests. Too arbitrary proposals and too selfish behaviour usually fail to win the confidence and cooperation of others. A senior diplomat emphasised that most countries also strive to implement agreements which they have negotiated and signed, a core principle of the notion of justice as a balanced settlement of conflicting claims. They do their utmost to avoid losing credibility from failing to deliver on their commitments, because '[i]t will cost them dearly. Everyone will know it, it will show. If then later something serious comes along, these countries' signatures just won't be worth anything . . . they won't be trusted' (Björkbom, 1997b).

This is not to suggest that ethical principles and behaviour have no inherent value or that they are simply used tactically for narrow self-interests. Arguments about justice and fairness would not carry any weight, and could therefore not be instrumental in promoting an agreement or otherwise make a difference, unless parties saw them as genuine and compelling. For example, the President of the 1995 NPT Review and Extension Conference worked hard to formulate a package agreement balancing different concerns and principles, and insisted on using the consensus rule to adopt the decision about extending the Treaty. This enhanced the moral authority of the Treaty and thus served the overarching goal of the Conference to strengthen the nuclear non-proliferation regime as far as possible. Unless seen as morally significant in its own right, the display of consensus could not have had this effect.

Operationalising the meaning of justice and fairness

The first two chapters referred to different approaches to justice and fairness found in the academic literature. Most of these concentrate on a particular aspect of negotiation, usually the outcome or the bargaining process. They tend to endorse a single criterion of assessment; for example, the extent to which concessions are reciprocated and whether agreements split the difference or distribute benefits proportionally to the parties' BATNAs. We also noted two broader competing theories defining justice as 'mutual advantage' and as 'impartiality', respectively. How then do negotiating parties themselves, as opposed to academics, define and operationalise justice and fairness? How do their notions compare in particular with that of justice as a balanced settlement of conflicting claims?

In the complex circumstances surrounding the cases in this volume, concepts of justice and fairness were both substantial and procedural. They included elements of both impartiality and mutual advantage, and conformed well with the discussed motivation to take such concepts into account in the negotiation process. They also lent support to the idea of justice as a balanced settlement of conflicting claims, although negotiators themselves tended to emphasise some considerations more such as the interests of parties, mutual gains and reciprocity. The substantial concepts were naturally more specific to each negotiation and issue area than the procedural ones, which played a role across the different cases.

In the European acid rain talks, the substantial content given to justice and fairness included 'no harm' to one's neighbours and 'polluter pays'. At the same time, contrary to the polluter pays principle, emission reduction obligations were differentiated based on economic ability. One negotiator recalled that there was 'hardly any debate about it, as the differentiation was indeed considered an issue of justice and fairness' (Keiser, 1997). Influential notions in the Uruguay Round of the GATT were non-discrimination understood as equal treatment (in terms of market access, competition and pricing), but also the differentiation of obligations according to individual trade, development and financial needs. The latter principle resulted in provisions for the LDCs which allowed them, as noted, to liberalise more slowly at a pace favouring their own industries and suitable to their stage of development. One meaning given to fairness in the Israel–PLO talks was equality in treatment, conditions and resources between the two sides. It impacted upon the negotiations over their new economic relations and the question of water access. Finally, the unacceptability of indiscriminate and massive harm, a danger posed by nuclear weapons, was a substantial norm underlying the NPT talks.

Procedural notions of justice and fairness were very influential in the four cases. They partly involved the parties' interests, joint gains and reciprocity, which are considerations also in the notion of justice as a balanced settlement of conflicting claims. Clearly, *taking account of the interests and concerns of parties* was seen as essential. Their own situations influenced what they genuinely held to be right and appropriate, particularly in the initial stages of bargaining. Requesting them to act against their own interests was regarded as not only unrealistic, but unfair. One delegate to the Uruguay Round talks on trade in services stated that 'putting the abstract notion of fairness against economic self-interest . . . [is] building a theoretical construct which was not there' (Zutshi, 1998). Another delegate in the same talks pointed out that justice and fairness influenced the outcome, in the sense that parties left the negotiations 'believing that they got an agreement that benefits their countries, rather than having been forced to accept a deal that was not beneficial' (Hellström, 1998). The Chair of the acid rain talks within the UN-ECE stressed that '[n]o party will agree to terms which do not serve its own interests. Justice and fairness figure into this, because it would be unfair to ask parties to agree to something which doesn't benefit or even harms their own interests' (Björkbom, 1997b). In a similar vein, in negotiating with the PLO Israel held that asking a country to compromise its national security interests, lower its living standard or accept other net losses in favour of another was excessive and unreasonable.

Fairness was not connected with the unconstrained pursuit of self-interest. It rather meant representing, protecting and promoting needs and interests of *all* parties concerned (Shohat, 1997; Earle, 1998; Tran, 1998). The process and the ultimate agreement should deliver *joint gains*. But each party should also receive its 'fair share' and a sound balance of benefits should be established between parties. Related to this was the strong emphasis placed on *reciprocity*: 'The purpose of

221

any negotiation is to produce an outcome that yields overall reciprocal benefits. Therefore parties seek a political and legal conclusion that establishes a balance of benefits to all countries, which means reciprocal benefits . . . All parties feel that they need a balance of concessions from the negotiations; that is, they require reciprocity from other parties' (Self, 1998). Negotiators associated a fair negotiation process with a good amount of give-and-take (Yeutter, 1998). Those interviewed generally said that they had looked for 'adequate' or 'sufficient' commitments from other parties and then responded with concessions of their own, so as to arrive at an agreement considered balanced overall (Hawes, 1998). Unlike many models and approaches reviewed in the first two chapters negotiators rarely insisted on precisely equal or comparable concessions, especially not when the parties' ability to reciprocate was very different. This corresponds well to the notion of 'diffuse reciprocity' and the overall concept of justice as a balanced settlement of conflicting claims.[3] In the Uruguay Round of the GATT, many parties were eventually expected to make the best possible concessions given their level of development (Falkenberg, 1998). The least-developed countries were exempted from having to reciprocate some trade liberalising measures in any way at all. Even the US sought reciprocity in the sense of 'concessions here and there, all of which added up to a balance of concessions' and not the same measures by all parties (Self, 2000a).

Three other procedural notions were prominent in the four areas of international negotiation: the exercise of free will and avoidance of coercion, the obligation to implement and comply with freely negotiated agreements, and the establishment of a balance between competing interests and principles. The use of force and coercion to make a party accept a particular concession or agreement was clearly seen as illegitimate. One interviewee gave the example of how parties to the Comprehensive Test Ban Treaty (CTBT) talks bypassed the Conference on Disarmament and its consensus rule by submitting the final draft treaty to the UN General Assembly for approval. Their purpose was to avoid India, an opponent to the draft, blocking its adoption: 'India was treated unfairly in the CTBT negotiations because a solution was forced on them that was not forced on anybody else. The rules of the game were changed. That was unfair'

---

[3] See the discussion on reciprocity in the section 'Procedural issues' in chapter 2, pp. 39–43 above.

(Sinclair, 1998). Conversely, the voluntary acceptance of an arrangement was taken to be a major element of justice and fairness. A senior arms control negotiator held, for example, that the NPT is not discriminatory because participation in it is 'entirely voluntary' (Weston, 1998). Many negotiators suggested that a party's acceptance of and signature on an agreement *per se* was an indication of free will and the absence of force. They did not mention poor alternatives or other subtler forms of pressure and constraints which might exist, and which are important in the notion of justice as a balanced settlement of conflicting claims and some other reviewed approaches. Other than in (pro-)Palestinian circles, they were rarely highlighted as relevant although they can clearly leave a party, a weak one in particular, with little or no choice but to agree.

The obligation to honour negotiated commitments emerged as an influential principle in three of the cases. Protests over the alleged failure of some parties to deliver fully on their obligations became particularly bitter in the NPT and the Israel–PLO talks. Moreover, in these talks, the same countries had secured favourable terms for themselves, at least in the eyes of other parties. In both the NPT Review and Extension Conference and the Uruguay Round, the erring parties were seen as free-riding on the adherence by others and as undermining their benefits to be had from the agreement. Objections to nuclear states' inadequate steps under the NPT meant that the renewal decision had to be linked to a strengthened review process, to ensure a more evenhanded implementation of the Treaty in the future. US resentment over insufficient trade liberalising measures on the part of some countries required the Uruguay Round to apply the MFN principle on a conditional basis for the first time ever.

Finally, there was a widespread emphasis placed on 'balance' which corresponds well with the overarching concept of justice set forth in the first two chapters. What was eventually balanced to different degrees was the parties' conflicting interests, claims and perceptions of fairness, and ultimately the benefits to them to be had from a particular cooperative venture. Across the cases 'balancing' took place in every stage of the process, starting with the agenda-setting for the GATT and the NPT talks. It became most noticeable and influential in the final stages of negotiation, however, when several principles representing different understandings of a reasonable solution were combined. Since the procedure led to package agreements which virtually all parties could accept, it could be mistaken for a purely calculating and pragmatic approach. It is clear, however, that the parties concerned regarded the act of balancing as fundamental to fairness. They saw it as an ethical, as much as a practical, way of proceeding in a situation of moral ambiguity. In every case the parties evoked competing principles and claims. Most of these would have established justice or fairness in some particular respect, but not in others. None emerged as superior on its own; that is, as capable of taking account of all the relevant factors in tackling the complex issues at hand. Thus, high-level participants in the four cases reported that they had accepted the final agreement as fair although they might not be satisfied with every aspect of it: its various principles and provisions established some overall balance between the obligations, rights and interests of the parties.

What factors influence the role of justice and fairness, and the choice of principle?

The introductory chapter noted approaches in the literature which hold that parties will accept moral constraints only when there is interdependence or a balance of forces between them. One theory specifies that parties are more likely to be motivated to act justly (i.e., on impartial grounds which cannot reasonably be rejected) when they require the voluntary approval and collaboration of others (Barry, 1989a, 1995). This was the situation in the cases covered here. However, they also point to other important circumstances. These affected not only the extent to which justice and fairness played a role *per se*. They also influenced the choice among and weight attached to particular principles in the bargaining process and in the ultimate agreements, and the way in which they were interpreted and applied. We shall recall eight factors.

The *need to gain the approval and cooperation of parties* and to reach an agreement helps to explain the influence of several principles, and the relative weight attached to each. It was a key consideration behind the emphasis on the duty of compliance and on universality in the 1995 NPT Conference. It largely explains Israel's recognition of Palestinian water rights: 'The Israeli government realised that if the Palestinians didn't have water, there would be no peace . . . therefore, concessions on water were made' (Rouyer, 1997). It was also a factor behind the decisions to differentiate emission reduction obligations according to economic ability in the second sulphur protocol talks, and to differentiate trade liberalising measures according to level of development in the Uruguay Round. A US trade negotiator explains: '[T]he services negotiations . . . allowed a country's level of development to be considered with regards to the commitments to be made. This was controversial in the US, but had the US not conceded on this, there would never have been an agreement' (Self, 1998). Conversely, some notions which appeared to have little support and to threaten an agreement were either reinterpreted and addressed in an alternative way, or ignored altogether. For example, financial and technology transfers to poorer polluting countries was the central fairness issue for many participants in the acid rain talks. Nevertheless, the chair steered them away from the matter, being convinced that formal discussion of it would lead to stalemate, and it was never completely resolved (Wuester, 1997d).

The meaning given to justice and fairness by negotiators points to other factors, such as the significance of *interests and mutual benefit*. Principles which failed to address the concerns of parties and to benefit them in a balanced way seldom became influential. They should not impose costs and burdens solely on one party, but act as a constraint which ensured that one party's pursuit of its interests would not damage those of another. We have seen many examples of how *internal politics* and interest groups can in turn influence a country's definition of its concerns and positions. In the case of the interim talks, addressing justice as defined by the Palestinians and much of the international community would have tilted the balance heavily against Israel. Therefore, Israeli negotiators emphasised the notion of protecting interests and improving conditions on both sides in a mutually gainful manner. We noted that Palestinian participants accepted the ultimate agreements, based on this approach, as reasonable under the circumstances and that their major charges of injustice related instead to the delays or failures to implement them fully.

A third factor which impacted upon the role of justice and fairness in the preceding cases was *the institutional and normative context*. The acid rain and the NPT talks took place in the shadow of principles and norms incorporated in earlier agreements. The common references to the existence of 'regimes' in these two areas indicate their strength. In all cases except Israel and the PLO, the setting allowed the chair of the talks, as a representative of the organisation hosting them, to *exercise leadership* and to steer the course of the process. In each case the chair engineered initiatives which influenced what principles were reflected in the final outcome. Furthermore, the fact that decision-making by consensus is an established rule in the GATT/WTO and the preferred method of work at NPT Review Conferences reinforced the need in the Uruguay Round and the 1995 NPT Conference to formulate terms which parties could accept as balanced and fair. The chief US negotiator on services in the former case pointed out: 'The GATT meets requirements of fairness quite well. It is practically impossible to do anything . . . without consensus, and that gives all countries – big and small – veto power . . . a fair degree of equality when it comes to things like decision-making' (Self, 1998). He also added that 'the ability to block consensus can make it very difficult for the WTO to carry on its business positively' (Self, 2000b).

The normative setting did indeed permeate the GATT talks in the most far-reaching way. One expert explains: 'The GATT is essentially a contract. What parties give up is the freedom to break the rules . . . and what they gain is the assurance that other parties will play by the rules. Therefore, fairness and justice are inherent in contractual relations' (Winham, 1998). As in previous rounds, the parties to the Uruguay Round were from the outset expected to adhere to and promote norms specified in the GATT treaties. The significant issues and disputes which arose stemmed from these norms including reciprocity and balanced concessions, non-discrimination in market access, preferential treatment of LDCs, and transparency. Moreover, the arguments about fairness which appeared credible and became influential were related to GATT norms, and could be supported and justified by them. The Israel–PLO talks were instead marked by the absence of clearly applicable and agreed norms; for example, concerning water rights and the equitable utilisation of water resources.

Another factor in the four cases was *the larger political environment.* Intergovernmental talks are never conducted in isolation but take place in a wider bilateral or international context, which affects what happens inside the negotiating room. In the acid rain and the arms control talks, the end of the Cold War altered dramatically their aims and prospects, and the political relations among parties. It bolstered the role which considerations of justice and fairness could play. By contrast, suicide bombings and a worsening security situation undermined Israel–PLO relations and led to experiences of injustice in terms of delays and failures to deliver on negotiated commitments. Apart from the official agenda, delegates also come with their own issues and goals, even in different areas and from other ongoing negotiations, which they seek to further. For example, in the second sulphur protocol talks, eagerness to gain entry into the EU was a likely reason behind Eastern and Central European countries being so forthcoming and refraining from insisting on formal cost-sharing.

The availability of *sufficient knowledge and expertise* had an obvious impact in the acid rain case. For the first decade of these talks, the uncertainties surrounding the science of air pollution led parties to undertake emission cuts which they did not consider fair. The development of better data in due course permitted the adoption of a more sophisticated approach, involving the use of critical loads, and also undermined the ability of countries to justify inaction on grounds of uncertainties about the benefits of environmental protection. One participant noted: 'with the use of critical loads, we have in effect introduced an element and a criterion of fairness due to cost–benefit considerations being included' (Kakebeeke, 1997). In the Uruguay Round of the GATT, the provision of new expertise reduced uncertainties and facilitated the application of norms of free and fair trade to the services sector.

Finally, *relative power and power relations* were influential. Israeli principles guided the interim talks far more than those of the Palestinians. The US concept of fair trade could not be ignored in the Uruguay Round and was reflected considerably in the Final Act. US arguments about the choice of a baseline year which would be fair to itself marked the conclusion of the talks on a nitrogen oxides protocol. However, the presence of power inequalities did not preclude a role for ethical considerations, as commonly thought. Nor did the supposedly powerful parties control the negotiation process, although they had more influence than others. On many occasions negotiators acted upon principles which benefited weaker parties such as LDCs, countries undergoing economic transformation, non-nuclear weapons states, and the Palestinians. A high-level negotiator in the Uruguay Round explained: 'The developed countries were wary of clauses for special treatment for LDCs, as . . . it allowed for free-riding. However, they also recognised that the concerns of the LDCs had to be accommodated if they were to participate in the talks' (Hawes, 1998).

The cases shed light on the question of whether justice and fairness act as an independent force. Such considerations do often constrain the behaviour of negotiators, including what they can ask for and pursue with credibility and effectiveness. Proposals which appear too self-serving and cannot be supported by some widely accepted principle rarely go far. Thus, Japan's arguments about food security in the Uruguay Round were seen largely as a tactical effort to protect the country's rice monopoly. Despite its economic power, these claims were not taken so seriously and were not nearly as successful as those of food-importing LDCs. However, there is little evidence to suggest that parties voluntarily sacrifice vital interests in the name of justice or fairness. A chief delegate to the 1995 NPT conference stated: 'National security concerns are always the prime motivations for negotiators . . . they would not support anything that threatened the national security of their country, even to be fair to another party' (Earle, 1998). They rather regard the protection of such interests as fundamental to fairness. Vital interests and concerns influence what a party will regard as the most applicable principles in a particular situation, and how it will interpret and seek to implement those principles.

We have noted that in the initial stages, negotiators tended to emphasise narrower concerns of their own countries. As the process continued, their interests and notions of fairness were usually modified and expanded to mean addressing and balancing the concerns of all parties. When vital interests and notions of fairness did conflict, however, parties would compromise on the latter with reluctance. Despite the conviction of many non-nuclear states that the NPT is discriminatory, they have remained parties to it. On another front, the head of the Pakistani delegation to the CTBT talks described the process as follows: 'The argument about non-proliferation and disarmament ran through the negotiation until the end. The bargain became worse and worse for developing countries . . . the treaty became more and more unequal [between the five Western NWS and the LDCs] and more unattractive from an equity point of view, but Pakistan was stuck because it was either this treaty or no treaty. The primary Pakistani objective was to stop India, and Pakistan decided to support the Treaty at least to stop India' (Akram, 1998). However, Pakistan had still not signed the CTBT by early 2000, arguing that it could not reasonably do so until India also signed the Treaty.

Looking ahead

The preceding chapters have demonstrated that ideas about justice and fairness can have almost any conceivable impact. They may serve as external referents guiding the bargaining dynamics, or become subject to negotiation themselves. They influence the positions and proposals brought to the table, the exchange and evaluation of concessions, and the formulation of agreements. They may trigger the onset of dialogue and facilitate its progress, or cause deadlocks and stalemates which bring the entire process to the brink of collapse. They may constrain the freedom of action of parties, or be used and abused tactically in the pursuit of individual advantage. They may prompt parties to sign and comply with an agreement, or provoke condemnations which threaten its very existence and effectiveness.

Negotiators are ultimately motivated, however, to act upon grounds which others can accept as justified so as to reach and maintain cooperative agreements. Their frequent endorsement of impartial notions, such as justice as a balanced settlement of conflicting claims, means that a widely respected agreement can be reached. It entails that the voices and interests of weaker parties are taken more into account than if such values had not operated. It is perhaps on these two counts that justice and fairness make the greatest difference in international negotiations.

This study has examined how negotiators actually define the concepts, and how they handle conflicting notions of what is right or appropriate. It has drawn extensively on the first-hand experiences and knowledge of senior participants, and covered and compared four cases. These represent major areas of international affairs but differ enormously when it comes to the nature of the issues, the number of parties involved and their power relations, the institutional setting, the normative and political context, and so on. This approach has yielded a number of insights, notably that concepts of justice and fairness assume nuanced and multifaceted meanings in the details of real complex talks which cannot be reduced to a single standard or principle. The head of the US delegation to the CTBT negotiations put it as follows: 'There are so many criteria for what is fair, that the outcome is always a muddle' (Ledogar, 1998). It has also shown that a number of factors affect how far such values determine the bargaining process and the outcome, and how they are interpreted and applied.

However, the study has not generated empirical evidence to ascertain the extent to which its conclusions hold true beyond the cases and areas here covered. This brings us to the subject of what directions future work could usefully take. Detailed analysis of cases in other areas would be very valuable, for the special characteristics of each clearly influence the place of justice and fairness. Additional empirical data could shed light on the relative importance of each factor here identified as affecting the role and meaning which these values assume. It could also reveal new significant aspects. For example, all the cases in this volume were part of long-term processes of negotiation in which the parties had become interdependent and expected future cooperation. To what extent does this make a difference? Do justice and fairness play a lesser role in one-time, *ad hoc* encounters between parties which do not plan to meet again? Do they play a greater role in large-scale multilateral negotiations given the need to win the approval of more parties? Does the nature of the issues matter, for example whether they involve shared global resources or solely the private (national) assets of the parties? Moreover, different cultures emphasise different ethical principles within their societies. How, if at all, is this reflected in an international negotiating context?

A question for policy is how negotiators themselves can enhance the perceived justice of their activities. We have noted many possibilities in the preceding pages: the construction of a broad agenda which widens the scope for balanced agreements, the inclusion of all voices and concerns in the bargaining process, the use of the consensus rule and avoidance of coercive tactics, the exercise of enlightened and effective leadership, the formulation of agreements based on several principles and linkages between issues, measures to ensure and demonstrate compliance with negotiated commitments, and so on. But it should be possible to say more about this.

For the negotiation field, one fundamental matter takes priority: to reveal fully the ways in which just and fair negotiations are indeed 'better'. Although policy-makers, like philosophers, dispute what justice is and requires, it is commonly thought that such negotiations produce more effective solutions to conflicts. In fact, there is still little systematic evidence to dissect what exactly we mean by this or in what sense it is actually true. The cases in this volume were old enough to demonstrate that justice and fairness mattered both before, during and after the formal talks and the signing of an agreement. Perceptions about the unfairness of earlier agreements resulted, among other things, in demands for the use of new criteria (the acid rain talks), improved compliance (the NPT talks) and better consideration of the interests of weaker parties (the GATT talks). They are too recent, however, to contribute evidence on the question of how the handling of justice and fairness issues in the bargaining process affects the outcome and its durability in the long term. Can attention to these values compromise rather than promote timely and efficient solutions to problems under negotiation? Will a party's judgment of the process and the outcome matter years and even decades down the road, and influence its decisions concerning compliance? Such issues have clear implications for policy, and for the sorts of contributions that research can make in support of practitioners. They will be central in the cases here discussed, and time will show how they will play out.

Bibliography

Primary documents

'Arrangement Regarding International Trade in Textiles' (Multifiber Arrangement). GATT Doc. No. TEX.NG/1. Entered into force in January 1974

'1979 Convention on Long-Range Transboundary Air Pollution and its Protocols'. Economic Commission for Europe, United Nations, Geneva, October 1996 (ECE/EB.AIR/50)

'Convention on the Prohibition of the Development, Production and Stockpiling of Bacteriological (Biological) and Toxin Weapons and on Their Destruction (Biological Weapons Convention)'. Published in J. Goldblat, *Arms Control. A Guide to Negotiations and Agreements*. Oslo and London: International Peace Research Institute and Sage Publications, 1996

'Convention on the Prohibition of the Development, Production, Stockpiling and Use of Chemical Weapons and on Their Destruction (Chemical Weapons Convention)'. Published in J. Goldblat, *Arms Control. A Guide to Negotiations and Agreements*. Oslo and London: International Peace Research Institute and Sage Publications, 1996

'Council Directive on the Limitation of Certain Pollutants into the Air from Large Combustion Plants'. *Official Journal of the European Communities*, L336. Brussels: Commission of the European Communities, 7 December 1988 (88/609/EEC)

'The Critical Load Concept and the Role of Best Available Technology and Other Approaches'. Report of the Working Group on Abatement Strategies, September 1991. Geneva: Economic Commission for Europe, United Nations (EB.AIR/WG.5/R.24/Rev.l)

'The Critical Loads and Levels Approach and Its Application in Preparation of the New Sulfur Protocol'. Report by the Bureau of the Working Group on Effects for a special session in Oslo, 13–14 June 1994. Geneva: Executive Body for the Convention on Long-Range Transboundary Air Pollution, Economic Commission for Europe, United Nations, 3 May 1994 (EB.AIR/R.85)

232

'Declaration of Principles on Interim Self-Government Arrangements'. Jerusalem: Israeli Ministry of Foreign Affairs, September 1993

'Draft Final Act Embodying the Results of the Uruguay Round of Multilateral Trade Negotiations'. GATT Doc. No. MTN.TNC/W/FA (20 December 1991)

'Economic Principles for Allocating the Costs of Reducing Sulphur Emissions in Europe'. Report submitted by the delegation of The Netherlands for the 5th session of the Group of Economic Experts on Air Pollution. Geneva: Executive Body for the Convention on Long-Range Transboundary Air Pollution. Economic Commission for Europe, United Nations, 26–28 June 1989 (EB.AIR/GE.2/R.26, 19 May 1989)

'Extension of the Treaty on the Non-Proliferation of Nuclear Weapons'. Decision adopted at the 1995 NPT Review and Extension Conference, New York, 17 April–12 May 1995 (NPT/CONF.1995/32/DEC.3)

'The Final Act Embodying the Results of the Uruguay Round of Multilateral Trade Negotiations'. Signed by ministers in Marrakesh on 15 April 1994. Geneva: GATT, 1995 (GATT 94/4)

'General Agreement on Tariffs and Trade'. Opened for signature on 30 October 1947

'General Agreement on Trade in Services'. In 'The Final Act Embodying the Results of the Uruguay Round of Multilateral Trade Negotiations'. Signed by ministers in Marrakesh on 15 April 1994. Geneva: GATT, 1995 (GATT 94/4)

'International Strategies to Combat Air Pollution Reviewed by the Executive Body at its Third Session, Helsinki, 8–12 July'. Press Release, 12 July 1985. Geneva: Economic Commission for Europe, United Nations (ECE/ENV/7)

'Israeli–Palestinian Interim Agreement on the West Bank and the Gaza Strip – September 28, 1995'. Jerusalem: Information Division, Israeli Ministry of Foreign Affairs, November 1995

'Joint Implementation under the Oslo Protocol'. Report by the Chairman of the Open-Ended Group of Experts. Working Group on Strategies (16th session, 19–23 February 1996). Geneva: Economic Commission for Europe, United Nations, 23 November 1995 (EB.AIR/WG.5/R.57)

'Legality of the Threat or Use of Nuclear Weapons'. Advisory Opinion, International Court of Justice, General List No. 95, 8 July 1996

'Mid-Term Meeting'. Report on the results adopted by the Trade Negotiations Committee at its mid-term review held in Montreal on 5–9 December 1988 and in Geneva on 5–8 April 1989. GATT Doc. No. MTN.TNC/11 (21 April 1989)

'Ministerial Declaration on the Uruguay Round'. GATT Doc. No. MIN. DEC (20 September 1986)

'Opening of Negotiations on the Framework Agreement on Permanent Status, November 8, 1999'. Document available *via* the website of the Embassy of Israel, London, at http://www.israel-embassy.org.uk/web/pages/peace.htm

'Positions and Strategies of the Different Contracting Parties to the Convention on Long-Range Transboundary Air Pollution Concerning the Reduction of Sulphur Emissions or their Transboundary Fluxes'. Geneva: Economic Commission for Europe, United Nations, 6 August 1985 (ECE/EB. AIR/7)

'Principles and Objectives for Nuclear Non-Proliferation and Disarmament'. Decision adopted at the 1995 NPT Review and Extension Conference, New York, 17 April–12 May 1995 (NPT/CONF.1995/32/DEC.2)

'Progress Report by the Chairman of the Task Force (Professor David Pearce) on Economic Aspects of Abatement Strategies' of 9 January 1997 to the Working Group on Strategies, section IV on 'burden sharing'. Geneva: Economic Commission for Europe, United Nations (EB.AIR/WG.5/R.70)

'Protocol Concerning Safe Passage between the West Bank and the Gaza Strip', signed by Israel and the PLO on 5 October 1999 in Jerusalem. Document available *via* the website of the Embassy of Israel, London, at http://www.israel-embassy.org.uk/web/pages/peace.htm

'Protocol on Economic Relations between the Government of the State of Israel and the PLO, representing the Palestinian people', 29 April 1994. Jerusalem: Israel Information Service Gopher, Information Division, Israel Foreign Ministry

'Protocol to the 1979 Convention on Long-Range Transboundary Air Pollution Concerning the Control of Emissions of Nitrogen Oxides or their Transboundary Fluxes'. First revised edition. New York and Geneva: United Nations, May 1995 (ECE/EB.AIR/21/Rev.1)

'Protocol to the 1979 Convention on Long-Range Transboundary Air Pollution on Further Reduction of Sulphur Emissions and Decision on the Structure and Functions of the Implementation Committee, as well as Procedures for its Review of Compliance'. Geneva: Economic Commission for Europe, United Nations, 1994 (ECE/EB.AIR/40)

'Recommendations of the Council on Guiding Principles Concerning International Economic Aspects of Environmental Policies'. Document C(72) 128, 6 June 1972. Paris: Organization for Economic Cooperation and Development

Records of UN-ECE Senior Advisers on Environmental and Water Problems, Working Party on Air Pollution Problems, 19th and 20th Sessions, 10 April 1990–22 May 1991. Geneva: Economic Commission for Europe, United Nations (ENVWA/WP.1/R.23&24 and Add.1; 25–32)

'Resolution on the Middle East'. Adopted at the 1995 NPT Review and Extension Conference, New York, 17 April–12 May 1995 (NPT/CONF.1995/32/RES/1)

'The Sharm el-Sheikh Memorandum on Implementation Timeline of Outstanding Commitments of Agreements Signed and the Resumption of Permanent Status Negotiations', signed by Israel and the PLO on 4 September 1999 in Sharm el-Sheikh, Egypt. Document available *via* the website of the Embassy of Israel, London, at http://www.israel-embassy.org.uk/web/pages/peace.htm

'The State of Transboundary Air Pollution'. Report prepared within the framework of the Convention on Long-Range Transboundary Air Pollution. Air Pollution Studies, No. 12. Geneva: Economic Commission for Europe, United Nations, 1996 (ECE/EB.AIR/47)

'Strategies and Policies for Air Pollution Abatement'. 1994 major review prepared under the Convention on Long-Range Transboundary Air Pollution. Geneva: Economic Commission for Europe, United Nations, July 1995 (ECE/EB.AIR/44)

'Strengthening the Review Process for the Treaty'. Decision adopted at the 1995 NPT Review and Extension Conference, New York, 17 April–12 May 1995 (NPT/CONF.1995/32/DEC.1)

'Tackling Air Pollution from Lawnmowers to Jumbo Jets'. UN-ECE Press Release, 28 November 1996, by Lars Nordberg, Deputy Director, Environment and Human Settlements Division. Geneva: Economic Commission for Europe, United Nations

'Treaty on the Non-Proliferation of Nuclear Weapons'. Washington, DC: US Arms Control and Disarmament Agency (obtained from http://www.acda.gov/treaties/npt1.htm (undated))

'The Wye River Memorandum', signed by Yassir Arafat and Benjamin Netanyahu on 23 October 1998 in Washington, DC. Document available *via* the website of the Embassy of Israel, London, at http://www.israel-embassy.org.uk/web/pages/peace.htm

Books, articles and interviews (references in the text)

References to individuals interviewed indicate primarily the positions and affiliations they had at the time of giving the interview or making a statement used in this study.

Adams, J. S. (1965) 'Inequity in Social Exchange'. In L. Berkowitz, ed., *Advances in Experimental Social Psychology*, Vol. II. New York: Academic Press

Ahnlid, A. (1996) 'Comparing GATT and GATS: Regime Creation under and after Hegemony'. *Review of International Political Economy*, Vol. 3, No. 1, Spring

Akao, Nobutoshi (1998) Permanent Representative of Japan to international organisations and to the GATT, Geneva, and chief negotiator for Japan in the Uruguay Round of the GATT (in 1993 and 1994), personal interview on 6 May 1998

Akram, Munir (1998) Ambassador, Head of the Pakistani delegation to the negotiations (from 1994 to 1996) within the Conference on Disarmament leading to the Comprehensive Test Ban Treaty (CTBT), personal interview on 26 June 1998

Albin, C. (1991). 'Negotiating Indivisible Goods: The Case of Jerusalem'. *Jerusalem Journal of International Relations*, Vol. 13, No. 1, March, pp. 45–76

Albin, C. (1992) 'Fairness Issues in Negotiation'. Working Paper WP-92–88, December. Laxenburg, Austria: International Institute for Applied Systems Analysis

Albin, C. (1995) 'The Global Security Challenge to Negotiation: Towards the

New Agenda'. In C. Albin, ed., *Negotiation and Global Security: New Approaches to Contemporary Issues*. Special issue of *American Behavioral Scientist*, Vol. 38, No. 6, May

Albin, C. (1997a) 'Is There a Place for Justice and Fairness in International Negotiations? Theoretical and Empirical Observations'. In H. Kimura, ed., *International Comparative Studies of Negotiating Behaviour*. Kyoto, Japan: International Research Centre for Japanese Studies

Albin, C. (1997b) 'Securing the Peace of Jerusalem: On the Politics of Unifying and Dividing'. *Review of International Studies*, Vol. 23, No. 2, April, pp. 117–42

Albin, C. (1997c) 'Negotiating Intractable Conflicts'. *Cooperation and Conflict*, Vol. 32, No. 1, March, pp. 29–77

Albin, C., ed. (1999) 'Negotiating Effectively: The Role of Non-Governmental Organisations'. Special issue of *International Negotiation*, Vol. 4, No. 3

Al-Sharif, Nabil (1997) Palestinian National Authority's Water Commissioner, Chairman of the Palestinian Water Authority, and a core member of the Palestinian delegation to the multilateral talks and the bilateral interim talks on water, communication in writing on 7 September 1997

Amann, M. *et al.* (1992) 'Strategies for Reducing Sulfur Dioxide Emissions in Europe'. Background paper prepared for the UN-ECE Task Force on Integrated Assessment Modelling, 3–5 June 1992, Bilthoven, The Netherlands. Laxenburg, Austria: International Institute for Applied Systems Analysis, 27 July

Ashrawi, H. (1995) *This Side of Peace. A Personal Account*. New York: Simon and Schuster

Axelrod, R. (1984) *The Evolution of Cooperation*. New York: Basic Books

Bailey, P., Gough, C. and Millock, K. (1996) 'Prospects for the Joint Implementation of Sulphur Emission Reductions in Europe'. *Energy Policy*, Vol. 24, No. 6, pp. 507–16

Baram, Yam (1997) journalist for *Middle East International*, personal interview on 7 August 1997

Barry, B. (1965) *Political Argument*. London: Routledge & Kegan Paul

Barry, B. (1989a) *Theories of Justice*. Berkeley, CA: University of California Press

Barry, B. (1989b) 'Can States be Moral?'. In B. Barry, *Democracy, Power and Justice. Essays in Political Theory*. Oxford: Clarendon Press

Barry, B. (1995) *Justice as Impartiality*. Oxford: Clarendon Press

Bartos, O. (1974) *Process and Outcome of Negotiations*. New York: Columbia University Press

Baskin, G. (1993) 'The West Bank and Israel's Water Crisis'. In G. Baskin, ed., *Water: Conflict or Cooperation*. Israel/Palestine: Issues in Conflict, Issues for Cooperation. Vol. II, No. 2, March. Jerusalem: Israel/Palestine Centre for Research and Information

Beitz, C. (1979) *Political Theory and International Relations*. Princeton, NJ: Princeton University Press

Ben Meir, Meir (1997) Israel's Water Commissioner (since January 1997), involved in the negotiations over the interpretation and implementation of the interim agreements on water, personal interview on 27 August 1997

Benton, A. and Druckman, D. (1973) 'Salient Solutions and the Bargaining Behaviour of Representatives and Nonrepresentatives'. *International Journal of Group Tensions*, Vol. 3, pp. 28–39

Bergman, L., Cesar, H. and Klaassen, G. (1992). 'Efficiency in Transboundary Pollution Abatement: A Scheme for Sharing the Costs of Reducing Sulphur Emissions in Europe'. In J. J. Krabbe and W. J. M. Heyman, eds, *National Income and Nature: Externalities, Growth and Steady State*. Dordrecht, Boston and London: Kluwer Academic Publishers

Bernauer, T. (1993) *The Chemistry of Regime Formation: Explaining International Cooperation for a Comprehensive Ban on Chemical Weapons*. Aldershot: Dartmouth

Björkbom, Lars (1997a) Chair of the Working Group on Strategies (the Negotiating Committee) under the 1979 Convention on Long-Range Transboundary Air Pollution (LRTAP) of the UN Economic Commission for Europe (UN-ECE), previously Head of the Swedish delegation to the negotiations under this Convention, and participant in the negotiations of all the protocols under the Convention, personal interview on 10 July 1997

Björkbom, Lars (1997b) personal interview on 15 July 1997

Björkbom, Lars (1997c) 'Protection of natural ecosystems from transboundary air pollution in Europe'. Paper for SCOPE UK meeting on effective use of the sciences in sustainable land management at the Royal Society, 21 February 1997

Björkbom, Lars (1997d) communication in writing on 10 November 1997

Björkbom, Lars (1997e) communication in writing on 28 November 1997

Björkbom, Lars (1998a) communication in writing on 8 January 1998

Björkbom, Lars (1998b) communication in writing on 4 February 1998

Björkbom, Lars (1998c) communication in writing on 6 April 1998

Björkbom, Lars (2000) communication in writing on 24 February 2000

Boehmer-Christiansen, S. and Skea, J. (1991) *Acid Politics: Environmental and Energy Policies in Britain and Germany*. London: Belhaven Press

Boutwell, J. and Mendelsohn, E. (1995) *Israeli–Palestinian Security: Issues in the Permanent Status Negotiations*. Cambridge, MA: American Academy of Arts and Sciences

Braithwaite, R. B. (1955) *Theory of Games as a Tool for the Moral Philosopher*. Cambridge: Cambridge University Press

Brams, S. (1990) *Negotiation Games. Applying Game Theory to Bargaining and Arbitration*. New York: Routledge, Chapman and Hall

Breen, J. (1993) 'Agriculture'. In T. Stewart, ed., *The GATT Uruguay Round. A Negotiating History (1986–1992)*. Vol. I: *Commentary*. Deventer, The Netherlands: Kluwer Law and Taxation Publishers

Brodet, David (1997) Israel's former Budget Director, Director-General of Israel's Ministry of Finance (since January 1995), and member of the

Israeli delegation to the interim talks on economics with a leading role in negotiating the details of the 1994 Paris Protocol under the general direction of A. Shohat (see below), personal interview on 30 October 1997

Brown, C. (1997) *Understanding International Relations*. London: Macmillan Press

Chossudovsky, E. (1988) *'East–West' Diplomacy for Environment in the United Nations: The High-Level Meeting within the Framework of the ECE on the Protection of the Environment, A Case Study*. New York: United Nations Institute for Training and Research

Churchill, Robin (1997) Reader in Law at Cardiff Law School, University of Wales, and co-leader of research project on 'Effectiveness of Legal Agreements to Protect Global Commons', personal interview on 21 July 1997

Churchill, R. R., Kütting, G. and Warren, L. M. (1995) 'The 1994 UN ECE Sulphur Protocol'. *Journal of Environmental Law*, Vol. 7, No. 2, pp. 169–97

Clapp, J. (1994) 'Dumping on the Poor'. Occasional Paper No. 5, Global Security Programme. Cambridge: University of Cambridge

Collins, L. (1995) 'Water Rights Negotiations Move Along a Very Slippery Road'. *Jerusalem Post*, 29 July

Cooley, J. (1994) 'Agreement on Water'. *Middle East International*, 29 April

Cross, J. (1978) 'Negotiation as a Learning Process'. In I. W. Zartman, ed., *The Negotiation Process. Theories and Applications*. Beverly Hills, CA and London: Sage Publications

de Zeeuw, Aart (1998) (The Netherlands), Chair of the Negotiating Group on Agriculture within the Uruguay Round (from 1986 to 1990), personal interview on 18 February 1998

Deutsch, M. (1973) *The Resolution of Conflict: Constructive and Destructive Processes*. New Haven, CT: Yale University Press

Deutsch, M. (1975) 'Equity, Equality, and Need: What Determines Which Value Will Be Used as the Basis of Distributive Justice?' *Journal of Social Issues*, Vol. 31, No. 3, pp. 137–50

Dhanapala, J. (1995) 'The 1995 Review and Extension Conference of the Nuclear Non-Proliferation Treaty. The Outcome of the Conference'. *Disarmament*, Vol. 18, No. 3, pp. 1–14

Dhanapala, Jayantha (1998) President of the 1995 Nuclear Non-Proliferation Treaty (NPT) Review and Extension Conference and UN Under-Secretary-General for Disarmament Affairs, New York, formerly Ambassador of Sri Lanka to the US, personal interview on 29 June 1998

Doherty, A. (1994) 'The role of NGOs in UNCED'. In B. Spector, G. Sjöstedt and I. W. Zartman, eds, *Negotiating International Regimes: Lessons Learned from the United Nations Conference on Environment and Development*. London: Graham & Trotman

Drake, W. and Nicolaidis, K. (1992) 'Ideas, Interests, and Institutionalisation: "Trade in Services" and the Uruguay Round'. *International Organization*, Vol. 46, No. 1, Winter

Druckman, D. (1990) 'The Social Psychology of Arms Control and Reciprocation'. *Political Psychology*, Vol. 11, No. 3

Druckman, D. and Bonoma, T. V. (1976) 'Determinants of Bargaining Behaviour in a Bilateral Monopoly Situation II: Opponent's Concession Rate and Similarity'. *Behavioral Science*, Vol. 21, pp. 252–62

Druckman, D. and Harris, R. (1990) 'Alternative Models of Responsiveness in International Negotiation'. *Journal of Conflict Resolution*, Vol. 34, No. 2, June

Earle, Ralph (1998) Ambassador, Acting Head of the US delegation to the 1995 NPT Review and Extension Conference (with US Vice-President Al Gore as the nominal Head and US Secretary of State Madeleine Albright as the official Vice-Head), personal interview on 30 June 1998

Earley, P. C. and Lind, E. A. (1987) 'Procedural Justice and Participation in Task Selection: The Role of Control in Mediating Justice Judgments'. *Journal of Personality and Social Psychology*, Vol. 52, pp. 1148–60

Eckhoff, T. (1974) *Justice: Its Determinants in Social Interaction*. Rotterdam, The Netherlands: Rotterdam University Press

El-Araby, Nabil (1998) Ambassador, Egypt's Permanent Representative to the United Nations, Deputy Head and later Head of Egypt's delegation to the 1995 NPT Review and Extension Conference, personal interview on 14 July 1998

Elmusa, Sharif (1996a) Member of the Palestinian delegation to the Washington Peace Talks on the Middle East (from 1991 to 1993), principal advisor to the Palestinian delegation in the secret Israel–PLO talks in Oslo and in the interim talks on water, personal interview on 9 February 1996

Elmusa, S. (1996b) *Negotiating Water: Israel and the Palestinians*. Final Status Issues Study. Washington, DC: Institute for Palestine Studies

Elmusa, S. and El-Jafaari, M. (1995) 'Power and Trade: The Israeli–Palestinian Economic Protocol'. *Journal of Palestine Studies*, Vol. 24, No. 2, Winter, pp. 14–32

Elster, J. (1989) *Solomonic Judgements. Studies in the Limitations of Rationality*. Cambridge: Cambridge University Press

Epstein, P. (1997) 'Beyond Policy Community: French Agriculture and the GATT'. *Journal of European Public Policy*, Vol. 4, No. 3, pp. 355–72

Evron, Y. (1994) *Israel's Nuclear Dilemma*. London: Routledge

Falkenberg, Karl (1998) First Secretary of the EC delegation to the Uruguay Round of the GATT and then Head of the EC unit in charge of the negotiations on trade in services, personal interview on 27 April 1998

Farer, T. (1995) 'New Players in the Old Game: The De Facto Expansion of Standing to Participate in Global Security Negotiations'. In C. Albin, ed., *Negotiation and Global Security: New Approaches to Contemporary Issues*. Special issue of *American Behavioral Scientist*, Vol. 38, No. 6, May

Faure, G. O. and Rubin, J. Z. (1993) 'Organizing Concepts and Questions'. In G. Sjöstedt, ed., *International Environmental Negotiation*. Newbury Park and London: Sage Publications

Fennell, W. *et al.* (1993) 'Tropical Products'. In T. Stewart, ed., *The GATT Uruguay Round. A Negotiating History (1986–1992)*. Vol. I: *Commentary*. Deventer, The Netherlands: Kluwer Law and Taxation Publishers

Fischer, S. *et al.*, eds (1994) *Securing Peace in the Middle East: Project on Economic Transition*. Cambridge, MA: MIT Press

Fisher, R. and Ury, W. (1981) *Getting to Yes. Negotiating Agreement Without Giving In*. New York: Penguin Books

Foa, U. and Foa, E. (1975) *Resource Theory of Social Exchange*. Morristown, NJ: General Learning Press

Fraenkel, A. (1989) 'The Convention on Long-Range Transboundary Air Pollution: Meeting the Challenge of International Co-operation'. *Harvard International Law Journal*, Vol. 30, pp. 447–77

Frost, M. (1986) *Towards a Normative Theory of International Relations*. Cambridge and London: Cambridge University Press

Gauthier, D. (1986) *Morals by Agreement*. Oxford: Clarendon Press

Ghose, A. (1997) 'Negotiating the CTBT: India's Security Concerns and Nuclear Disarmament'. *Journal of International Affairs*, Vol. 51, No. 1, pp. 239–61

Ghose, Arundhati (1998) Ambassador, Permanent Mission of India to the United Nations, Geneva, and India's Representative to the Conference on Disarmament, personal interview on 9 July 1998

Gibbard, A. (1990) *Wise Choices, Apt Feelings: A Theory of Normative Judgment*. Oxford: Clarendon Press

Gleick, P. (1993) *Water in Crisis*. Oxford: Oxford University Press

Gold, D. (1995) 'Minefields in the Talks are on Land and Water'. *Jerusalem Post*, 14 July, p. 11

Goldblat, J. (1996) *Arms Control. A Guide to Negotiations and Agreements*. Oslo and London: International Peace Research Institute and Sage Publications

Golt, S. (1988) *The GATT Negotiations 1986–90: Origins, Issues and Prospects*. London: British–North America Committee

Goosen, Peter (1998) Ambassador, Permanent Mission of South Africa to the United Nations, Geneva, South Africa's Minister of Disarmament at the time of the 1995 NPT Review and Extension Conference, personal interview on 8 July 1998

Gouldner, A. (1960) 'The Norm of Reciprocity: A Preliminary Statement'. *American Sociological Review*, Vol. 25, No. 2, April

Gross Stein, J., ed. (1989) *Getting to the Table: The Processes of International Prenegotiation*. Baltimore, MD: Johns Hopkins University Press

Grubb, M. *et al.* (1993) *The Earth Summit Agreements. A Guide and Assessment*. London: Earthscan Publications and the Royal Institute of International Affairs

H'Maidi, Mohammed (1997) Member of the Palestinian delegation to the interim talks on water and Head of the Palestinian delegation to the negotiations over environmental issues, personal interview on 19 August 1997

Habeeb, W. M. (1988) *Power and Tactics in International Negotiation*. Baltimore, MD: Johns Hopkins University Press

Haddad, Marwan (1997) Consultant to the Palestinian delegation in the interim talks on water, personal interview on 13 October 1997

Haigh, N. (1989). 'New Tools for European Air Pollution Control'. *International Environmental Affairs*, Vol. 1, pp. 26–37

Hathaway, D. (1987) *Agriculture and the GATT: Rewriting the Rules*. Washington, DC: Institute for International Economics

Hawes, David (1998) Permanent Representative of Australia to the GATT, Co-Chairman (from 1991 to 1992) and then Acting Chair of the Group of Negotiations on Services in the Uruguay Round of the GATT, personal interview on 26 March 1998

Hazboun, S., Mitwasi, T. and El-Sheikh, W. (1994) 'The Economic Impact of the Israeli–PLO Declaration of Principles on the West Bank, Gaza Strip and the Middle East Region'. Israel/Palestine Issues in Conflict, Issues for Cooperation, Vol. III, No. 1. Jerusalem: Israel/Palestine Centre for Research and Information

Hellström, Mats (1998) Formerly Sweden's Minister of Trade (from 1983 to 1986) involved in the pre-negotiations leading up to the Uruguay Round of the GATT and in the Uruguay Round talks over services, then Minister of Agriculture and Chair of the Negotiating Group on Agriculture in the Uruguay Round (in 1990), personal interview on 5 March 1998

Hemmi, K. (1994) 'The Japanese Perspective'. In Ingersent, K., Rayner, A. and Hine, R., eds, *Agriculture in the Uruguay Round*. New York: St Martin's Press

Hillman, J. (1994) 'The US Perspective'. In Ingersent, K., Rayner, A. and Hine, R., eds, *Agriculture in the Uruguay Round*. New York: St Martin's Press

Hirsch, M., Housen-Couriel, D. and Lapidoth, R. (1995) *Whither Jerusalem? Proposals and Positions Concerning the Future of Jerusalem*. Dordrecht: Kluwer Law International

Hirschfeld, Yair (1997) Professor of Middle Eastern History at Haifa University, initiator of and lead participant in the secret Israel–PLO talks in Oslo, personal interview on 25 August 1997

Hobbes, T. (1991) *Leviathan*. Edited by R. Tuck. Cambridge: Cambridge University Press

Homans, G. (1961) *Social Behaviour*. New York: Harcourt, Brace, Jovanovich

Hopkins, R. (1993) 'Developing Countries in the Uruguay Round: Bargaining under Uncertainty and Inequality'. In Avery, W., ed., *World Agriculture and the GATT*. London: Lynne Rienner Publishers

Hulleileh, Samir (1997a) Director-General of the Palestinian Authority's Trade Department of the Ministry of Economics, and Palestinian Co-ordinator for the Working Groups on banking, insurance and tourism in the interim negotiations over economic issues with Israel, personal interview on 5 November 1997

Hulleileh, S. (1997b) 'Negotiating Economic Agreements: A Palestinian

Perspective'. In *Diplomacy and Conflict Resolution in the Middle East.* Proceedings of a seminar held in 1997. Jerusalem: Palestinian Academic Society for the Study of International Affairs

Hurewitz, L. (1993) 'Textiles'. In T. Stewart, ed., *The GATT Uruguay Round. A Negotiating History (1986–1992).* Vol. I: *Commentary.* Deventer, The Netherlands: Kluwer Law and Taxation Publishers

Hutton, J. and Halkos, G. 'Optimal Acid Rain Abatement Policy for Europe'. *Energy Economics,* Vol. 17, No. 4, pp. 259–75

Iklé, F. (1964) *How Nations Negotiate.* New York: Praeger Publishers

Ingersent, K., Rayner, A. and Hine, R. (1994) 'The EC Perspective'. In Ingersent, K., Rayner, A. and Hine, R., eds, *Agriculture in the Uruguay Round.* New York: St Martin's Press

Jagusiewicz, Andrzej (1997a) Staff member of the UN-ECE, Geneva, and member of the Polish delegation to the negotiations leading to the 1988 Sofia Protocol, personal interview on 17 September 1997

Jagusiewicz, Andrzej (1997b) personal interview on 11 November 1997

Jaramillo, Felipe (1998) Ambassador (Colombia), Chair of the Group of Negotiations on Services in the Uruguay Round of the GATT, personal interview on 7 April 1998

Jensen, L. (1963) 'Soviet–American Bargaining Behaviour in Post-War Disarmament Negotiations'. *Journal of Arms Control,* Vol. 1, October

Jensen, L. (1983) 'Soviet–American Behaviour in Disarmament Negotiations'. In Zartman, I. W., ed., *The 50 Per Cent Solution.* New Haven and London: Yale University Press

Jilek, Pavel (1997) Deputy Director of the Air Protection Department, Ministry of the Environment, Czech Republic and Czech delegate to the Working Group on Strategies under the LRTAP Convention, and Sochor, Vladimir, Czech delegate to the UN-ECE Task Force on Economic Aspects of Abatement Strategies, joint answers provided in writing on 16 September 1997

Joffe, L. (1996) *Keesing's Guide to the Middle East Peace Process.* London: Cartermill International Ltd

Johnson, R. (1995a) 'Indefinite Extension of the Non-Proliferation Treaty: Risks and Reckonings'. A Report of the 1995 NPT Review and Extension Conference, New York, 17 April to 12 May, 1995. *Acronym Report,* No. 7, September

Johnson, R. (1995b) 'Security Assurances'. *Acronym NPT Update,* No. 14, 4 May

Johnson, R. (1998) 'Reviewing the Non-Proliferation Treaty: Problems and Processes'. A Report of the Second Preparatory Committee Meeting of the 2000 Review Conference of the NPT, Geneva, 27 April to 8 May 1998. *Acronym Report,* No. 12, September

Jones, D. Gareth and Harris, Robyn J. (1997) 'Contending for the Dead'. *Nature,* Vol. 386, 6 March

Josling, T. E., Tangermann, S. and Warley, T. K. (1996) *Agriculture in the GATT.* London: Macmillan Press

Jurrjens, R. and Sizoo, J. (1997) *Efficacy and Efficiency in Multilateral Policy Formation: The Experience of Three Arms Control Negotiations.* The Hague: Kluwer Law International

Kakebeeke, William (1997) Special Advisor, Ministry of the Environment, The Netherlands; member of the Dutch delegation (from 1977 until 1994) to the negotiations leading to the 1979 UN-ECE LRTAP Convention and the subsequent negotiations under this Convention; Vice-Chairman of the negotiations leading to the 1988 Sofia Protocol, personal interview on 25 July 1997

Kantor, Shmuel (1997) Advisor to Israel's Water Commissioner Meir Ben Meir, member of the Israeli delegation to the interim talks on water, and Head of several sub-committees of the Israeli–Palestinian Joint Water Committee, personal interview on 29 August, and communication in writing on 8 September and 13 October 1997

Kasperson, R., Derr, P. and Kates, R. (1983) 'Confronting Equity in Radioactive Waste Management: Modest Proposals for a Socially Just and Acceptable Program'. In Kasperson, R., ed., *Equity Issues in Radioactive Waste Management.* Oelgeschlager, Gunn and Hain Publishers

Keiser, Volkert (1997) Directorate-General for the Environment, Air and Energy Directorate, Air Quality and Acidification, The Netherlands; Head of the Dutch delegation in the UN-ECE Executive Body and the Working Group on Abatement Strategies (since 1992), communication in writing on 1 October 1997

Kelley, H., Beckman, L. and Fischer, C. (1967) 'Negotiating the Division of a Reward under Incomplete Information'. *Journal of Experimental Social Psychology,* Vol. 3, pp. 361–98

Kemp, G. and Harkavy, R. (1997) *Strategic Geography and the Changing Middle East.* Washington, DC: Carnegie Endowment for International Peace and the Brookings Institution

Khalidi, A. S. (1996) Senior Advisor to the Palestinian delegation in the interim talks on security issues, and Research Associate at the Royal Institute for International Affairs, Chatham House, London, personal interview on 8 February 1996

Kinarti, Noah (1997) Leading member of the Israeli Labor Party, Senior Advisor to former Prime Minister Yitzhak Rabin, and Head of the Israeli delegation to the interim talks over water (until August 1995), personal interview on 20 August 1997

Klaassen, G. (1996) *Acid Rain and Environmental Degradation: The Economics of Emission Trading.* Cheltenham: Edward Elgar Publishing

Klaassen, Ger (1997) Staff member of the International Institute for Applied Systems Analysis, Austria, during the negotiations of the 1994 Second Sulphur Protocol, and involved in the Group of Economic Experts in developing economic models for this protocol, personal interview on 22 July 1997 (his statements reflect his own personal opinion)

Klaassen, G., Amann, G. and Schöpp, W. (1992) 'Strategies for Reducing

Sulfur Dioxide Emissions in Europe Based on Critical Sulfur Deposition Values'. Background paper prepared for the UN-ECE Task Force on Integrated Assessment Modelling, 30 November–2 December 1992 in Geneva. Draft, November 1992. Laxenburg, Austria: International Institute for Applied Systems Analysis

Krasner, S. D., ed. (1983) *International Regimes*. Ithaca, NY: Cornell University Press

Kuttab, D. (1994) 'Agreement on Currency'. *Middle East International*, 21 January, p. 10

Lammers, J. (1991) 'The European Approach to Acid Rain'. In D. B. Magraw, ed., *International Law and Pollution*. Philadelphia, PA: University of Pennsylvania Press

Lang, W. (1995) 'Negotiation in the Face of the Future'. In C. Albin, ed., *Negotiation and Global Security: New Approaches to Contemporary Issues*. Special issue of *American Behavioral Scientist*, Vol. 38, No. 6, May

Lax, D. and Sebenius, J. (1986) *The Manager as Negotiator. Bargaining for Cooperation and Competitive Gain*. New York and London: The Free Press

Lazar, F. (1990) 'Services and the GATT: US Motives and a Blueprint for Negotiations'. *Journal of World Trade*, Vol. 24, No. 1, January, pp. 135–45

Ledogar, Stephen L. (1998) Ambassador, Head of the US delegation to the negotiations (from 1994 to 1996) within the Conference on Disarmament leading to the CTBT, personal interview on 25 June 1998

Leigh-Phippard, H. (1997) 'Multilateral Diplomacy at the 1995 NPT Review and Extension Conference'. *Diplomacy and Statecraft*, Vol. 8, No. 2, July, pp. 167–90

Levy, M. (1993) 'European Acid Rain: The Power of Tote-Board Diplomacy'. In P. Haas, R. Keohane and M. Levy, eds, *Institutions for the Earth: Sources of Effective International Environmental Protection*. Cambridge, MA: MIT Press

Levy, M. (1995) 'International Co-operation to Combat Acid Rain'. *Green Globe Yearbook*. Oxford: Oxford University Press

Levy, Mark (1997) Visiting Lecturer, Williams College, Massachusetts, personal interview on 14 July 1997

Lind, E. A. and Tyler, T. R. (1988) *The Social Psychology of Procedural Justice*. New York: Plenum

Magraw, D. B., ed. (1991) *International Law and Pollution*. Philadelphia, PA: University of Pennsylvania Press

Mahmood, T. (1995) 'Nuclear Non-Proliferation Treaty (NPT): India and Pakistan'. *Pakistan Horizon*, Vol. 48, No. 3, July, pp. 81–100

Makovsky, D. (1996) *Making Peace with the PLO*. Boulder, CO: Westview Press

Maltz, J. (1995) 'The Paris Economic Protocol One Year On: An Israeli Perspective'. *Peace Economics*, Economist Intelligence Unit, 3rd Quarter

Mason, R. 'Joint Implementation and the Second Sulfur Protocol'. *Review of European Community and International Environmental Law*, Vol. 4, No. 4, December, pp. 296–303

Masri, M. (1997) 'The Future of External Trade in Palestine: Summary'. Nablus

(West Bank): Centre for Palestine Research and Studies, Economics Department

McCormick, J. (1989) *Acid Earth. The Global Threat of Acid Pollution*. London: Earthscan Publications

Morgenthau, H. (1948) *Politics Among Nations*. New York: Knopf Publishers

Morgenthau, H. (1971) *Politics in the Twentieth Century*. Chicago and London: University of Chicago Press

Moyes, A. (1987) *Common Ground: How Changes in the Common Agricultural Policy Affect the Third World Poor*. Oxford: Oxfam

Murlis, J. (1995) 'Critical Loads: The Policy Background'. In R. W. Battarbee, ed., *Acid Rain and its Impact: The Critical Loads Debate*. London: Ensis Publishing

Murphy, E. (1995) 'Stacking the Deck: The Economics of the Israeli–PLO Accords'. *Middle East Report*, May–June/July–August

Murphy, Michael (1998) Department of Land Economy, University of Cambridge, UK, personal interview on 24 February 1998

Nardin, T. (1983) *Law, Morality, and the Relations of States*. Princeton, NJ: Princeton University Press

Nash, J. F. (1950) 'The Bargaining Problem'. *Econometrica*, Vol. 18

Nayyar, D. (1988) 'Some Reflections on the Uruguay Round and Trade in Services'. *Journal of World Trade*, Vol. 22, No. 5

Nitze, William (1997) Assistant Administrator, Office of International Activities, Environmental Protection Agency, Washington, DC; member and at times Chair of the US delegation to the negotiations under the UN-ECE LRTAP Convention (from 1987 to 1990), personal interview on 18 July 1997

Nordberg, Lars (1997) Deputy Director, Environment and Human Settlements Division, Secretariat of the UN-ECE, Geneva, personal interview on 18 June 1997

Novik, Nimrod (1997) Senior Aide to Shimon Peres, engaged in the interim talks with the PLO, and Senior Vice-President of the Merhav Group of Companies, Israel, personal interview on 25 August 1997

Nunes, Tovar (1998) Member of Brazil's delegation to the Uruguay Round talks over services (from 1988 to 1991), personal interview on 7 May 1998

O'Brien, W. (1991) *Law and Morality in Israel's War with the PLO*. New York and London: Routledge Publishers

O'Connor, H. (1992) 'Explaining the Quagmire of the Agricultural Negotiations in the Uruguay Round'. Discussion paper in Economics and Econometrics, No. 92/14, Department of Economics, University of Nottingham, December

O'Neill, O. (1986) 'Rights to Compensation'. *Social Philosophy and Policy*, Vol. 5, No. 1

O'Neill, O. (1991) 'Transnational Justice'. In D. Held, ed., *Political Theory Today*. Cambridge: Polity Press

Ozanne, J. (1993) 'Israelis, Palestinians Split on Economic Policy'. *Financial Times*, 21 October

Pacheco, A. (1995) 'Oslo II and Still No Water'. *Middle East International*, 3 November, pp. 18–19

Park, C. (1987) *Acid Rain. Rhetoric and Reality.* London and New York: Methuen & Co.

Peres, S. (1993) *The New Middle East.* Shaftesbury, Dorset: Element Books

Piaget, J. (1948) *The Moral Judgment of the Child.* Glencoe: Free Press

Poloniecki, Jan (2000) Department of Public Health Sciences, St George's Hospital Medical School, London, personal interview on 22 February 2000

Poloniecki, J., Atkinson, R., de Leon A. P. and Anderson, R. (1997) 'Daily Time Series for Cardiovascular Hospital Admissions and Previous Day's Air Pollution in London, UK'. *Occupational and Environmental Medicine*, Vol. 54, No. 8, pp. 535–40

Prasnikar, V. and Roth, A. (1992) 'Considerations of Fairness and Strategy: Experimental Data from Sequential Games'. *Quarterly Journal of Economics*, August, pp. 865–88

Pruitt, D. (1981) *Negotiation Behaviour.* New York: Academic Press

Pundik, Ron (1997) Executive Director, Economic Cooperation Foundation, Tel Aviv, participant in the secret Israel–PLO talks in Oslo and in the drafting of the first version of the 1993 Declaration of Principles (DoP), personal interviews on 12 August 1997 and 9 July 1998

Q'Awash, Fadel (1997) Deputy Head of the Palestinian Water Authority, personal interview on 9 September and communication in writing on 6 October 1997

Quigley, J. (1995) 'Jerusalem in International Law'. Paper presented at a conference on 'The Current Status of Jerusalem and the Future of the Peace Process', organised by the International Campaign for Jerusalem, London, 15–16 June 1995

Qureshi, A. (1996) *The World Trade Organization. Implementing International Trade Norms.* Manchester: Manchester University Press

Ramaker, Jaap (1998) Ambassador, Chair of the negotiations within the Conference on Disarmament leading to the CTBT (the later stages of the talks), personal interview on 7 July 1998

Rapkin, D. and George, A. (1993) 'Rice Liberalisation and Japan's Role in the Uruguay Round: A Two-Level Game Approach'. In W. Avery, ed., *World Agriculture and the GATT.* London: Lynne Rienner Publishers

Ravenhill, J. (1993) 'When Weakness is Strength: The Lomé IV Negotiations'. In I. W. Zartman, ed., *Europe and Africa: The New Phase.* Boulder, CO: Lynne Rienner Publishers

Rawls, J. (1958) 'Justice as Fairness'. *Philosophical Review,* Vol. 67, pp. 164–94

Rawls, J. (1971) *A Theory of Justice.* Cambridge, MA: Harvard University Press

Rawls, J. (1982) 'Social Unity and Primary Goods'. In A. Sen and B. Williams, eds, *Utilitarianism and Beyond.* Cambridge: Cambridge University Press

Rayner, A. J., Ingersent, K. A. and Hine, R. C. (1993) 'Agriculture in the

Uruguay Round: An Assessment'. *Economic Journal*, Vol. 103, November, pp. 1513–27

Reyna, J. (1993) 'Services'. In T. Stewart, ed., *The GATT Uruguay Round. A Negotiating History (1986–1992)*. Vol. II: *Commentary*. Deventer, The Netherlands: Kluwer Law and Taxation Publishers

Rhodes, C. (1993) *Reciprocity, US Trade Policy, and the GATT Regime*. Ithaca and London: Cornell University Press

Ricardo, D. (1819) *On the Principles of Political Economy and Taxation*. First US edition, Georgetown, DC: Joseph Milligan

Rittberger, V., ed. (1993) *Regime Theory and International Relations*. Oxford: Clarendon Press

Roche, D. (1997) 'An Analysis of the First Preparatory Committee Meeting for the 2000 Review of the Non-Proliferation Treaty'. New York, 7–18 April 1997. Santa Barbara, CA: Nuclear Age Peace Foundation

Rodan, S. (1995a) 'Water Dispute: No Immediate Solution on Tap'. *Jerusalem Post*, 21 July

Rodan, S. (1995b) 'Divided Waters, Part I'. *Jerusalem Post*, 1 September

Rosencranz, A. (1988) 'The Acid Rain Controversy in Europe and North America: A Political Analysis'. In J. E. Carroll, ed., *International Environmental Diplomacy*. Cambridge: Cambridge University Press

Ross, J. and Wasserman, J. (1993) 'Trade-Related Aspects of Intellectual Property Rights'. In T. Stewart, ed., *The GATT Uruguay Round. A Negotiating History (1986–1992)*. Vol. II: *Commentary*. Deventer, The Netherlands: Kluwer Law and Taxation Publishers

Rothchild, D. (1997) 'Ethnic Bargaining and the Management of Intense Conflict'. In D. Rothchild, ed., *Ethnic Bargaining: Conflict Management in Pluralistic Societies*. Special issue of *International Negotiation*, Vol. 2., No. 1, pp. 1–20

Rouyer, Alwyn (1997a) Professor of Political Science at the University of Idaho, personal interview on 25 August 1997

Rouyer, A. (1997b) 'The Water Issue in the Palestinian–Israeli Peace Process'. *Survival*, Vol. 39, No. 2, Summer, pp. 57–81

Rubin, J. Z. and Brown, B. (1975) *The Social Psychology of Bargaining and Negotiation*. New York and London: Academic Press

Rubin, J. Z. and Zartman, I. W. (1995) 'Asymmetrical Negotiations: Some Survey Results that may Surprise'. *Negotiation Journal*, Vol. 11, No. 4, October, pp. 349–64

Said, E. (1995) *Peace and Its Discontents*. London: Vintage (Random House)

Sampson, E. (1975) 'On Justice as Equality'. *Journal of Social Issues*, Vol. 31, No. 3, pp. 45–64

Sanders, B. (1995) 'The 1995 NPT Review and Extension Conference: An Overview'. *Contemporary Security Policy*, Vol. 16, No. 3, December, pp. 421–8

Sayigh, Yezid (1996) Advisor to the Palestinian delegation to the Washington Peace Talks on the Middle East (from 1991 to 1993) and participant in the negotiations over the implementation of the Gaza–Jericho agreement in 1994, personal interviews on 7 and 15 February 1996

Scanlon, T. (1982) 'Contractualism and Utilitarianism'. In A. Sen and B. Williams, eds, *Utilitarianism and Beyond*. Cambridge: Cambridge University Press

Schelling, T. (1960) *The Strategy of Conflict*. Cambridge, MA: Harvard University Press

Schott, J. and Buurman, J. (1994) *The Uruguay Round: An Assessment*. Washington, DC: Institute for International Economics, November

Schott, J. and Mazza, J. (1986) 'Trade in Services and Developing Countries'. *Journal of World Trade Law*, Vol. 20, No. 3, May–June

Sebenius, J. (1984) *Negotiating the Law of the Sea*. Cambridge, MA: Harvard University Press

Self, Richard (1998) Ambassador, the chief US negotiator on services throughout the Uruguay Round, overseeing the drafting of the text of the General Agreement on Trade in Services (GATS) and the market access commitments of more than ninety countries, personal interview on 29 April 1998

Self, Richard (2000a) communication in writing on 18 February 2000

Self, Richard (2000b) communication in writing on 23 February 2000

Sen, A. (1992) *Inequality Reexamined*. Oxford: Oxford University Press

Shohat, Avraham (1997) formerly Israel's Minister of Finance and Head of the Israeli delegation to the interim talks on economics, personal interview on 31 October 1997

Shue, H. (1992) 'The Unavoidability of Justice'. In A. Hurrell and B. Kingsbury, eds, *The International Politics of the Environment*. New York: Oxford University Press

Sidgwick, H. (1901) *The Methods of Ethics*. 6th edition. London: Macmillan and Co

Simpson, John (1998) Professor of International Relations, University of Southampton, UK, personal interview on 9 June 1998

Sinclair, Don (1998) Ambassador, member of the Canadian delegation to the 1995 NPT Review and Extension Conference, and a 'Friend of the Chair' in the negotiations within the Conference on Disarmament leading to the CTBT, personal interview on 2 July 1998

Singer, Joel (1996) Legal Advisor, Israeli Ministry of Foreign Affairs, Jerusalem, and member (from 1993 to 1996) of the Israeli delegation to the interim talks with the PLO, personal interview on 18 March 1996

Sjöstedt, G. (1991) 'Trade Talks'. In V. Kremenyuk, ed., *International Negotiation. Analysis, Approaches, Issues*. San Francisco and Oxford: Jossey-Bass Publishers

Sjöstedt, G. (1996) 'Leadership in Multilateral Negotiations: Crisis or Transition?' Paper presented at the Symposium on Comparative Studies of Negotiating Behaviour, International Research Centre for Japanese Studies, Kyoto, 27–30 August 1996

Sjöstedt, Gunnar (1998) Senior Research Fellow, Swedish Institute of International Affairs, Stockholm, and Associate Professor of Political Science, University of Stockholm, personal interviews on 6 and 7 April 1998

Sjöstedt, G. and Spector, B. (1993) 'Conclusion'. In G. Sjöstedt, ed. (1993) *International Environmental Negotiation*. Newbury Park and London: Sage Publications

Slater, R. (1993) *Rabin of Israel. A Biography.* London: Robson Books

Sliggers, Johan (1997) Expert on air pollution, Air and Energy Department, Ministry of Housing, Spatial Planning and Environment, The Hague, The Netherlands, and member of the Dutch delegation to the talks leading to the 1994 Second Sulphur Protocol and to later talks over heavy metals, NO_x and VOCs, personal interview on 1 August 1997

Sliggers, J. and Klaassen, G. (1992) 'Cost Sharing for the Abatement of Acidification in Europe: The Key to a Protocol'. Draft paper prepared for the session of the UN-ECE Task Force on Economic Aspects of Abatement Strategies, Geneva, 3–4 December 1992

Sliggers, J. and Klaassen, G. (1994) 'Cost Sharing for the Abatement of Acidification in Europe: the Missing Link in the Sulphur Protocol'. *European Environment*, Vol. 4, Part 1, pp. 5–11

Snyder, G. and Diesing, P. (1977) *Conflict Among Nations.* Princeton, NJ: Princeton University Press

Sokolovsky, Valentin (1997) Head of the Soviet/Russian delegation (from 1978 until 1991) to the negotiations leading to the UN-ECE LRTAP Convention and subsequent negotiations under this Convention, Head of the UN-ECE Working Group on Abatement Strategies (from 1989 to 1991), and since 1992 adviser to the Minister of the Russian State Committee on the Protection of the Environment and Natural Resources, communication in writing on 27 August 1997

Spector, B. (1992a) 'Post-Negotiation: Is the Implementation of Future Negotiated Environmental Agreements Threatened?' Working Paper No. 92–22, February 1992. Laxenburg, Austria. International Institute for Applied Systems Analysis

Spector, B. (1992b) 'The Post-Agreement Negotiation Process: The Problems of Ratifying International Environmental Agreements'. Working Paper No. 92–90, December. Laxenburg, Austria: International Institute for Applied Systems Analysis

Spector, B., Sjöstedt, G. and Zartman, I. W., eds (1993) *Negotiating International Regimes: Lessons Learnt from UNCED.* London: Graham and Trotman

Sprinz, Detlef (1997) Senior Fellow, Potsdam Institute for Climate Impact Research, Germany, and observer of the UN-ECE negotiations leading to the 1994 Second Sulphur Protocol, personal interview on 25 July 1997

Sprinz, D. and Vaahtoranta, T. (1994) 'The Interest-Based Explanation of International Environmental Policy'. *International Organization*, Vol. 48, No. 1, Winter, pp. 77–105

Stern, J. (1994) 'Co-operative Security and the CWC: A Comparison of the

Chemical and Nuclear Weapons Non-Proliferation Regimes'. *Contemporary Security Policy*, Vol. 15, No. 3, December, pp. 30–57

Stewart, T. *et al.* (1993a) 'Antidumping'. In T. Stewart, ed., *The GATT Uruguay Round. A Negotiating History (1986–1992)*. Vol. II: *Commentary*. Deventer, The Netherlands: Kluwer Law and Taxation Publishers

Stewart, T. *et al.* (1993b) 'Safeguards'. In T. Stewart, ed., *The GATT Uruguay Round. A Negotiating History (1986–1992)*. Vol. II: *Commentary*. Deventer, The Netherlands: Kluwer Law and Taxation Publishers

Susskind, L. (1990) 'A Negotiation Credo for Controversial Siting Disputes'. *Negotiation Journal*, October, pp. 309–14

Susskind, L. (1994) *Environmental Diplomacy. Negotiating More Effective Global Agreements*. Oxford and New York: Oxford University Press

Susskind, L. and Cruikshank, J. (1987) *Breaking the Impasse. Consensual Approaches to Resolving Public Disputes*. New York: Basic Books

Sweet, J. (1993) 'Who's Afraid of Acid Rain?' *Energy Economist* (Financial Times), November, pp. 15–19

Tamari, S. (1996) *Palestinian Refugee Negotiations: From Madrid to Oslo II*. Final Status Issues Paper. Washington, DC: Institute for Palestine Studies

Tamari, Salim (1997) Director, Institute for Jerusalem Studies, East Jerusalem, Associate Professor of Sociology at Birzeit University, and Palestinian Coordinator of the Refugee Working Group in the multilateral peace talks, personal interview on 18 August 1997

Touval, S. and Zartman, I. W., eds (1985) *International Mediation in Theory and Practice*. Boulder, CO: Westview Press

Tran, Van-Thinh (1998) Head of and chief negotiator for the EC permanent delegation to the Uruguay Round of the GATT in all areas (from 1979 to 1994), personal interview on 25 March 1998

Tsur, Gideon (1997) Israel's Water Commissioner (until 1996) and member of the Israeli delegation to the interim talks on water, personal interview on 6 October 1997

Tsur, Ya'akov (1997) Israel's Minister of Agriculture (from 1992 to 1996) and a principal Israeli negotiator in the final stages of the interim talks leading to the 1995 Taba Agreement, personal interview on 16 September 1997

Usher, G. (1995) *Palestine in Crisis. The Struggle for Peace and Political Independence after Oslo*. London: Pluto Press

Walster, E., Walster, G. W. and Berscheid, E. (1978) *Equity: Theory and Research*. Boston, MA: Allyn and Bacon

Walton, R. and McKersie R. (1965) *A Behavioral Theory of Labor Negotiations*. New York: McGraw-Hill

Watkins, K. (1991) 'Agriculture and Food Security in the GATT Uruguay Round'. *Review of African Political Economy*, No. 50, pp. 38–50

Weaver, R. and Abellard, D. (1993) 'Functioning of the GATT System'. In T. Stewart, ed., *The GATT Uruguay Round. A Negotiating History (1986–1992)*. Vol. II: *Commentary*. Deventer, The Netherlands: Kluwer Law and Taxation Publishers

Weiss, E. (1989) *In Fairness to Future Generations*. Tokyo: United Nations University

Weiss, F. (1995) 'The General Agreement on Trade in Services 1994'. *Common Market Law Review*, Vol. 32, pp. 1177–225

Weissbrodt, David (1982) 'A New United Nations Mechanism for Encouraging the Ratification of Treaties'. *Human Rights Quarterly*, Vol. 4, pp. 333–52

Welch, D. (1993) *Justice and the Genesis of War*. New York: Cambridge University Press

Westdal, C. (1995) 'The Nuclear Non-Proliferation Treaty (NPT) Review and Extension Conference: A Canadian Perspective'. Presentation by Ambassador for Disarmament Christopher Westdal to the Standing Committee on Foreign Affairs and International Trade, House of Commons of Canada, 35th Parliament, 1st Session, 20 June 1995. Published in *Canadian Disarmament Digest*, 10 April 1996

Weston, Michael (1998) Ambassador, Head of the UK delegation to the 1995 NPT Review and Extension Conference and Head of the UK delegation to the negotiations within the Conference on Disarmament leading to the CTBT, personal interview on 16 July 1998

Williams, M. (1997) Member of the UK delegation to the negotiations under the UN-ECE LRTAP Convention (since 1993), personal interview on 31 July 1997

Winham, G. (1989) 'The Prenegotiation Phase of the Uruguay Round'. In J Gross Stein. ed., *Getting to the Table: Processes of International Prenegotiation*. Special issue of *International Journal*, Vol. 44, No. 2, Spring

Winham, Gilbert (1998) Professor, Department of Political Science, Dalhousie University, Nova Scotia, Canada, personal interview on 30 April 1998

Wuester, H. (1992) 'The Convention on Long-Range Transboundary Air Pollution: Its Achievements and its Potential'. In T. Schneider, ed., *Acidification Research: Evaluation and Policy Applications*. Proceedings of an International Conference, Maastricht, The Netherlands, 14–18 October 1991. Amsterdam: Elsevier Science Publishers

Wuester, Henning (1997a) Secretary to the Working Group on Strategies under the UN-ECE LRTAP Convention (since the beginning of the negotiations of the 1994 Second Sulphur Protocol), UN-ECE, Geneva, personal interview on 24 June 1997

Wuester, Henning (1997b) personal interview on 18 July 1997

Wuester, Henning (1997c) communication in writing on 10 November 1997

Wuester, Henning (1997d) communication in writing on 11 December 1997

Wuester, Henning (1997e) communication in writing on 12 December 1997

Wuester, Henning (2000) communication in writing on 1 March 2000

Yeutter, Clayton (1998) Former US Trade Representative and former US Secretary of Agriculture involved in the pre-negotiations leading up to the Uruguay Round of the GATT, and then in the formal Uruguay Round talks (from 1986 to 1991), personal interview on 8 March 1998

Bibliography

Young, H. P. (1991) 'Fair Division'. In H. P. Young, ed., *Negotiation Analysis*. Ann Arbor, MI: University of Michigan Press

Young, H. P. (1994) *Equity. In Theory and Practice*. Princeton, NJ: Princeton University Press

Young, H. P. and Wolf, A. (1992) 'Global Warming Negotiations: Does Fairness Matter?' *Brookings Review*, Vol. 10, pp. 46–51

Zaluar, A. and Monteleone-Neto, R. (1997) 'The 1972 Biological Weapons Convention: A View from the South'. *International Review of the Red Cross*, Vol. 38, No. 318, May–June

Zartman, I. W. (1991) 'The Structure of Negotiation'. In V. Kremenyuk, ed., *International Negotiation. Analysis, Approaches, Issues*. San Francisco: Jossey-Bass Publishers

Zartman, I. W. (1995) 'The Role of Justice in Global Security Negotiations'. In C. Albin, ed., *Negotiation and Global Security: New Approaches to Contemporary Issues*. Special issue of *American Behavioral Scientist*, Vol. 38, No. 6, May

Zartman, I. W. and Berman, M. (1982) *The Practical Negotiator*. New Haven and London: Yale University Press

Zartman, I. W., Druckman, D., Jensen, L., Pruitt, D. and Young, H. P. (1996) 'Negotiation as a Search for Justice'. *International Negotiation*, Vol. 1, pp. 79–98

Zartman, I. W., ed. (1983) *The 50 Per Cent Solution*. New Haven and London: Yale University Press

Zureik, E. (1996) *Palestinian Refugees and the Peace Process*. A Final Status Issues Paper. Washington, DC: Institute for Palestine Studies

Zurek, Janusz (1997) Head of the Department of Environmental Policy, Institute of Environmental Protection, Warsaw, and member of the Polish delegation to the negotiations leading to the Helsinki, Sofia and Oslo (Second Sulphur) Protocols under the UN-ECE LRTAP Convention, communication in writing on 8 October 1997

Zutshi, B. K. (1998) Ambassador, Head of India's delegation to the GATT (from June 1989 to October 1994); India's chief negotiator in the Uruguay Round talks over services, agriculture and intellectual property rights; Chair of the GATT Council of Representatives (in 1992); and Chair of the Contracting Parties to the GATT (in 1993), personal interview on 21 April 1998

Other sources

Acid News, No. 2, April 1993; No. 4, October 1993; No. 1, February 1994

Al Quds (East Jerusalem), 27 February 1998

Aristotle, *Nicomachean Ethics*. Translated, with introduction and notes, by Terence Irwin. Indianapolis: Hackett, 1985

'Developments in the Law. International Environmental Law', *Harvard Law Review*, Vol. 104, pp. 1487–639

The Economist, 16 May 1998, 18 October 1997, 15 November 1997

252

'Israel's Nuclear Weapons Continue as Stumbling Block', *ACRONYM NPT Update*, No. 5, 21 April 1995

Jerusalem Journal of International Relations, Vol. 13, No. 1, March 1991 (special issue on pre-negotiation)

Jerusalem Post: 'PA to be Given 30 Per Cent of Withheld Funds', 19 August 1997, p. 1; 'The Closure: Security Boost or Ticking Bomb?', 22 August 1997; 'Water Issue Resolved in Cairo', 21 April, 1994; 'Husseini Warns of Violence over Jerusalem', 7 April 2000

Middle East International, 8 September, 1995; 6 October 1995; 3 November 1995

Middle East Monitor, Vol. 5, No. 10, October 1995

MidEast Mirror: 'Economic Ties', 17 November 1993, p. 9; 'Economic Union', 24 November 1993, p. 14; 'Open Economic Market Agreed with the PLO', 16 December 1993, pp. 22–4; 'Economic Talks in Paris Reach Impasse on Customs Policy', 22 April 1994, p. 10; 'Paris Talks', 13 April 1994, p. 6; 'Autonomy Talks', 15 December 1993, p. 4; 'Peres, Buoyed by Pace of Cairo Talks, Expects Rabin to Meet Arafat "Very Soon"', 23 February 1994, p. 2

Nuclear Proliferation News, No. 24, 17 May 1995

Palestine Report (East Jerusalem): 'Separation Due to Irreconcilable Differences' (by M. Jamal), 15 March 1996, p. 12; 'Dependence on Israel Unhealthy', 14 June 1996, pp. 6–7; 'Paris Protocol: Null and Void', 26 April 1996, pp. 12–13; 'Water Rights Latest Obstacle in Peace Talks', 4 August 1995, pp. 4–5

'Report on Third Review Conference of the Biological and Toxin Weapons Convention', *Quarterly Review, Arms Control and Disarmament* (Foreign and Commonwealth Office), No. 23, October 1991

Risk: Health, Safety and Environment, Vol. 7, No. 2, 1996

Safeguards to Prevent Nuclear Proliferation. Nuclear Issues Briefing Paper 5, March. Melbourne: Uranium Information Centre

The Middle East and North Africa 1997. London: Europa Publications

The Palestinian Monetary Authority and the Banking System: Summary. Nablus (West Bank): Centre for Palestine Research and Studies (CPRS), Economics Department, December 1996

'Water after Oslo II: Legal Aspects of Water in the Occupied Territories'. *Palestine Yearbook of International Law*, Vol. 8, 1994–5

West Bank and Gaza Update (World Bank Resident Mission, West Bank and Gaza), March 1998 issue

Index

CAMBRIDGE STUDIES IN INTERNATIONAL RELATIONS